WORK-STUDY PROGRAMS
FOR ALIENATED YOUTH

A Casebook

Professional

Guidance

Series

COUNSELING ADOLESCENTS

THE COUNSELING RELATIONSHIP

GUIDANCE SERVICES

GUIDANCE TESTING

OCCUPATIONAL INFORMATION

WORK-STUDY PROGRAMS
FOR ALIENATED YOUTH

WORK-STUDY PROGRAMS FOR ALIENATED YOUTH

A Casebook

by **GEORGE W. BURCHILL**

Assistant Professor of Education,
University of Redlands, Redlands, California

formerly Assistant Professor of Education,
University of Wisconsin, Madison, Wisconsin

SCIENCE RESEARCH ASSOCIATES, INC.
CHICAGO

LIBRARY OF CONGRESS CATALOG CARD NUMBER: 62-20756

Reorder No.: 5-78

PHI DELTA KAPPA

PROFESSIONAL FRATERNITY FOR MEN IN EDUCATION

Commission on the Role of the School
in the Prevention of Juvenile Delinquency

Eighth Street and Union Avenue, Bloomington, Indiana

A project designed to identify and illustrate
outstanding work-study programs aimed at
the prevention of delinquent behavior
and at the rehabilitation of alienated youth

COMMISSION MEMBERS

ROBERT J. HAVIGHURST, cochairman
  University of Chicago, Chicago, Illinois

HOWARD C. SEYMOUR, cochairman
  Phoenix High School and Junior College District,
  Phoenix, Arizona

MACK P. MONROE
  Jackson Junior High School, Detroit, Michigan

LINDLEY J. STILES
  University of Wisconsin, Madison, Wisconsin

C. C. TRILLINGHAM
  Los Angeles County Schools, Los Angeles, California

The project is supported by a grant from the Ford Foundation.

Published for Phi Delta Kappa by
Science Research Associates, Inc., 259 East Erie Street, Chicago 11, Illinois

Foreword

Descriptions of nine work-study programs for secondary students are presented in this casebook. They are reported as examples of ways in which eight public school systems and one group of private individuals are combining classroom experience and job experience for certain youngsters to prevent them from becoming alienated from their society. The Phi Delta Kappa Commission on the Role of the School in the Prevention of Juvenile Delinquency hopes that knowledge of the methods will benefit educators planning or evaluating similar programs.

The history of the commission's concern about alienated youth and about the responsibilities of the nation's schoolmen for providing schoolwork curriculums goes back to April 1961. In that month Robert J. Havighurst and Lindley J. Stiles, members of the commission on juvenile delinquency prevention, issued "A Statement of National Policy for Alienated Youth" in the *Phi Delta Kappan.*[1] After its publication an appeal was made to the fraternity members for information regarding school-related work programs in U.S. educational systems. The response was overwhelming. Over fifteen hundred were reported. From these, the commission chose approximately twenty-five to consider for inclusion in a casebook that the Ford Foundation agreed to finance. This was the foundation's contribution to Phi Delta Kappa's program of illustrating what is being done in schools utilizing work-study programs to prevent youngsters from developing predelinquent tendencies or to rehabilitate children who have already manifested such tendencies.

A final screening of the programs was accomplished by Phi Delta Kappans who visited schools that were using the selected work-study plans. Finally, the writer visited schools with programs

---

1. Robert J. Havighurst and Lindley J. Stiles, "A Statement of National Policy for Alienated Youth," *Phi Delta Kappan,* April 1961, pp. 283–91.

selected on the basis of these criteria: applicability to alienated youth, relation to school and community, organization, proven success, and representativeness (geographic and size).

Thus, after a year's study the programs were identified. They are presented as examples of what is being done in nine settings to help young people develop into good citizens through school curriculums based on a combination of study and work.

In compiling this report the writer is indebted to many persons. He particularly appreciates the guidance of commission members Howard C. Seymour, Robert J. Havighurst, Lindley J. Stiles, Mack P. Monroe, and C. C. Trillingham; the work of Phi Delta Kappan visitors R. R. Edelman, Paul D. Shriver, and C. E. Wilson; the help of the individuals associated with the programs reported: Cedric Boeseke, Paul Driscoll, George W. Eyster, Herman Goldberg, Merle B. Karnes, Phillip H. Mahoney, Milan Wight, Gerald Gordon, Bernard C. Greene, who was also a visitor, and many of their colleagues who helped interpret the programs to the investigator; the research assistance of Coral Varo and Ernestine M. Wittig; the editorial review of Mary L. Burchill and Donna L. Simkins; and finally the friendly co-operation of the children the writer visited in classrooms and on work stations.

GEORGE W. BURCHILL

Introduction

Thirty to forty years ago, a young person unsuccessful in school or lacking the incentive to learn could achieve adult status by going to work. Today this is largely impossible. Ever since World War II, employers have shifted away from hiring the young, inexperienced worker. Laborsaving devices have multiplied, requiring skilled, experienced operators. With older persons in the market for work, job opportunities for the adolescent are scarce. Laws restricting the employment of minors have been enacted. The values of formal education have been extolled. (The public *expects* youth to be in school.) The result is that young people are being squeezed out of those experiences that may be their only sources of gaining recognition, security, and standing with peers, parents, and other adults.

Frustrated by a lack of success in school and thwarted by a failure to obtain work, a sizable percentage of these young people become hostile and aggressive. They strike out against society. The bewildered and more passive look to an easier yet less acceptable way of gaining status. Havighurst and Stiles see the problem in this way:[1]

> An increasing minority of youth (15 per cent of the total population but as high as 40 per cent in given communities, depending upon their composition) fail to move satisfactorily toward competent adulthood and become so frustrated by negative influences in their homes and school environments that they rebel—thus they may be properly described as alienated. Such individuals have high potentiality for delinquency.
>
> Alienated youth can be identified with reasonable accuracy by the time they are ten to twelve years old.

1. Robert J. Havighurst and Lindley J. Stiles, *A Statement of National Policy for Alienated Youth* (reprinted from *Phi Delta Kappan*, April 1961).

In spite of the fact that alienated youth are or could be known by age twelve, previous efforts to provide them appropriate highways to competent adulthood have been concentrated on boys and girls of ages fifteen and sixteen and upward, the point at which they drop out of school. At this age, delinquency patterns have already been established.

These young people have the same goals as their associates. But for those associates, school is a means of reaching the goals. Most young persons want jobs and money. Earning a living—a symbol of success regardless of the route to employment—is a way of achieving status. Adolescents, like adults, want to dress appropriately and to acquire cars, television sets, and other material advantages of our high standard of living. Boys want girl friends, the chance to select a suitable one and to marry and raise a family. Girls want jobs, the chance to make friends and to earn money to increase their own attractiveness. Both dislike depending on their parents for handouts even if resources in the family permit.

What does the young person do when these desires are unsatisfied in either school activities or employment? This is the question that prompted Phi Delta Kappa, an educational fraternity, to appoint in 1960 a commission on juvenile delinquency. President Charles Foster charged the members of this commission to study the problem and to take whatever steps necessary to promote a program which would help to meet the needs of alienated youth.

The commission's first accomplishment was the issuance of "A Statement of National Policy for Alienated Youth." This prompted the decision to produce this casebook of outstanding school-related work programs for the purpose of stimulating school personnel throughout the country to expand existing programs and to create new ones. Fortunately, the Ford Foundation was sufficiently interested to grant the commission enough funds so that they could send qualified observers to each of the communities selected to analyze the worth of each program in depth.

The burgeoning population, the concentration of people in congested areas, the alarming number of school dropouts, and the explosiveness in juvenile crime have caused many agencies, institutions, and governmental units to become concerned. The federal government has already enacted legislation and appropriated funds to stimulate efforts to reduce juvenile delinquency. Phi Delta Kappa's commission on juvenile delinquency has decided to limit its activities to the school-related work-study program, recognizing that this is only one possible solution to a complicated problem. The commission believes that many young people now unsuccessful at school will live useful, productive lives if they are taught the values inherent in work and if job opportunities are provided. It hopes that these descriptions of work-study plans will focus attention on trends in our economy that are admittedly depriving youth of opportunities to attain acceptable goals.

The ingredients of a successful attempt to serve the work aspirations of unemployed youth in any community are, first, the imaginative leadership of schoolmen; second, the support of school boards; next, co-operation of management and labor; and last, the interest of parents and the respect and endorsement of the community. A variety of work-experience programs is needed. Some youth can profit from a term of duty in a live-in work camp. Others can best be served by a combination of part-school and part-work programs. Still others can profit from a full-time work program while living at home. The age, maturity, and needs of each adolescent should determine the type of program in which he is most likely to be successful. Certainly, interesting and rewarding activities can be offered those young persons now largely unstimulated by conventional academic school activities. Surely a variety of school-related work experience ought to be available for pupils at an earlier age.

In colonial times the ever present challenge to every family was to complete the chores of home and community in time to free the young for education. Today the challenge is how to retain in the daily activities of youth enough opportunity to work and to learn those values that derive from work. This is not a plea to return to the good old days, nor is there implied a return to the cumbersome, time-consuming labor of colonial times or to that period when the young of the nation were subject to exploitation. Our task is to apportion a share of the work of the world to our young persons under appropriate controls and in proper dimensions. There must exist a smooth transition from school to work and from work to school and a real recognition of the importance of each in meeting the needs of different individuals. Work experience is one way, the commission believes, of reducing the number of young persons who under present conditions are alienated.

> HOWARD C. SEYMOUR
> Cochairman,
> Phi Delta Kappa Commission on the
> Role of the School in the Prevention
> of Juvenile Delinquency

Table of Contents

CONTENTS

Introduction to the Cases

THE PROBLEM
OF JUVENILE DELINQUENCY

A recent public opinion poll has shown
juvenile delinquency to be among the three
top concerns of the American public.
Only defense and peace ranked higher.[1]

The above statement is not distorted. During recent years the rate of delinquency among the nation's youth has accelerated significantly. In 1957 the number of juvenile delinquency court cases was double that reported in 1948. More than 600,000 juvenile offenses were serious enough to require court action. They involved approximately half a million individual youngsters, or almost 2.3 per cent of all children living in the United States in the ten-to-seventeen-year age group.[2]

Review of data pertinent to delinquency and its recent emphasis reveals the existence of a real problem. The entire nation is concerned. Almost all communities have felt the impact of this social phenomenon. Police are handling more cases, juvenile detention homes are overcrowded, and retraining schools are taxed almost beyond capacity. Moreover, the rapid rise in the number of detected

1. Dorothy E. Bradbury, "The Children's Bureau and Juvenile Delinquency," *Juvenile Delinquency, Facts and Facets*, No. 1 (Washington, D.C.: Government Printing Office, 1960), p. 3.

2. Richard I. Pertman, "Delinquency Prevention," *Juvenile Delinquency, Facts and Facets*, No. 4 (Washington, D.C.: Government Printing Office, 1960), p. 3.

cases cannot be attributed solely to natural repercussions of an expanded youth population. The increase in the number of minors arrested by civil authorities has far outstripped the increase in the nation's youth population.[3]

Regardless of the approach to the situation, juvenile delinquency is one of the United States' most vexing problems. The behavior of this young population is a manifestation of some of society's pressures. To complicate the problem, delinquency among children cannot be easily anticipated or contained. It does not know any geographic boundaries. Despite its notoriety as primarily a big-city condition, it is recognized in more and more small communities, which are becoming aware of the appearance of unacceptable behavior among children. In 1957 and 1958 juvenile delinquency increased twice as fast in towns with populations of less than 25,000 as it did in more heavily populated communities.[4] Increased mobility of the nation's population, changes in group mores, and rapid transportation and communications compound the difficulty of confining such social problems to any locale. Delinquency as a national concern arises from the accumulated difficulties of countless towns and cities.

In addition to the known juvenile delinquents, a host of others remain undetected. Statistics indicate that as many as 1.7 million children come to police attention annually. About three-quarters of these youngsters, guilty of violations not warranting court action, are dealt with in a variety of ways receiving little publicity—referrals to local social agencies, for example.[5] Many of these youthful offenders are from middle- and higher-income-level families. Their presence in the huge group of the nation's potential delinquents points up the range of youngsters vulnerable to this bane of today's society.

Although the children should be the facet of the problem on which attention is focused, the enormous costs of juvenile delinquency also require attention. The Federal Bureau of Investigation estimates the cost of all crime in the United States to be $20 billion. Much of this amount is attributable directly to juvenile delinquency, since research indicates that most adult criminals possess records of crimes commited during their youth. The less obvious

---

3. *Ibid.*, p. 7.

4. *Report to the Congress on Juvenile Delinquency*, (Washington, D.C.: Government Printing Office, 1960), p. 4.

5. Pertman, *op. cit.*, p. 4.

costs of delinquency are even larger than the actual crime costs. Facilities and staffs serving delinquents—police courts, detention homes, and institutional physical equipment—add approximately $200 million to the total expense. Consider also the more than $115 million in annual losses experienced by the public in property damage resulting from destructive juvenile behavior and the staggering costs of delinquency are apparent.[6]

Not surprisingly, the combined monetary and personal costs— personal unhappiness, unproductive years, family distress—have caused the public to note the alarming spread of juvenile delinquency between 1950 and 1960. Concern is so widespread and intense that Congress itself has been studying the problem. In the 1959 session more than twenty bills concerned with various aspects of juvenile delinquency were introduced.[7] The appearance of congressional fact-gathering committees and federal laws pertaining to juvenile delinquency cannot be viewed as unusual. Throughout United States history, social problems commonly become national issues whenever they grow beyond local and state control. Juvenile delinquency has reached this level.

HISTORICAL PERSPECTIVE OF JUVENILE DELINQUENCY IN THE UNITED STATES

Juvenile delinquency in America is not a new development. In colonial days it appeared in the form of "unruly, vicious and criminal children."[8] In keeping with the rigid puritanical views of the era, youthful offenders were subject to the same penalties as adults. Confinement of children along with grownups in prisons and workshops was common. They were treated as "miniature adults" until well into the 1800's. Fortunately, the impact of America's reform movement did much to change such harsh methods. Gradually, through the efforts of early leaders, society's concept of justice for juveniles was altered. Young criminals began to be recognized as children requiring treatment different from that of adults.

New correctional institutions for children appeared as the first signs of this new movement's progress. In 1825, New York City's House of Refuge for Children became a model looked to by other

---

6. *Ibid.*, p. 8.
7. Bradbury, *op. cit.*, p. iii.
8. *Report to the Congress on Juvenile Delinquency*, p. 7.

communities. Massachusetts established one patterned after it in 1847, and by 1875 most of the states had similar institutions for delinquent girls and boys. Unfortunately, these facilities were far from today's ideal. Their major function was confinement rather than rehabilitation. Hiding society's ills was still the accepted method of handling such social problems. These early institutions stood for hard work and rigid discipline. Wrongdoers were regarded as needing punishment rather than help. Despite the inadequacies as measured by present standards, the children's homes of the 1800's were nevertheless a real improvement over the prisons of the preceding period. Their acceptance by the public was a major step in improving the plight of America's maladjusted young people.

A noteworthy advance in the legal handling of delinquents occurred in 1899, when Illinois enacted the first juvenile court law in the United States.[9] The law held that treatment of delinquent youngsters should be similar to that of neglected or dependent children. Furthermore, the statute stated specifically that the circumstances leading to a child's appearance in court required that the child be treated with understanding and be guided and protected rather than punished or blamed. Illinois' concern for the lot of socially outcast boys and girls led the way to rapid improvement in the juvenile delinquency laws of other states.

National attention began to be focused on incorrigible children as a result of interest by individual states. In February 1909, hearings began in Washington regarding the need for a federal bureau devoted to children and their concerns. Distinguished Americans such as Jane Addams spoke in its behalf. She stressed the importance of establishing such a bureau primarily for the implications it would have in the field of combating juvenile delinquency. William James, dean of American philosophers, also supported the establishment of such a bureau. In his arguments for it, he urged the use of "work corps" to channel the vitality and enthusiasm of problem youth into acceptable paths.[10]

The early decades of the twentieth century witnessed an awakened interest in crime among children. The influence of Jane Addams and William James helped change attitudes. People began to view juvenile delinquency as a social problem rather than a criminal one. Changes in the thinking of many citizens led the way to changing "reform" schools into training schools charged with a

9. Bradbury, *op. cit.*, p. 1.

10. *Report to the Congress on Juvenile Delinquency*, p. 11.

rehabilitative function. State laws pertaining to those institutions and the children to be served by them appeared in such great numbers that by 1917 only three states did not have laws relating to juvenile criminals and juvenile court procedures.

The nation's awareness of juvenile problems and of improved methods of combating them came none too soon. Post-World War I days were characterized by a sharp rise in juvenile delinquency in America; the 1920's were fraught with difficulties with children and the law. This was an era somewhat comparable to the present one— a period of postwar prosperity and rising living standards resulting from rapid advancements in science and technology, rural-to-urban population shifts, and increased emphasis on material goals and possessions.[11] During these turbulent days the federal Children's Bureau, under the direction of Grace Abbott, led the way in researching the causes of juvenile delinquency and the methods for its prevention. This office, established by Congress in 1912 as a result of the recognition "that children are the most important of the Nation's resources and that the Government should foster their development and protection,"[12] acted as a clearinghouse to disseminate information about delinquency to agencies and individuals concerned with young offenders. It paid particular attention to non-juvenile court procedures involving children. Some of the findings reached by Miss Abbott and her dedicated staff led them to conclude that "much yet remains to be done if the ideal of the juvenile court movement—that delinquent children are to be placed under redeeming and not degrading influences—is to be realized."[13]

The influence of the bureau continued well into the depression days of the 1930's. Increased problems appeared, created by hundreds of thousands of adolescents and young adults experiencing the traumata of home environments blighted by the effects of widespread unemployment. Social and moral hazards threatened the nation's children. Concern heightened to the point that congressional investigating committees, at the urging of the Children's Bureau, established work for this endangered population by creating the Civilian Conservation Corps and the National Youth Administration.[14] These government agencies helped establish prototypes for school-work programs of later eras. In fact, the government's

---

11. *Ibid.*, p. 20.
12. Bradbury, *op. cit.*, p. 6.
13. *Ibid.*, p. 6.
14. *Ibid.*, pp. 8–9.

continued influence on delinquency prevention can be traced to this period when the Justice Department established a commission on juvenile delinquency. This group was maintained throughout the 1940's as an advisory resource for legislation relating to delinquency.[15] National groups have done much to educate the public about causes of delinquency and effective methods for combating its development. Such knowledge, unfortunately, is not complete. While research has been done on the problem, more is needed before juvenile delinquency in the United States can be understood completely.

POSSIBLE CAUSES OF DELINQUENCY

Delinquency among children has been attributed to numerous causes. Some investigators contend that it stems from foundational imbalances in society; others consider it an exaggerated development of the adolescent maturation process; still others reason that it is a form of mental illness, emanating from parent-child disharmony or psychological imbalance within the organism.[16]

Identifying the cause of behavior is always difficult. In the case of juvenile delinquency, this is especially true. The difficulty, however, has not deterred researchers from studying the phenomenon. Some of their findings are helpful to persons interested in preventing delinquency; other findings do not lend themselves to practical application. For the most part, conclusions reached by investigators still require subjective evaluation to determine their reliability and validity. With these considerations noted, attention can be better focused on causes of juvenile delinquency.

In support of societal imbalance as a causal factor, research indicates that juvenile delinquency rates are highest in deteriorated areas of large cities. In this climate, many sociologists maintain, subcultures of youth of low-income families are formed. These groups appear, they reason, as members' reactions to their deprived societal state. Seemingly rejected by the larger society, youngsters develop values differing from those of the middle and upper classes. This value system, in many instances, is established by young persons who stress the importance of antisocial acts considered delinquent by the prevailing culture. Thus, in the underprivileged en-

---

15. *Report to the Congress on Juvenile Delinquency*, p. 8.
16. *Ibid.*, p. 20.

vironment, delinquency might be considered as behavior patterns established by maladjusted children expressing their basic conflicts with their society.[17] This partial explanation of delinquency among deprived children, however, does not appear to be equally valid when applied to more privileged youngsters.

Increasingly, the fact that delinquency in the United States is not limited to the lower classes is being recognized. Recent studies conducted with sample populations of college students and young adults living substantial community roles revealed that almost two-thirds of the group had at some time committed acts classed as felonies under their state statutes.[18] Explanations for such findings are not readily apparent. Some authorities consider the appearance of maladjustment in well-to-do youngsters a reflection of their parents' emphasis on material and occupational progress. Such parental values, in homes lacking strong family bonds, may be a cause for misbehavior in certain children. Also, evidence suggests that many middle-class children emulate the behavior patterns of their less privileged peers for thrills. This rebellion against adults is most likely to be expressed by children whose parents' standards of conduct are inconsistent with their own behavior, or whose homes possess two social standards: one for children and another for adults.[19]

Erik Erikson, a psychoanalyst noted for his research in child development and anthropology, offers reasons for believing that delinquency stems from distorted developmental patterns in youth. At a conference held by the Children's Bureau in May 1955, he proposed the thesis that personality development evolves through a series of childhood psychosocial crises. Each of these traumatic events stems from the individual's biological and social needs to sense himself and his environment. Avoidance of such experiences, he believes, may jeopardize the proper psychological development of the individual.[20] Consequently, adolescence, commonly characterized by biological turmoil and social confusion, is a crucial time in a child's development into adulthood. Erikson contends that a child, during this phase, needs to reconcile his self-concept of what he is with his vision of what he is to be as an adult. In addition, he must reconcile his image as perceived by himself with the image as he imag-

---

17. *Ibid.*, pp. 5–7.

18. Pertman, *op. cit.*, pp. 6–7.

19. *Report to the Congress on Juvenile Delinquency*, p. 20.

20. Helen L. Witmer, "Delinquency and the Adolescent Crisis," *Juvenile Delinquency, Facts and Facets*, No. 11 (Washington, D.C.: Government Printing Office, 1960), pp. 1–2.

ines others perceive it. The struggle to achieve acceptable self-understandings and role acceptance may result in extreme and even bizarre behavior by some youngsters. In some cases it might take the form of delinquent behavior adopted to experiment with adult expectations. In other words, a search for identity during the adolescent years may cause certain children to perform antisocial roles as compensation for their inability to perform satisfactorily in acceptable roles relegated to them by their society.

In addition, as Havighurst points out, "the turmoil and conflict which accompany the adolescent crisis is further complicated by the task of achieving emotional independence of parents and other adults, making it difficult for the adolescent to rely on these older sources for guidance."[21] Thus, during these transitional years children may find themselves unable to accept adult leadership, yet unable to lead. Behavior based on confused understanding of role may easily become unacceptable. Furthermore, in recent years, adults' overconcern with the adolescent role often pressures some youngsters into a premature experimentation with negative roles. If left to their own concerns, perhaps more children might experiment with roles, either intellectually or through experience, prior to crystallizing their values.

The final interpretation of delinquent behavior as a manifestation of poor mental health of some children is clarified somewhat in this quotation from a joint report to Congress by the National Institute of Mental Health and the Children's Bureau.

> Psychological difficulties of youth and delinquent behavior are related and overlapping areas; but they are not the same thing. Psychological disturbance is a cause for only a proportion, and it must be said an undetermined proportion, of all delinquency. Some delinquency is "normal" in that it develops out of identifications which children make with their own neighborhood or groups within it. There are groups that are rebellious and defiant toward the norms and life patterns which the majority in the adult community accepts for itself and proposes as models for children and youth. Immediate rewards and psychological satisfaction of acceptance by their peers lead children and youth under such conditions to participate in what . . . may be delinquent behavior on a basis that is quite understandable in terms of the individual's sense of personal worth.

> On the other hand, some kinds of psychological disturbance can predispose children and youth toward delinquent behavior. The child who has been subjected to hostility, rejection, or other unfavorable adult attitudes

---

21. Robert J. Havighurst, *Development Tasks and Education* (New York: David McKay & Co., 1948), p. 242.

toward him may learn to hate and mistrust the adult world. . . . His method of attack may take the form of violating the norms society officially protects; thus, he becomes a delinquent.[22]

The difficulty of identifying the causes leading children to delinquent behavior varies with authorities and research findings. Common elements of cause, however, do predominate in the three major approaches to explaining antisocial behavior of some young people. For those unable to accept any of the three noted explanations, synthesis of segments from the pure theories is possible. The eclectic consideration of the cause of delinquency appears to have most meaning for school people concerned with its prevention. As an example, here is the way in which personnel of the Kansas City School District (a description of their school-work experiment is included in this casebook) summarized the cause of delinquency.

A chain of circumstances which makes a juvenile delinquent appears to be the following:

1. Boys want to grow up so as to gain the rewards of manhood, as well as to satisfy the expectations of their families and teachers and friends. They see before them two alternative patterns of adult success: (a) a steady job, good pay, automobile, girl friends or wife, etc.; (b) progress through high school which leads to (a) or progress through high school and college leading to (a). The channel through school is becoming more and more the *only* avenue to successful status. Boys see fewer and fewer young men getting a good job, etc., without high school graduation. All kinds of boys want the status of young manhood with job, money, etc. Some boys want the job and the money as soon as possible. Other boys are content to wait for these things while taking a slow journey through high school and college. Lower-class boys tend to want the job and the adult status as early as possible.

2. Certain boys have difficulty in growing up through the channel offered by the school. About 15 per cent of all boys fall in this group. They tend to have below-average intellectual ability, to come from lower-class homes, and to have a history of failure and misbehavior in school. By the age of thirteen or fourteen they are generally quite clearly visible to teachers and to their agemates. As recently as 1930, most of these boys could quit school and go to work in the city or on a farm, with a reasonably clear pathway for growth into manhood ahead of them. But the changes in employment opportunity for boys since 1920 have blocked this avenue of growth. In that year, 48 per cent of boys aged fourteen to seventeen in Chicago were employed. In 1940, only 10 per cent of boys in this age range were employed, and that proportion is even smaller today.

---

22. *Report to the Congress on Juvenile Delinquency*, p. 2.

3. These boys react to their failure to grow up successfully through the school in two ways: (a) They look for alternative pathways to adulthood with little success. They seek jobs but have difficulty in finding and holding them. They secure automobiles and other symbols of manly status as early as possible. (For instance, there is the Montana study in which it was found that most high-school-age boys who owned cars were from working-class families and were failing in school.) (b) Alternatively, they seek certain gratifications that make their failure to grow up more tolerable, such as the excitement of fighting and drinking, the "easy" profits of stealing, and sexual activities. These activities do not help them grow up, but they fill the gap of the adolescent years until the boys become old enough and mature enough to make some sort of adult adjustment.[23]

The school's awareness of the danger of delinquency among youth is not enough. Knowledge of the causes is necessary. Armed with such knowledge, education can help prevent development of antisocial behavior in children. The role of the school in the process is an important one. During recent years, schools have assumed leadership. The history of work-study education programs is ample evidence of American education's willingness to accept such responsibilities.

SOME EFFORTS TO MEET THE PROBLEMS OF JUVENILE DELINQUENCY

Many, including Erikson, contend that juvenile delinquency is overemphasized in American culture. Erikson further maintains that society is too eager to assign the label of delinquent to almost any deviant adolescent behavior.[24] Many juveniles, he states, act out personal conflicts in unacceptable ways or experiment with roles branded by adults as delinquent. The emphasis on such ephemeral occurrences causes some children to adopt behavior patterns consistent with the self-concepts these pressures impose on them. Research indicates that much adolescent misbehavior is most appropriate to their developmental growth. In a sense, reality testing by defying adult authority can be considered a normal transitory phase of maturation even among youngsters of the slum subcultures that harbor the bulk of the nation's bona fide delinquents. This is not to suggest that society should approve the transgres-

---

23. School District of Kansas City, "A Work-Study Program To Reduce Juvenile Delinquency, Kansas City Public Schools" (December 12, 1960), p. 17.

24. Witmer, op. cit., p. 4.

sions of the young. Rather, adults should know causes of children's misbehavior and should maintain in proper perspective both the emphasis on the offending acts and the punishment meted out for these acts.

Society's charge to respond to youth's problems in a constructive way also carries with it preventive responsibilities. Maladjustment of young people is caused. Delinquent behavior, as a by-product of disorder in the young person's psychological constitution, can foretell offenses. Consequently, an alert population must anticipate the dangers faced by their progeny. Continual research aimed at understanding the cause of alienation among children should be encouraged. Adolescents must be helped to meet the problems associated with their developing self-concepts. They must also be assisted to channel their energies into acceptable outlets within their environment. Youngsters need sensitive adult assistance to develop attitudes that will encourage a satisfactory transition to adult life. Such a preventive approach can enhance successful development of individual youngsters and the total society.

Work-study education is an accepted method of helping alienated young people to achieve satisfactory adjustment during adolescence. Curriculums based on academic preparation and supervised work experience can satisfy some adolescents' needs for recognition. In these programs, youngsters may develop feelings of individuality by occupying roles meaningful to themselves, to their peers, and to adults. Identification with work may provide many youngsters with an avenue for recognizing their approaching maturity with its concomitant responsibilities. The maturation process may be enhanced by appropriate personal and educational-vocational preparation.[25]

Various work-experience programs are offered in the United States. Many are aimed at providing worthwhile experiences for nondelinquents as well as delinquents. They are offered to young persons at many age levels. For example, at the elementary school level, a systematic plan of regular work that some hundred boys and girls perform at home is guided by Potomac State College educators.[26] Many programs exist on the junior and senior high school levels. Besides those included in this casebook, countless schools offer varied programs. Some are well known: Detroit's Job Upgrading Program, Philadelphia's Youth Achievement Plan, and Baltimore's program are examples.

---

25. *Ibid.*, p. 6.
26. Lindley J. Stiles, "Work-Experience Programs of the United States" (address presented at Work-Study Program of Kansas City Schools, August 14, 1961), p. 32.

Work-education programs not associated with schools also merit attention. Many have a philosophical base providing for non-alienated as well as maladjusted children. Camps for delinquent youth have been patterned after the Civilian Conservation Corps of depression days.[27] The camps' success hinged on informal organization. Young men could study academic subjects and involve themselves in physical tasks to gain good work habits and proper attitudes toward themselves, their fellows, and their authority figures. The value of these experiences convinced federal and state agencies that camp environments helped rehabilitate young offenders. At present, year-round camps for delinquent youth are operated by fifteen states and the federal government.[28] Other camps are provided for both nondelinquent and delinquency-prone youngsters. Michigan's work camps for nondelinquents are widely known, as are the California rehabilitation camps for delinquent youth. Some camps, such as the Shaker Village Work Camp and those maintained by the American Friends Service Committee, stress community service and recreation.[29]

Varied philosophies of the cause and cure of delinquency give rise to varied techniques to help youth adjust within their society. Many of the effective techniques need exploration. Attention, however, must be turned to this study's objectives: to explore briefly the rationale behind programs of education and work for alienated youngsters as a preventive or rehabilitative experience, and to present examples of school-affiliated work-study programs.

SCHOOL-RELATED WORK-STUDY PROGRAMS

Social and civic agencies are rapidly becoming unable to cope with the numbers of juveniles needing attention. The agencies are, for the most part, understaffed and possess inadequate facilities. Specialized personnel are their greatest need. Between 1952 and 1957 the number of juvenile probation officers in the United States increased 46 per cent while juvenile delinquency increased 82 per cent.[30] These particular staff shortages are not the only ones add-

---

27. George H. Weber, *Camps for Delinquent Boys* (Washington, D.C.: Government Printing Office, 1960), p. 1.

28. Stiles, *op. cit.*, p. 25.

29. *Ibid.*, p. 24.

30. *Report to the Congress on Juvenile Delinquency*, p. 8.

ing to the problem. Psychiatrists, psychologists, and social workers are also in short supply. The severity of the need is evident in this statement made by Mrs. Katherine B. Oettinger, chief of the Children's Bureau:

> The states are falling further and further behind in dealing with delinquency. Everywhere existing programs in local communities need strengthening. As a country, we are confronted with an almost total lack of training on the part of personnel already employed in serving delinquent youth. And, in addition, no pool of trained workers exists to fill vacancies, and the lack of training resources contributes a major roadblock in improving the quality of existing services.[31]

Shortages in the number of agencies and professional staff workers to combat juvenile delinquency have created a new conceptual trend relating to socially maladjusted children. The nation is turning its attention to noncorrective methods of preventing the rise of new crops of delinquents. With a philosophy of prevention and rehabilitation as a foundation, schools have been singled out to help improve the condition of the nation's young people. The school, after all, is the social institution most appropriate for implementing this objective. Schools have helped attain this goal in the past and promise to make even greater contributions in the future. The way in which schools appear to be best able to prevent certain youngsters from developing delinquent behavior patterns is through curriculums combining work and study.

Work-study programs in American public schools are not new. Earlier in this section, a number of cities were cited because they have effective programs. Many more exist. Some 1500 U.S. school districts offer some form of work-study program as a part of their curriculum. The philosophies, structures, and methods vary widely. A few programs are primarily aimed at preventing delinquency; more are less specific in their approach.

In view of the small number of programs designed to meet the unique needs of alienated youth, the commission on juvenile delinquency of Phi Delta Kappa has called the nation's attention to the plight of alienated children and to the importance of school-related work-study programs in rehabilitating them.

Defining its terms, the commission suggests that work-study programs should meet the criteria listed in 1957 by DeWitt Hunt:

> The student performs socially useful tasks at a level of proficiency commensurate with his own highest ability.

---

31. Bradbury, *op. cit.*, p. 30.

The work performed is supervised by a qualified school official.

Credit is based on both quantitative and qualitative judgments of the work done, and it is granted toward high school graduation; it thus becomes part of the student's personnel record.

The work-experience for credit must be gained during school-released time.

The student may or may not receive remuneration for the work done.

The co-ordinator or supervisor should meet the students enrolled in the work-experience program in a special class in which problems of public relations and job success are considered.

Local, state, and federal labor laws and regulations pertaining to the employment of youth are observed.

Care is taken that no exploitation of student labor results.

The controlling purposes of work-experience programs may range from guidance and general education to vocational education for a specific occupation.[32]

The commission has added these criteria:

It will commence at age thirteen or fourteen and continue to age eighteen, though many boys will graduate from it a year or two before age eighteen.

It will attempt to teach boys elementary work disciplines: punctuality, ability to take orders from a boss, ability to work co-operatively with others in a team, responsibility on the job.

It will lead directly into stable adult jobs.

It will be part of the public school program, with the curriculum adapted to the intellectual level, the interest in practical endeavors, and the work-experience program of alienated youth.[33]

Furthermore, the commission recommends that programs be organized into stages commensurate with children's maturation levels. It suggests the inclusion of three stages:

The first stage would be to work in groups, under school supervision, completely or partially outside of the labor market. For example, boys might work in groups in parks, school grounds, alleys, beaches, thus contributing to community housekeeping. Or boys might work in a "sheltered workshop" in the school, which would contract for jobs with local business and industry, e.g., stuffing envelopes with advertising

---

32. DeWitt Hunt, *Work-Experience Education Programs in American Schools* (Bulletin 1957, No. 5, U. S. Department of Health, Education, and Welfare, Washington, D.C.), p. 8.

33. Robert J. Havighurst and Lindley J. Stiles, "A Statement of National Policy for Alienated Youth," *Phi Delta Kappan*, April 1961, p. 289.

material; simple assembly jobs, such as collecting nuts and bolts into packages for sales; processing material with a simple machine. The difficulty with the sheltered workshop idea for boys is that similar facilities are badly needed for handicapped adults and for old people who need employment.

A second stage should be part-time work on an individual basis with employers in private or public business or industry. Here the boys would be more nearly "on their own" in the labor market, but they would still work under close supervision by the school.

The final stage would be full-time employment in a stable job, aided by some guidance and supervision on the part of school or employment service personnel.

The corollary school program provided for alienated youth would need to be adapted, in content, methods of instruction, and learning materials, to the ability and orientation of youth involved. The content would need to be appropriate to the goals of instruction and to the age level of the pupils. At the same time it would, in most cases, need to be presented in textbooks and other learning materials at a lower reading level, and with less abstractness, than is common for high school courses. Instruction would need to be characterized by practical approaches to problems, shop or laboratory experience, and an extensive use of audio-visual aids. A close relationship between the program of the school and work experiences would be desirable.[34]

The commission, aware that suggestions are sometimes difficult to comprehend without illustration, selected the following nine cases as examples of existing work-study programs that incorporate within their design, function, or operation many of the elements necessary for successful work-study programs for alienated youth.

---

34. *Ibid.*

CASE ONE: *Flint, Michigan*

The Community Schools, Flint, Michigan

THE JUNIOR HIGH SCHOOL
REHABILITATION PROGRAM

THE VOLUNTARY
WORK-EDUCATION PROJECT
FOR HIGH SCHOOL DROPOUTS

Two rehabilitative programs for alienated youth
presented as examples of services
offered to a community by a board of education
combining with a philanthropic foundation
for the purpose of using the public schools
to intensify and expand opportunities
in education, health, and recreation
for each of its citizens

Two experimental work-study programs in Flint community schools exemplify new approaches to rehabilitating alienated children. The Junior High School Rehabilitation Program is designed to replace the traditional work-study program functioning in the Flint schools since 1954. Its objective is to rehabilitate alienated boys and girls by helping them change their attitudes and behavior so that they can attend regular school classes. The procedure is to remove alienated youth from regular classes and to reschedule them into special classes meeting at the end of the normal school day. The aim in these classes is to help the youngsters attain desired behavior through counseling by teams of professional staff members. According to the rationale, after-school classes permit the fullest utilization of the school's physical facilities and personnel. When youngsters acquire realistic self-understandings and appreciation of their responsibilities to others, they resume regular study programs during school hours.

The second program—The Voluntary Work-Education Project for High School Dropouts—is a continuation of the work-study program that provides practical methods of helping sixteen- to twenty-year-old dropouts become employable, find jobs, and become self-supporting workers. To attain such goals, the schools provide daily classes where students improve their educational level while working on jobs to upgrade themselves for future employment. The flexible curriculum provides individual instruction and counseling for each participant. On-the-job training is gained on part-time community work assignments. Constant supervision by school personnel and community employers helps students develop good work habits and healthy attitudes toward themselves and others. Placement assistance for either part-time or full-time work is provided. Finally, through student follow-up, school personnel offer children the final support necessary for their successful transition to work roles. Both programs are small but important parts of Flint's community schools. They reflect the system's philosophy of education that has as its basic premise community betterment through improvement of individual citizens.

Flint is virtually a one-industry city, since 82,000 of its 200,000 residents work in General Motor's factories. In the expanding metropolitan center of almost 300,000 persons, the people are of many different ethnic and racial backgrounds, representing more than 50 distinct national groups. About 12 per cent of the population is Negro. A large proportion of the citizens is transient. High rates of in- and out-migration started in the stark depression days when in one four-year period Flint experienced a complete turnover of one-third of its population. While today's residents are not nearly as mobile as formerly, people in certain sections of the city are still highly mobile. During the 1960-61 school term, for instance, one attendance district had a 100 per cent pupil change.

In a city characterized by diversity in its people and lack of diversity in its economy, any approach to strengthening community life should not lie in accenting existing conditions. Rather, a unifying philosophy stressing integration of individuals into the community is appropriate. Such is the belief of Flint's citizens: improving themselves and their living conditions through a total community approach. Their program of total community betterment has numberless goals, including

> improving the quality and variety of education offered to children and adults; providing more effective programs of health and recreation; enriching personal and social life in the community; and developing a deeper sense of personal identity, responsibility, and commitment to the community and its many complex problems of adjustment and growth.[1]

An ongoing objective of the Flint schools is to reduce or eliminate alienation among children. Because of their philosophy, this goal is not primary. The people of Flint do not believe social problems can be sliced into easy-to-get-at projects. They believe total community improvement is obtained by uplifting each individual. Betterment may take the form of helping someone experience intellectual stimulation, gain physical or mental health, or progress economically. Their philosophy holds that eventual reflections of an individual citizen's improvement are seen in eventual reduction of civic and social problems. The institution they use to achieve their objectives is the community school.

Flint's community school concept started in 1935 when Charles S. Mott, wealthy industrialist and former mayor of Flint, donated $6000 to the Flint Board of Education. The money was used to make five schools' facilities available to children and adults during early evening hours. The first participants' enthusiasm convinced Mott that the residents were eager for such help. As a result, he established the Mott Foundation to make money available for—

> Making possible experimental pilot programs without using tax money until they have proved themselves to be beneficial. Successful programs would be taken over by other agencies or supported by regular school taxes.
>
> Establishing and sustaining special community services and community school programs. These would include enrichment classes for children; adult education offerings; a school-community health program; a children's health center and dental clinic; a community-wide recreation program; youth service programs; a co-operative safety program; and individual community activities at each school.[2]

The Mott Foundation became a partner with the Flint Board of Education in community improvement. From the modest initial

---

1. *The Community School in Action: The Flint Program* (a joint project of the Mott Foundation and the University of Chicago), Preface I.

2. Board of Education, *Flint Community Schools*, p. 3.

grant of $6000, foundation contributions reached $1 million of the 1961 school budget of $15 million.

The philosophy underlying the Mott Program of the Flint Board of Education resulted from the community's awareness that it possessed social problems of varying degrees of intensity. Crime, juvenile delinquency, mental illness, broken homes, racial and religious prejudices among its citizenry, and school dropouts were just a few. The solutions, in Flint as in many other places, often seemed impossible to achieve because of citizens' apathy. Often suitable personal and material resources went unused. Therefore, the board adopted the approach of using the schools—established and accepted institutions—to improve the community by educating people of all ages to understand the problems with which they were confronted. With such understanding, the schools could also provide professional people to help identify the city's problems and deal with them. Thus, they believed the community could be improved through education. Such a philosophy is based on the assumption that problems of a community, state, or nation are the problems of human relations. The philosophy is most evident in the adoption of the term *community school*. Its definition in Flint is consistent with that recognized by Michigan educators:

> The community school recognizes that education cannot be separated from the influences of community life. It is the responsibility of the community school to improve the community—the quality of living—in order to improve the quality of education. . . . The community school differs from the traditional school in the degree to which programs in curriculum and extended services to the community actually reflect the belief in and the use of the schools as an agency for community improvement—in the neighborhood, state, national or international community.[3]

The philosophy sets the program's objectives. Education is the core and the process by which the philosophy is implemented.

Education, therefore, is the basis for these objectives:

Education knows no age limits, no racial or social barriers, no point of perfection.

Education is the privilege of all, the property of him who seeks it.

Education is the means of understanding our fellow man, the hope of assisting him.

Education holds the answer to all personal and community problems.[4]

---

3. Michigan Association of School Administrators, Community School Committee, *Developing Community Schools in Michigan* (1959–60), p. 2.

4. Board of Education, *Flint Community Schools*, p. 1.

In effect, the philosophy recognizes the values of a community as the values of people. To implement their philosophy, Flint's leaders determined to turn the public elementary schools into community schools, relatively small social units with which inhabitants of the sprawling city could identify themselves. They were to be places where individuals could learn about themselves, about their fellow humans, and about the ways in which they might work together. Some of the specific reasons given by the Flint officials for the selection of the public school system to be the community schools are these:

> The public school has played a traditional role of common denominator in our society.
>
> The physical plans of schools are ideally suited for community education, recreation, and other services. Representing as they do a huge community investment of tax dollars, their use avoids costly duplication of facilities.
>
> If experimental programs can be proved feasible within a public school system, the transition from a private support is relatively easy. Public schools are geographically located to serve as natural, accessible neighborhood centers.[5]

The Mott Program operates through existing facilities. Each of the forty community schools is used as a center providing educational and recreational programs for all ages.

The school programs differ, since they are based on the desires of the people. As a result, the community program has many facets. It was developed over the years and is in constant flux. Flint recognizes that a community's requirements vary with time and individuals, and that its entire program of education must likewise fluctuate.

Descriptions of the programs available would fill the balance of this casebook, and undoubtedly another one. Flint's philosophy is, however, that through its total community approach it reaches and does something with its alienated youngsters. The contention is that any contact with family members is an avenue of communication permitting alienated youth to be drawn within reach of the community schools. The following programs are the two phases of education designed especially to provide alienated young people with school-work experience: The Junior High School Rehabilitation Program and the Voluntary Work-Education Project.

---

5. *Ibid.*, p. 4.

THE JUNIOR HIGH SCHOOL REHABILITATION PROGRAM

This program was developed to replace a project in effect in Flint schools since 1954. The original program provided work experience for junior and senior high school boys identified as potential dropouts. The curriculum consisted of basic school subjects adapted to students' interests and levels. Subjects were taught in conjunction with work experience in the school district. The boys attended morning classes and worked for the remainder of the school day at activities such as refinishing school furniture, building instructional aids, and maintenance tasks that included cleaning, painting, and laying brick or cement blocks. The program was tried in six junior high schools and in two senior high schools. Approximately thirty boys were involved each year.

In 1960 a school committee surveyed the program and determined that it was worthwhile. Boys' school attendance had improved and participants had learned certain work skills and proper habits of work. Few boys had dropped out either through court action or voluntarily. The committee concluded, however, that the project was limited. Members contended that physical facilities were inadequate and that the professional staff was restricted, both in number of persons and in the variety of competencies. Finally, they recognized that the program was not providing for enough boys and did not include any provisions for alienated girls.

The Junior High School Rehabilitation Program, proposed to replace the work-study curriculum, was based on the premise that shortages of classrooms and the problems of co-ordinating efforts of staff members had prevented the operation of effective work-study curriculums during the regular school hours. Since conditions were not expected to improve, the committee suggested establishment of an after-school rehabilitation program. In the new plan, students would report to school at the beginning of the first afternoon instructional period. During the afternoon they would study regular nonacademic courses: physical education, industrial arts, shop, music, arts and crafts, and homemaking. After school the alienated youngsters would report to special double-period classes where instruction would be in two core areas: reading-English-social studies and mathematics-science-health. Instruction would utilize any acceptable methods, depending on the number and kinds of students and the teachers' skills. Ideally, the program would be flexible, with constant focus on class members' needs. Rather than be subject-centered, it would keynote individualized instruction.

A significant advantage of the plan as proposed is that many resource people would be able to participate in teams working with alienated youth. Teachers of the special classes would co-ordinate the teams, assuming responsibilities for seeking the services of counselors, deans, administrative staff members, and other classroom teachers to make up the teams. Since the work would take place in late afternoons, the individuals would be more readily available to participate than if work-study activities were carried on during the regular school day. Team members would pool information for the teachers. Thus, a teacher would present a case, work it through with the team, and use their suggestions in his work with the pupils.

The general objective of the program is to help each child change attitudes and behavior sufficiently to permit his resumption of a regular school program. There is no time limit for the rehabilitation process. Specifically, the objectives are to help each child attain:

Improved attitudes toward community and self

Improved basic academic skills

Improved social skills—appearance, manners, speech, and social participation

Flint school officials believe the number of students eligible for the program is a small proportion of the junior high school enrollment. As a function of the small number and in accord with the philosophy of individualized instruction and guidance, class sizes are to be limited to no more than fifteen students.

To be eligible for the program, students must be referred by classroom teachers, administrators, or members of regional counseling teams.[6] According to the plan, referred boys and girls would be screened by committees in each junior high school, composed of the dean of counseling, dean of students, visiting teacher, police counselors, nurses, referring teacher, and the teacher of the special class. Approval also must come from the director of pupil personnel services for the Flint Community Schools. Parents must grant their approval as the final step in the process.

Pupils enrolled in any other special program will not be eligible for the work-study curriculum. Likewise, mentally handicapped children are not eligible.

---

6. In Flint, greater utilization of professional staff people is accomplished by assigning guidance personnel, special teachers, nurses, attendance officers, principals, and other professionals to regional teams that pool their resources in staffing cases of any students in their high school, junior high school, or elementary district.

Teachers of the special classes would be selected, the plan states, from the junior high school faculty. The criteria to be used in selecting them, ranked in order of importance, include:

Personality characteristics (sensitivity to individual student needs, patience, sense of humor, sincerity, friendliness, adaptability)

Job competence (skill in language arts and arithmetic skills, creativeness, enthusiasm, ability to handle problem boys and girls)

The teachers in each junior high school would be selected by committees consisting of the principal, dean of counseling, dean of students, and a Flint Board of Education consultant.

Teachers selected would undergo in-service training in workshops devoted to particular sections of the curriculum as well as in periodic conferences with specialists in reading, arithmetic, and guidance.

The program would be evaluated twice each semester. The screening committee would review the students' progress. Mid-term evaluation would consist of subjective appraisals of each student by the special teacher regarding the child's attitudes toward work, school, and classmates. The final evaluation would include measurement by appropriate standardized tests of each youth's achievement in basic skills. Changes in students' attitudes and social behavior would be judged by all the school personnel involved in each school's program. The final test of the program's effectiveness would be measured by the number of students successfully rehabilitated. To qualify under this definition, students would have to resume regular study programs and pursue them successfully without unusual staff assistance.

THE VOLUNTARY WORK-EDUCATION PROJECT

This is another experimental program, established in 1961 to help sixteen- to twenty-year-old dropouts become employable, responsible citizens. The Flint Board of Education recognizes the school dropout as a critical community problem. Such children, the board asserts, possess fewer qualifications than their contemporaries for a labor market requiring individuals to have more education and more salable skills. A school dropout can rarely compete for other than unskilled entrance jobs. Dropouts frequently advance beyond alienated stages of behavior into stages that are without question socially unacceptable. In 1960, for example, a study of early school leavers was conducted by school officials, personnel of the Michigan Employment Security Commission, and community leaders. This group concluded that school dropouts should be encouraged to return to school where an instructional work-study program would enable them to upgrade themselves in their work roles.

The program developed from the committee's findings places special emphasis on two areas: school-job adjustment and work experience.

School-Job Adjustment Training

This phase involves informal classes conducted for daily three-hour periods. Classwork consists of a curriculum based on vocational objectives. Activities such as training in how to prepare for a job interview, filling out application forms, and role playing in job interviews are stressed. Emphasis is on the importance of personal grooming, the development of social graces, and the practice of wise health measures. Discussion guides and units are constructed to help students learn to appreciate the values of work and their contributions to society. All students continue their academic preparation by enrolling in either senior high school or adult classes.

Work Experience

This portion consists of practical, subsidized work experience. School personnel locate community employers who provide supervised work experience for the dropouts. Each job is set up on a six-week minimum time schedule. The employer pays each student regular wages. Jobs include clerical assistant, institutional aid, custodian, cafeteria helper, stock clerk, and assignments associated with service and unskilled trades. Specific job training is not a primary goal. Instead, jobs are selected to help dropouts develop desirable work habits applicable to any work situation.

The instructor conducts daily classes for the program participants. Teaching takes place in informal workshops without rigid class periods and schedules. Training is adapted to individual needs and capacities, with an emphasis on vocational and personal counseling. Many of the more adaptable participants find jobs within a few weeks after beginning the program. In such instances there is no follow-up of their work progress. Most students, however, are placed in supervised work stations by arrangement with employers. The most important function of the jobs is to provide students with work experience under realistic conditions to enable them to develop good work habits and attitudes.

The instructor visits program participants during the first six months that they are on regular part-time or full-time jobs.

Thus the school personnel are able to continue counseling young workers through this critical period. Sympathetic supervision and close co-operation between employers and instructors help prepare the dropouts for full-time employment. While this is a noncredit program, appropriate notations on students' transcripts certify to their participation in the course.

The job-upgrading approach to helping school dropouts improve their personal, economic, and vocational status sets the overall objectives for this phase. These are:

To provide practical means of helping such youngsters become more employable

To help students find jobs

To enable them to become self-supporting workers

Less obvious objectives stem from Flint's total approach to community improvement. The school-work experiences provided for this particular group of young citizens prevent them from developing antisocial behavior patterns resulting from educational and vocational inadequacies.

To be eligible for the program, boys or girls must have been dropouts for a minimum of thirty days. There is no upper time limit. Students must be aged sixteen to twenty and must be identified for admission by any individual or by referral from any public private, or social agency. Entrance requirements are set low, so that objectives may be easier to achieve.

The pilot stage of the program involved one staff member whose responsibilities included teaching, visiting students on jobs, and co-ordinating resource people. The co-ordinator, a well-known professional athlete before becoming a teacher, undoubtedly has many advantages in his association with the program for adolescent youth. Flint school officials are quick to point out, however, that they consider his success to be a function of his professional and personal qualities rather than of his athletic reputation.

The plan for evaluating this project calls for yearly appraisals of each participant's progress. Student success will be measured by the individual's personal adjustment and his ability to acquire and hold a job. The employer's estimate will be used to evaluate the latter criteria, while the co-ordinator judges the adjustment factor. As the project continues, follow-up studies of all students will be conducted.

Already, though, there are some indications of accomplishment. Consider Dave, who dropped out of junior high school because of repeated failures and low grades. When he joined the Voluntary Work-Education Project, little or nothing could be done for him in terms of the three R's, but he was extremely interested in auto body repair. After four weeks of basic training, he was given a chance to work in a bump-and-paint shop five afternoons a week for six weeks. His employer was impressed with Dave's eagerness and the manner in which he performed his job. Later the same employer hired the boy as a full-time employee, an outcome common to many of the boys who helped themselves.

Another young person, Flora, had spent two years in the girls vocational school. As a child she had never experienced the security of a wholesome family life. Then she was introduced to the Voluntary Work-Education Project by a social worker. In the project, workers discovered that the teen-ager wanted to be a dental assistant. Through staff efforts, she received training and obtained work in a dentist's office, where she performed successfully all the duties of an apprentice dental assistant.

Or consider the story of Dallas, afflicted with polio while he was in first grade. As a child be became overly aware of his physical—and mental—disabilities. He became withdrawn; he did not do well in regular classes; and he did not participate in any extracurricular activities. During his junior year at Central Community High School, however, he was placed in the Voluntary Work-Education Project, where he was able to do the work assigned to him and was given the responsibility of being football manager. As a result, Dallas blossomed into a well-liked, respected citizen of Central. He was graduated recently and attended Flint Junior College, studying business administration for a semester. At last report, he was employed by a local store.

Flint authorities see in these cases signs that the program may be a success.

CASE TWO: *Mount Diablo*

Mount Diablo Unified School District, Concord, California

INSIDE-OUTSIDE
WORK EXPERIENCE

A two-phase program to provide high school
students with exploratory work experiences,
in in-school and out-of-school settings

Work-experience education was added to the high school curriculum of the Mount Diablo Unified School District in 1952. It has been developed into a comprehensive program built on the premise that high school students should be permitted to explore vocations through practical job assignments within the school and community.

The progressive program at Mount Diablo has two parts: inside work experience and outside work experience. Both are regular curricular offerings of the five district high schools. While the Mount Diablo program is not designed specifically for alienated youth, it has important implications for work-study programs for such children.

Inside work experience has two facets. Exploratory work-experience assignments permit youngsters to try out jobs in and around the school. General work-experience assignments, again in the school setting, help children acquire desirable work habits and attitudes. Both experiences earn school credit.

The outside work experience has three phases. Exploratory experience offers students opportunities to observe and sample a variety of community work assignments. General work experience parallels the inside phase of the program: students work on part-time jobs outside school, where they gain a realistic appreciation of work and healthy attitudes toward themselves and others. The third phase—vocational experience—is an extension of the vocational education program some students elect in school. On part-time jobs related to their vocational goals, they acquire realistic experience in work associated with their interests. As in the school program, work assignments in this phase earn credit toward graduation.

Work education is important to the young people of Concord and its suburbs, because these children live in communities that do not contain a great variety of job opportunities.

The towns are bedroom communities from which the students' parents commute to work in the San Francisco Bay area. Houses are for the most part new dwellings built for modern living, and there are not enough chores required for their maintenance to give young people a real appreciation of work and the rewards that can be obtained from well-performed jobs.

Mount Diablo school personnel are aware of the needs of their community, which has grown from 1373 residents in 1940 to 34,614 in 1961.[1]

The decision to add work education to the curriculum resulted from a survey of the work-study programs in the Oakland, San Francisco, and Los Angeles school systems. After evaluating these, the Mount Diablo staff evolved a two-pronged approach to work education: school and community experiences.

Mount Diablo's pilot program was barely under way when a California study of work education was conducted in the secondary schools of the state. During the period 1952–55 a state committee surveyed all the work-experience programs. Its recommendations to the California superintendent of public instruction resulted in legislation aimed at clarifying work-study programs in the education code. A state senate bill enacted in 1958 incorporated such programs into the regular curriculum of secondary schools.

The new law prompted Mount Diablo officials to weigh their pilot program against provisions of the state code. Their study in-

---

1. Mount Diablo Unified School District, *Plan for the Administration and Operation of a Work-Experience Program* (mimeographed report, March 16, 1959), p. 1.

cluded students enrolled in the last four years of high school, their parents, and the business establishments within the boundaries of the district. This survey helped officials refine the existing program and expand it to meet the special vocational needs of the students.

Underlying the resulting program was the philosophy of the Mount Diablo schools: that the major function of the district's schools is

> to provide students with experiences which develop a knowledge and appreciation of various vocational pursuits and give practice in those which best meet their individual needs, potentialities, capabilities, and interests.[2]

The objectives of the work-study curriculums are a direct extension of the philosophy. They are:

> To provide students with vocational guidance through opportunities to observe and sample systematically a variety of conditions of work for the purpose of ascertaining their suitability for the occupation they are exploring.

> To provide supervised part-time employment of pupils with the intent of helping them acquire desirable work habits and attitudes.

> To provide vocational learning opportunities for a pupil in supervised part-time employment in the occupation for which his course in school is preparing him.[3]

The purposes of work education as stated in the California School Law are also considered important objectives of the Mount Diablo program. The state charges schools to—

> Provide appropriate and continuous guidance services to the pupils throughout their enrollment in the Work-Experience Education Program.

> Assign a sufficient number of qualified certificated personnel to direct the program and co-ordinate jobs held by pupils with the school.

> Make certain that work done by pupils is of a useful educational nature. Ascertain, through the appropriate enforcement agency, that applicable federal, state, and local laws and regulations are followed.

> Evaluate, with the help of the employer and job supervisor, work done by a pupil; award credit toward graduation for work successfully

---

2. Milan Wight, *Report of Work-Experience Programs in the Mount Diablo Unified School District* (mimeographed report, 1961), p. 1.

3. California Administrative Code, Art. 13.1, Secs. 115.2–115.26.

accomplished; and enter pertinent facts concerning the pupil's work on the pupil's cumulative record.

Provide necessary clerical and instructional services.[4]

The work-education program constructed to accomplish these objectives functions under a citizens advisory committee within the educational service branch of the district's board of education. A full-time co-ordinator administers the program and supervises the school co-ordinators. The school co-ordinators—teachers released from classroom duties one period a day—oversee the inside work-experience program. One co-ordinator directs the outside work-experience program for all high schools in the district.

INSIDE WORK EXPERIENCE

The inside work-experience (IWE) program was set up original-ly to provide a laboratory situation for business-education students. Now it is open to noncommercial students who use it to explore jobs. This phase has two divisions: exploratory work experience and general work experience. Enrollment in these ranged between 10 and 13 per cent of total enrollment in the 1960–61 school year.

Exploratory work experience is designed to provide vocational guidance for individual students. Assignments in school offices permit them to observe job procedures and sample a variety of tasks in planned, supervised settings for an hour a day. Though they do not receive pay, they do receive school credits. Careful planning and supervision insure the creation of worthwhile learning situations for each child. Assignments are structured to permit pupils to explore all the jobs in any work area. Each inside work-experience co-ordinator supervises students and sees that they are not exploited on assignments. (See Appendix D, Example 1.)

General work experience provides students with supervised part-time employment aimed at helping youngsters acquire desirable work habits and attitudes. For these part-time assignments, in the school and performed on school time, students are not paid but they do receive school credits. Work stations need not be related to students' vocational goals, since the objective is to maintain this part of the program as a general exploratory experience.

Assignments in either part of the inside work-experience program are limited by rules for school credit established by the

4. *Ibid.*

Mount Diablo system in accordance with state regulations. Students are not permitted to receive more than twenty semester hours of school credit for work experience. They may, however, divide their credits between exploratory and general experiences and may earn a maximum of five semester hours each term in either phase.

Work education is scheduled by students as they would elect any other nonacademic course. To participate, a student must meet these requirements:

> Have attained at least sophomore standing.
>
> Be a full-time pupil. (For purposes of this section, a full-time pupil means a high school pupil enrolled in four or more subjects, including Work-Experience Education as one of such subjects.)
>
> Have parental or guardian approval.
>
> Have the approval of the counselor to enroll in the Work-Experience Education Program.
>
> Have a vocational or educational goal to which the Work-Experience Education chosen will, in the opinion of the school, contribute.[5]

Here are school regulations governing assignments:

> No student may be assigned to a study if he has an IWE assignment.
>
> No student may be assigned to IWE after the end of the first report period of any semester.
>
> No student should be assigned to the same job supervisor for more than one year. An exception may be made in the case of an office situation where the variety of tasks is great enough to provide additional learning.
>
> No student may be assigned to both IWE and the Outside Work-Experience program during the same semester.[6]

Jobs in the inside work-experience phase are located by each building co-ordinator on the basis of these criteria:

> EDUCATIONAL VALUE
> The job must be one that adds to the student's educational experience. Routine jobs, quickly learned with no additional value, are not acceptable for this program unless combined with other responsibilities to form a pattern for development.
>
> CHARACTER OF WORK
> An IWE job must be a series of tasks that cannot be accomplished in a normal classroom situation.

---

5. Milan Wight, *Work-Experience Adjustment Bulletin No. 2* (Mount Diablo Unified School District, May 1961).

6. *Ibid.*

TRAINING PROGRAM

The supervisor should have a training program and a definite interest in teaching the student and developing good work habits.

TRAINING FACILITIES

Training facilities should be available. There should be adequate equipment to provide a well-rounded program of training. For example, an office worker should be placed where a typewriter and other machines are available for on-the-job training and experience.

REGULARITY OF WORK

Training stations should provide a full period of work throughout the semester or year. Offices that have sporadic work loads or that can furnish only part-period work should be avoided.

SAFETY

Students should never be placed in jobs that are dangerous or likely to be detrimental to their health or physical well-being.[7]

OUTSIDE WORK EXPERIENCE

The outside work-experience (OWE) program was established to meet the needs of students desiring vocational experience during their last two years in high school, and its original intent has been maintained. Jobs provide students with vocational experiences in agriculture, office work, trade and industrial work, or distributive activities.

In the year-round program, students attend school for four hours and work regular part-time shifts during the remainder of each school day. Students must work two hours in class for each hour of release time from school.

There are three kinds of assignments: exploratory work education, general work experience, and vocational work experience.

Exploratory work experience introduces pupils to vocations. For specified hours during schooltime they work on community job assignments for which they receive school credit instead of pay. Close supervision insures co-ordination of the school and laboratory learning experiences.

General work experience helps students acquire good work habits and attitudes. Usually during school hours, pupils work in public or private settings outside the school. For the job assignments—which do not have to be related to students' occupational goals—they receive pay and school credits. In a recent school year, for instance, sixty students worked at thirty-two distributive jobs and earned $41,561.75.

---

7. *Ibid.*

Vocational work experience, similar to the companion courses in the in-school phase, extends students' vocational learning into out-of-school situations. Students work as part-time employees in fields related directly to their school curriculum and receive pay from the employer as well as credit from the school.

The categories of vocational work-experience assignments are:

Agricultural occupations—farms, food processing plants, farm implements or supply firms

Distributive occupations—retail, wholesale, and specialty sales, advertising, insurance, real estate, business management, traffic and transportation, interior decoration

Office occupations—offices including secretarial, accounting, bookkeeping, and general clerical positions

Trade and industrial occupations—establishments including jobs in machine trades, metal trades, auto mechanics, drafting, electronics, and woodworking trades[8]

Pupils usually work two hours a day for five semester hours of credit a semester but are limited to forty semester hours credit including that gained from inside work experience, and ten hours in any one semester. Those who work Saturdays may apply that time toward their total credit requirements.

The election of outside work activities by students also requires their regular counselor's approval. Then the co-ordinator places them on assignments and maintains liaison with the employer-supervisor.

To qualify for assignments, students must meet these criteria, approved by the superintendent of the district on January 30, 1956:[9]

AGE
Students should be at least sixteen years of age, so that they may be employed in a gainful occupation.

OCCUPATIONAL INTEREST
Students should have thought about what they are best fitted to do and should have made a preliminary decision on the best occupational area for them. Interest is vital for continued study and progress in the chosen occupation.

JOB OPPORTUNITIES
Selection should generally be made after consideration of work oppor-

8. Milan Wight, *Outside Work Experience* (Occupational Adjustment Bulletin No. 1, November 1960).

9. Mount Diablo Unified School District, "Superintendent of Schools Notice to Faculties" (January 30, 1956).

tunities and prospective part-time job or training stations that may be open to the work-experience trainee.

TRAINING STATION REQUIREMENT

Since work-experience students are required to work in a part-time job, the requirements and qualifications imposed by the employers in the community should be considered. Students should have these qualifications in order to enroll.

INTEREST IN THE TRAINING PROGRAM

Since this is not a program for the mere placement of students in jobs, but has a primary objective of training in school and on the job, students should have a definite interest in and desire to receive all the training that is provided.

HEALTH

No student should be allowed to enroll if the work experience on the job will be detrimental or harmful to his health or well-being. A combination of part-time work and school will usually be harder on a student than merely attending school full time.

POSSIBILITY OF ADVANCED SCHOOLING

Vocational education was originally intended for those students who could not attend school beyond the secondary level. Such students should probably be given the first chance to enroll in the work-experience program, if it is to help complete their period of formal schooling.

PAST SCHOOL RECORD

Carefully check the applicant's past school record of grades, attendance, honors, habits, and similar characteristics. These can be helpful in knowing students' background and in determining those who may benefit most by work experience. Out-of-school history and information may also be used. Information about a student's work experience might be one of the most important kinds of out-of-school information needed.

GRADE LEVEL IN SCHOOL

Students nearest to leaving school should be given the first opportunity to take advantage of this training. In a few cases, students below the eleventh grade may be old enough and eligible to enroll.

PERSONAL CHARACTERISTICS AND TRAITS

Students should possess traits that best fit them to their chosen occupation. Some of these include appearance, speech, intelligence, aptitudes, dependability, accuracy, and initiative. Many of these can be developed and may not be too important in the preselection process. Vocational aptitude and interest tests may help to give some of this information to the co-ordinator.

NEED FOR A PART-TIME JOB

The work-experience program is basically a training program and not one of placement. At times it may be desirable, however, to consider a student's need for employment, especially as this will occur immediately after he leaves school. Students who need regular employment should be given every opportunity to enroll, in preference to those who may not plan to go to work at all. Part-time work may help a student to stay in school who might otherwise have to drop out.

STUDENT HAVING OWN PART-TIME JOB
Some students who already have part-time jobs will report to the co-ordinator for admission to the program. If these jobs meet the qualifications and standards set up for a training station as listed in the "Criteria for Selection of Training Stations," there is no reason why such students should not be allowed to enroll.

PERMISSION OF PARENTS AND SCHOOL ADMINISTRATORS
Before final enrollment it is necessary to have the approval of parents, dean, counselor, work co-ordinator, and attendance office (work permit). Parents may be called by phone, visited in the home, or otherwise contacted. Signatures may be required on the training agreement.

These are criteria for selection of student training stations:

The employer or job supervisor must understand the educational objectives of providing work experience for the pupil.

The work station must offer a reasonable probability of continuous employment for the pupil during the work-experience period for which he is enrolled.

The employer must have adequate equipment, materials, and other facilities to provide an appropriate learning opportunity.

Overall working conditions must be such that they will not endanger the health, safety, welfare, or morals of the pupil.

The employer must provide adequate supervision to insure a planned program of the pupil's job activities in order that the pupil may receive maximum educational benefit.

The employer, as required by law, will provide adequate compensation insurance.

The employer must maintain accurate records of the pupil's attendance.

In addition to the above, OWE work stations shall further be subject to "Factors To Consider in the Final Selection of Training Stations." Copies of this material are available from the work-experience co-ordinator or a counselor.[10]

This phase attracts a smaller number of students than does the in-school experience, perhaps because of the nature of the assignments.

The jobs included in the program vary with employers' needs and young persons' interests. In addition to the stations noted in the explanation of vocational experience, this phase includes work in restaurants, retail groceries, stationery stores, clothing estab-

10. Wight, Bulletin No. 1.

lishments, department stores, and many service-related activities.

The criteria for in-school assignments are used to select work stations for this program. Jobs are carefully screened by the co-ordinator and teachers to insure that they are relevant to students' work in the classroom.

The program is a large one, well organized and well administered by the co-ordinator. The co-ordinator's duties are delineated in the superintendent's description of his job:

DUTIES OF THE DISTRICT CO-ORDINATOR
OF WORK-EXPERIENCE EDUCATION

The basic function of the work-experience education co-ordinator is to provide those services that are devoted to the occupational adjustment of students in the district. The co-ordinator works with students, parents, counselors, teachers, administrators, employers, and labor union representatives during work assignments and career conference activities. The-co-ordinator works closely with the consultants in instruction, guidance, and attendance and welfare in the development and operation of the program. More specifically, the co-ordinator of work-experience education shall—

Be directly responsible to the assistant superintendent, Educational Services.

Undertake those organizational and promotional activities necessary to establish a work-experience education program in the secondary schools of the district.

Co-ordinate the work-study assignments of those students assigned to OWE in all the high schools of the district.

Work with the IWE education co-ordinators in the establishment and operation of these programs in the high schools of the district.

Register and co-ordinate placement of those students interested in working on the work-experience program after school, during vacation, and full time.

Organize and develop a Christmas sales training and Christmas work program in the secondary schools of the district.

Assist in the development of work-experience records.

Conduct follow-up studies of graduates and relate to in-school surveys prior to graduation.

Assist in the development of advanced work-study programs.

Conduct career interest surveys among ninth- and twelfth-grade students in the high schools of the district.

Consult with teachers and principals in the establishment and co-ordination of career conference programs, vocational units of study, and job counselor conferences.

Consult with teachers and counselors regarding the vocational testing program.

Consult with attendance secretaries for the purpose of developing and operating a system of work-permit records for those students assigned to the work-experience education program.

Consult with librarians and teachers regarding sources and uses of occupational information.[11]

Duties of the five building co-ordinators of IWE are also specific. They are:

ORGANIZATION AND PROMOTION ACTIVITIES

Survey needs of the school for the establishment of work stations.

Obtain a job analysis from job supervisors in offices approved by the principal.

Prepare a catalog of job descriptions.

Prepare a summary of job stations by office and period.

Contact the job supervisors and explain IWE.

Assign students referred by the counselors to job stations.

Maintain continuing publicity on the accomplishments of the program.

Determine that state rules and regulations are followed in the operation of the program.

CO-ORDINATION

Place students in training stations approved for IWE.

Plan a schedule of related job experiences with job supervisors and agree on a system of supervision.

Carefully follow up students periodically to carry out training plans and to check on the process of work experience.

FOLLOW-UP AND EVALUATION

Report follow-up information to the principal and recommend curriculum and guidance adjustment for the work-experience program.

Make reports to the principal on the progress of the program.

Conduct conferences with individual students on personal achievement and job performance problems and make recommendations when needed for improvement.

OTHER DUTIES

Keep records of trainees and work-experience statistics.

Assist with other vocational guidance activities that affect the work-experience program.

---

11. Mount Diablo Schools, *Plan for Administration*, p. 8.

Work with the district co-ordinator of work-experience education in the development and operation of IWE.[12]

Evaluation of the Mount Diablo work-education program has been thorough. The study in 1957 included students in grades 9–12, their parents, and businesses within the school district. The major purpose was to determine the conditions under which the school personnel should offer a work-education program. The survey performed by the co-ordinator as part of his regular duties was designed to answer the following questions:

What are the employment patterns and needs of high school students?

What did parents consider to be the employment needs of their sons and daughters?

To what extent did employers in the Mount Diablo Unified School District employ or consider employing high school students, and under what conditions?

How should the Mount Diablo Unified School District modify its work-experience education program?[13]

The instruments consisted of a questionnaire, which was machine processed. Here are salient findings from the comprehensive survey.[14]

From the student survey:

The increasing population and the unique characteristics of the suburban area served by the district placed increased demands on the curriculum to prepare students for the competitive situation in the labor market.

Many students in the district planned further education that they planned to finance from part-time employment. Training and experience were considered necessary for such educational and occupational plans.

A smaller percentage than the national average of high school students was employed in the Mount Diablo Unified School District: 29 per cent compared with 40 per cent.

Most of the students who were employed worked less than ten hours per week.

Relatively few high school students were employed in sales, stock, and clerical jobs at the higher skill levels.

---

12. *Ibid.*, p. 7.

13. *Ibid.*

14. Mount Diablo Unified School District, *Survey Summary* (mimeographed copy).

High school students wanted to work but apparently were depending on a job coming to them. Very few applied for work.

Many students available for work had not developed skill through job-training classes. There appeared to be many undeveloped skills and interests of occupational significance to part-time employment and full-time careers.

The relationship of students' career interests to the distribution of employed workers was quite unrealistic. Considerably more students were planning careers in professional and technical work than could ever be absorbed in this work. More would be working in sales than indicated an interest in this area at the time.

More vocational counseling at an earlier age apparently was needed.

Many students failed to see the occupational significance of subjects being taken in high school.

Most students in high school obtained some kind of work experience while enrolled in school.

Better-organized vocational units of study and library usage appeared to be essential to learning about the labor market.

There were 13 per cent who indicated an interest in distributive education as part of their high school curriculum.

There were a substantial number of students who were willing to relate their classroom instruction to on-the-job training by enrolling in a special class.

Contrary to general belief, students were not primarily interested in work for the monetary return. For most students, work was exploratory.

Students needed training in the technique of how to prepare for and find a job.

Students needed help in evaluating their own personal characteristics and applying for work that would be of some long-range value to them.

From the parent survey:

The school district should continue to offer a diversified work-experience education program including directed work experience on and off campus for school credit, seasonal work such as Christmas sales training, summer work, and full-time work registration and placement. Many parents preferred after-school or vacation work and did not necessarily desire it to be an integral part of their son's or daughter's program for credit.

The school district should continue to offer the inside work-experience program and the 4-4 program for school credit as an integral part of the program of students who request it.

Most parents preferred their son or daughter to undertake further training beyond high school.

Parents felt that the curriculum of the secondary schools should provide subjects that would train specifically for part-time and full-time employment.

Typing and salesmanship were rated highest by parents as skill subjects students should take.

From the employer survey:

Most business establishments in the Concord area are small businesses employing few if any part-time employees.

Strong objection was expressed by some merchants to the limitations of the union contract as it applied to the employment of trainees and high school students.

The hours of work available to part-time employees were sufficient for school credit for work-experience students.

Most businesses could use part-time employees during the day when students could be released to work. Some had work schedules that did not lend themselves to a school program.

The greatest demand for part-time employees tended to occur toward the latter part of the week. It appeared that four to five days work might be available.

There were sufficient firms willing to employ students on the work-experience program to make the program economically feasible.

The community had few industrial but many retail establishments that were in need of part-time employees.

To insure continued evaluation, an annual follow-up of graduates is conducted. Personnel in the program are aware of the worth of ongoing research.

A glimpse at the students themselves illustrates the program's accomplishments. Consider the case of Mary, a junior girl who had been suspended from school a number of times for unauthorized absences. She was removed from one class: her appearance was sloppy. After entering the IWE program, she was assigned to a job station in the school kitchen. There the adult women workers expressed interest in her as an individual. Soon her appearance improved. Moreover, she was not absent from school or referred to the office for discipline. Her counselor noted:

The quality of her work and her willingness to accept responsibility on the job probably resulted from the full status given her as a worker on a real job. To date, her grades in academic subjects have not improved but her teachers indicate that she is making a real effort now.

Then there's Chuck, a bright sophomore. An only child, he lives with his mother, who works. Chuck's trouble came in the physical education program, where he could not get along with the coach. Ultimately he was removed from the program, but it was necessary to threaten him with police action to get him to school at all. The change in Chuck began the day he was assigned to independent study in the biology lab, to work with some girls who were performing research. On the first two days, according to reports from the instructor, the boy appeared pouting. On the third day he performed the job assigned to him smiling. He chatted some, too, as he made blood smears and labeled some biological specimens. And on the fifth day he even expressed the hope that he might one day work in a field of science himself.

Of course, not all students who benefit from Mount Diablo's program are in need of therapy. One bright student with many extracurricular activities reported that she had learned to be dependable and responsible in doing her work correctly without a supervisor being present to watch over her.

Another student reported:

The work I did in the office had to be done 100 per cent right, not like what we are satisfied to get away with in the classroom.

Dr. Ferd Diel, principal of Mount Diablo High School, summed up the program as follows:

Work experience helps in the adjustment of youngsters in an important developmental stage. They learn to adjust in real life situations. They achieve some degree of independence in which they must live with themselves and at the same time get along with other people.

CASE THREE: *Arrowhead Ranch*

Arrowhead Ranch, Moline, Illinois

A farm-home laboratory in which thirty-five boys
from ten to twenty live, work,
and study together

The paragraph below, from an article in the *Moline Dispatch* of
January 3, 1959, refers to a unique program for boys in trouble
with their society.

> Miracles—or the next thing to them—are made every day at Arrowhead
> Ranch. . . . The laboratory is a farm, a home, a school and above all,
> a healthy atmosphere. The material is boys. Most have been in minor
> scrapes with the law, are wards of the court, and products of broken
> homes. All are at Arrowhead to get their first chance at just about
> everything.

Arrowhead Ranch is a 430-acre farm in Rock Island County,
Illinois. On it live thirty-five boys who fit the definition of alienated
youth.

In a twenty-four-hour custodial care program, the boys are
helped to readjust their values and attitudes. They are admitted to

Arrowhead as wards of the courts or as incorrigibles headed for trouble with the law. After being accepted by the board of directors who oversee the institution, they are placed in the home-school-work environment. Each boy's program of study, his work assignment, and even his way of life is supervised by an especially competent staff of adults. Some are professionals; others are not. Each boy's stay at the ranch is determined by how rapidly he becomes socially adjusted. The underlying philosophy of Arrowhead requires that a boy be kept in the program only as long as it is beneficial to him. The staff, however, reviews each case after the minimum residence of one year.

The program of Arrowhead is an approach to working with alienated youth that differs from the other cases reported. Arrowhead is school-connected, but it is a private institution not located within a school setting. It has many relations with courts and law enforcement agencies as well as with the Moline public schools.

Arrowhead Ranch is a farm, similar in appearance to hundreds of others in the Midwest. Physical appearance, however, is the only attribute shared with other farms. Primarily, it differs from others because of its functions: it is a farm-home where boys from ten to twenty live, work, and study together. The farm provides the setting and also provides the work. The boys themselves, with the help of a sensitive staff of adults, provide the most important aspect of this unusual way of life—the social setting in which each learns to live with others.

Arrowhead—on the outskirts of the Quad Cities of Moline, East Moline, and Rock Island, Illinois, and Davenport, Iowa—by its very name suggests its bond with the area. These four communities are grouped along the banks of the Mississippi River on the sites of the ancient village of the Sac and Fox Indians. In frontier days the communities formed a four-cornered nucleus of trade associated with westward expansion. By 1854 the area had become a brisk commercial trade center dominated by railroads that had brought with them the heavy and medium industries of the next era. Even early in the twentieth century, the Quad Cities were beset by many of the social ills that accompany rapid urban development in a farming and trading area forced into the transitional phases associated with industrial development.

The patina of the present-day Quad Cities has developed from its potpourri past. Fragments of the social conditions associated with an old river town transformed into a railroad center are apparent in the lives of a people who are busy with many activities associated with manufacturing farm implements, iron and steel kitchen products, and providing a commercial center for a large surrounding rural population. In this setting, Arrowhead Ranch symbolizes the practical and real approach the residents of this area exhibit toward life.

The people are conservative. Their lives, for the most part, have not been easy. They react to personal and community problems in a straightforward way. They established Arrowhead Ranch as their method of coping with one of their social problems—what to do with certain young boys who manifest offensive behavior within their society.

The approach to their problem was direct. During the early 1940's a group of Rock Island County citizens became concerned about the increase in the number of young boys not able to conform to social requirements of personal behavior. Increased truancy in schools, heavier bookings of juveniles by local law enforcement agencies, and observations by key community adults that some boys were not "fitting in" led a group of concerned citizens to study this social phenomenon. Those first involved were practical people who because of their vocations or their community involvement could observe youngsters in various roles. A group of citizens, including the judge of the county court, a Rock Island physician, and a Moline school administrator, agreed to conduct an unofficial study of their county's problems.

Their objectives were practical: first, to determine whether many boys were unable to deal with the pressures of society without special help from concerned adults; and second, to formulate a method to help such deviant youngsters readjust to the demands of society. Their plan was this: The initial study would determine whether their concerns were justified and would provide the groundwork for the next step—attempting to solve the problem.

The action resulted in a two-year study that was not scientific in design but, at best, an observational approach to determine whether the number of socially maladjusted youth in the county warranted special plans to care for them. The techniques of the study, consequently, would not stand up to the criticisms of social researchers. The members of the committee merely asked key community leaders whether they had observed youngsters who did not appear to be fitting into their family, school, or community in an appropriate way. They pooled this information to estimate the number of alienated children, and they tried to determine ways in which the youngsters did not exhibit behavior expected of them by adults.

During its two-year study the committee met frequently, discussed findings, gave more direction to the investigation, and summarized important aspects of the adjustment problem of boys in trouble. Though the findings were as unscientific as the approach, they did have meaning. The committee discovered a population of boys who needed help and concluded that existing facilities could not offer the appropriate help.

The evidence convinced members that environmental conditions were the crucial elements enhancing the possibility that certain boys would develop predelinquent or even bona fide delinquent behavior patterns. As a result, they devoted the project to the possibility of providing a controlled home-study-work situation for youngsters either delinquency-prone or adjudged by law to be delinquent. Next they turned their attention to establishing a situation where they could create and maintain a reasonably controlled environment for alienated boys.

In contrast to most fact-finding committees, which normally vote themselves into oblivion after filing the report of their investigation, they considered themselves to be the best-prepared body to deal with their findings. Consequently they decided to oversee the project.

The assumption of new responsibility caused the group to act quickly. Problems were numberless. The initial task was to acquire a physical setting where they could establish the home-work-study environment. Their search for a facility turned them to the Rock Island County Convalescent Home on the outskirts of Moline. This was a long-established institution whose residents were housed in large brick buildings. It also contained a number of tumbledown, gazebo-like structures used years before to expose patients to "healing air" when the home also served the county as a tuberculosis sanitorium. The other structures on the two-hundred-odd acres were an old, sprawling farmhouse (vacant at the time) and nearby barns, chicken houses, and assorted animal pens.

Investigation of the county home revealed that the farmhouse could be used. With this facility available, the group incorporated the Rock Island County Farm School for Boys and became the board of directors. The legal workings necessary to obtain a nonprofit charter under Illinois law were completed by spring, 1945. During the months following acquisition of the building, committee members solicited their fellow citizens for financial help. Small contributions enabled them to make the old farmhouse livable. Two dormitories large enough to house thirty-five boys were set up on the second floor. Two small bedrooms for staff members were also constructed, by a modification of partitions. The bathroom was expanded to provide facilities for the residents. The first floor required little change except to equip it with cooking facilities adequate for a large number of people. A small apartment was set aside on this floor for a housemother. It adjoined a comfortably furnished living room that added to the homelike atmosphere. Other rooms provided office space for the director, dining space, and an area for two classes. Construction in 1949 provided additional classroom space.

At first the farmland was not available to the project. In 1953, however, the board of directors leased 280 acres from the county on a sharecrop basis, and the farm has continued to operate under this agreement. Recently an additional 150 acres, rented from a nearby resident, have been added. All of this land is cultivated by the boys.

The grounds have been improved too. A rose garden, of which the residents are very proud, has added to the beauty of the front lawn. A swimming pool, financed by contributions raised through the efforts of the woman doctor who oversees the physical health of the boys, was built in 1960.

In 1957 the name Arrowhead Ranch was substituted for the original name, Rock Island County Farm School for Boys. The new name was chosen to reflect the historical traditions of the area as well as to reduce the confusion caused by the original description. Many people had believed the project was a county-sponsored agency financed by county funds.

The farm itself provides one source of income, mainly from its dairy. The number of cattle on the premises varies from 50 to 130, depending on the season of the year. As a rule, a milking herd of approximately 45 cows is maintained to insure the ranch a monthly income. Income is bolstered during the marketing months by profits received from the sale of hogs. As of September 1961, 220 feeder pigs were being fattened for market.

The farm crops are the animal feeds of corn, hay, and alfalfa. A large vegetable garden is planted each year and is tended by the boys. Its importance is evident in a review of the ranch's budget. Only a small part of the money allotted to maintain the boys is spent for food. Careful planning by the residents and the farm manager has resulted in a variety of crops to insure them a yearlong supply of vegetables. The vegetables canned by the boys, ranch-raised meat, and dairy products leave little to be purchased other than the basic staples of flour, sugar, and a few commercial foods not available on the farm.

Counties sending boys to Arrowhead also provide income. If a youngster accepted by the ranch is a ward of Rock Island County, for instance, a monthly contribution of ninety dollars is made to the ranch. The payment is also required of any parent who received permission from the Intake and Placement Committee of the ranch to have his child placed in the care of the Arrowhead Ranch personnel.

In addition to the income from the farm and the boys' maintenance allowances, state financial aid is received by Arrowhead through the school lunch program. The Orphanage Act of the State of Illinois provides major salary support for the superintendent and for part of the salaries of the two men who teach at the ranch. The other staff members—the assistant superintendent, cook, farm manager, and housemother—receive their salaries from the operating budget.

As is common in any budget, not every expense can be anticipated. The board, aware of the variety of expenses for maintaining some thirty boys, sets aside certain unobligated funds to serve as a cushion. The original money earmarked for this purpose has grown to a sizable amount through contributions from individuals, groups, and the bequests from estates of friends of Arrowhead. The Benevolent Fund, as it is called, can be used to pay for eyeglasses, swimming lessons at the YMCA, and loans to any Arrowhead boys needing financial help for college. This fund, in the opinion of the directors, is one of their most important means of adding flexibility to the program of individualized attention for each boy.

Although the acquisition of the farm and the plan for its financing were important, they were not nearly as important as the philosophy the directors evolved to guide the program. Their knowledge of alienated youth was gained from study and their practical philosophy reflects this knowledge. This study convinced them that the boys not capable of living in a socially acceptable way in their communities needed help either in readjusting their values or in developing a socially acceptable value system. Since the boys were unable to achieve this alone, the directors committed themselves to provide an atmosphere in which the boys could achieve such goals. The ranch, contended the directors, should provide a homelike setting where boys, guided by a staff of capable, sensitive adults, would have the opportunity to work out or alter their value systems.

The philosophy was simple but far-reaching in its implications and laid the groundwork for objectives that have continued to offer direction to the program. They include the provision of an accepting, homelike atmosphere where each boy can feel he is important both to himself and to those with whom he lives and works; a program of studies adapted to individual needs so that each boy is permitted to continue his formal education on the level of his abilities; a work program for each youngster, to help him appreciate good work habits and become aware of his worth in society; a social-recreational program designed to help each boy satisfy his needs for social development; and a permissive religious atmosphere in which every boy is encouraged to develop his own faith.

Most of the boys admitted have been in trouble with police and are wards of the court, though not all have police records. If a judge recommends that a boy be admitted to Arrowhead, the case is reviewed by the Intake and Placement Committee, composed of five members selected from the board of directors. In addition, some boys are referred to the committee by parents or school authorities. Each youngster's case is reviewed completely; the review often involves attendance of probation officers as well as parents. If the committee concludes that the boy can be helped by an experience at Arrowhead, he is admitted for a minimum of one year.

Arrowhead does not admit boys who need unusual medical or psychiatric care or who have a history of incorrigibility that would require physical confinement. The most important single factor that keeps a boy out of Arrowhead, however, is lack of room. The facilities are designed for thirty-five, the number usually present.

The maximum stay is indefinite. Boys are kept until they can no longer profit from their life at Arrowhead, or until a parent or civil authority petitions for release of the boy. The committee discharges a boy after considering his case again. Appropriate placement of each boy leaving Arrowhead is carefully considered.

The program at Arrowhead follows the objectives closely. The home atmosphere of the ranch does not just happen. Arrowhead looks like a home; it feels like a home; and the house itself is a sprawling, comfortable structure.

The homelife of the boys at Arrowhead forms the backdrop of their schoolwork. Two male teachers, employed by the Moline public schools, instruct the boys in an eleven-month term. They offer a curriculum including all of the academic subjects taught in the Moline public schools, ranging from third-grade reading to twelfth-grade geometry. The two well-equipped classrooms are organized on a one-room-school basis, with boys grouped by age into two sections. Each boy has an independent study program. In a typical routine, the teacher moves from boy to boy, occasionally calling the attention of all the children to a particular task or subject. Both teachers appeared especially adept at determining the different levels of ability of the boys and at devising techniques to interest each youngster. Mathematical and scientific principles, for example, were explained in relation to the soapbox derby entries of the older boys. A butterfly and stamp collection helped boys of different ages develop scientific approaches to identification.

Classes are held Monday through Friday from 8:30 A.M. to 5:30 P.M. and on Saturday from 8:30 A.M. to noon. Schoolwork is presented on a long-day schedule to allow individual boys to be excused from classes for varying numbers of hours so that they can do their chores. Instead of holding all boys in class for a short day and then assigning all to work tasks, the staggered program permits boys and staff to adjust hours of work and study. In this way, each youngster benefits from more individual attention, receiving maximum supervision both in his work program and in his class activities.

All the reading material in the classrooms is selected to fit the interest patterns of boys. The teachers are careful to keep track of the individual programs to insure the easy transition of each boy back to the regular public school system when he leaves Arrowhead. Consequently, the units of study and the curriculum parallel those of the regular schools. If a boy completes all of his required school subjects for graduation, he may receive a Moline school diploma from Arrowhead.

Work assignments of each boy are commensurate with his age, interests, and abilities. New younger boys are often assigned to work supervised by the housemother. They work on household tasks such as dusting the furniture, vacuuming the rugs, washing the windows, helping with cooking, laundering, and removing the garbage.

Older boys are usually assigned regular farm chores. They are supervised by the farm manager, the superintendent, or the assistant superintendent.

The operation of a large dairy farm creates a host of jobs. Each boy first receives a careful explanation of his duties and responsibilities. If a boy starts to become lax in his responsibilities or superficial in the performance of his tasks, he is counseled by the person to whom he is assigned. Counseling in a practical, straightforward way also helps boys adjust to work responsibilities at Arrowhead. Far less time is spent attempting to analyze the deep psychological roots of problems faced by some of the boys than is spent helping them adjust to work experiences. This approach reflects the Arrowhead philosophy.

School and work are not the only activities of an Arrowhead boy. Each boy is involved in some sport, hobby, or social project outside of the class-work routine. During the winter months when farm responsibilities are lighter, the boys spend much of their time on hobbies. The staff's realistic attitude toward the social and athletic needs of youngsters assures each boy active outlets. Some youngsters concentrate on sports in formal and informal programs. A basketball court, baseball diamond, and swimming pool are facilities for their use. Others choose 4-H club projects associated with animals and plants. College students instruct and supervise the boys in these leisure-time activities.

On the writer's visit, one boy was grooming a pony for an approaching fair. Another was feeding a pig in hopes of developing a prize winner. Still another kept a flock of pigeons in one of the abandoned gazebos that had been converted into a functional dovecote. The boys' interest in animals is evident throughout the ranch. Dogs, cats, rabbits, and chinchillas are a few of their projects. Scrapbooks of pictures of prize-winning animals, vegetables, and stamp collections provide an enviable record that new boys quickly attempt to emulate.

One project that evokes great interest is the annual soapbox derby. A workshop is bulging with racers and parts. This was set up as a recreational woodshop for an evening program, because the person qualified to handle the course was available at that time. The purpose of the shop was to enable boys to use their creative abilities, to develop good work habits, to learn to work congenially with others in a shop situation, and to learn to handle shop tools and materials.

The shop has a therapeutic value: the work relaxes the boys physically and mentally and tends to help the emotionally disturbed boys who are not helped by playing games or watching TV.

Work in the shop is voluntary. And since the range of ages is wide, each boy works on projects suited to his age and ability. These include building models, birdhouses, knickknacks, bookshelves, flower stands, tie racks, and lamps.

One of the major annual projects is the building of soapbox racers. Boys who show manual dexterity, creativity, and ability to stay with a project are selected to build their own racers, supervised by the staff. Building a racer is complicated and requires a working knowledge of many woodworking hand tools as well as the application of academic knowledge. The result is that the boys see the program as a challenge and take pride in accomplishments and the good sportsmanship shown in the competition.

With so many activities, one wonders when the boys of Arrowhead have an opportunity to loaf. Their schedule has been deliberately designed to avoid too much free or unsupervised time, possibly a factor in incidents that led to their admission. Each boy, however, has a reasonable amount of free time. In the early evening on school days and on Sunday afternoon particularly, the boys are encouraged to relax in their own fashion. Each boy is expected to attend religious services of his own choice on Sunday mornings. If he has never attended church or Sunday school, he is encouraged to visit a number of different ones. An Arrowhead bus drops the boys off at the churches in the neighborhood. Provisions are also made for boys to attend particular instructional meetings held by certain religious groups during the week. In addition, they are permitted to join in the social activities of their church groups. Many of the older boys attend parties and youth group meetings in the community. Often the entire group of boys is invited to a church function or receives tickets for a play or concert in the Quad Cities area. They are always encouraged to attend such functions, and since the ranch owns its own bus, transportation is not a problem.

The staff attempts to help each youngster perceive the importance of religion in day-to-day life. Staff members are careful, however, to avoid unduly influencing a boy to favor a particular faith. This is left for the religious leaders who are frequent visitors to the ranch and who also have contact with the boys at religious services.

The comprehensiveness of the program at Arrowhead suggests that the staff is larger than it is. Hindered by budgetary limitations dating from its inception, the board of directors organized the program to make maximum use of a small staff. Professional help is solicited from the Moline school system. School personnel have been interested in the project from the start, when educators were a part of the original study team. When the program was established, the director of special services of the Moline schools agreed to co-ordinate the educational program at Arrowhead. The superintendent of the ranch supervises the home-work part of the program. Since it started, Arrowhead has had only two superintendents. Both were selected because of their teaching experience and knowledge of and sensitivity toward boys. An assistant superintendent possessing similar personal and professional traits acts as the head of the work-recreation-crafts program and assumes leadership responsibilities in the absence of the superintendent.

The two teachers were selected because of their professional competence and personal qualifications for the unique teaching situation at Arrowhead.

The housemother, cook, and farm manager were chosen because of their ability to relate to boys. The same criteria were applied to the selection of the two male students from nearby Augustana College who live at the ranch and augment the regular staff in supervising leisure-time activities.

The staff includes persons who serve as role models, who, according to psychologists, are important to young boys. The men and women who teach, supervise farm work, and give leadership to the program possess qualities that adolescent boys can perceive as desirable in adults.

On this unique staff, each person is competent in his own area and co-operates with the others to form a workable team. Definite rules and lines of responsibility are not apparent. Everyone pitches in and works. At harvesttime, for instance, the superintendent and assistant superintendent are as likely to be working on the hay wagon as they are to be in their office. The models they present to the boys as individuals and as a group of adults co-operating in a society are commendable.

Though the Arrowhead program is not systematically evaluated, the adjustment of boys is followed up by the superintendent for at least one year after their release from the ranch. The hope is that in the future sufficient funds and personnel will permit a full-time staff person to offer long-term help to boys leaving Arrowhead. Incidental follow-up, however, goes on all the time.

Typical is the case of Jerry, who came to Arrowhead when he was fifteen. This teen-ager was suffering from a dislike of school —a dislike common to many of the ranch boys. Conditions in his home were far from ideal. Jerry's relationship with his father was strained. Once, when the boy could no longer tolerate the abuse of his mother, he had even threatened his father's life. Ultimately the father was placed on a work farm for failure to support his family. Despite his problems, Jerry had one fine attribute: he loved to work in gardens and on farms. Because of his urban origin, however, he had little chance for gardening or farming at home. Since Jerry refused to attend school, authorities filed a petition of delinquency against him. Then he was referred to Arrowhead. There he was placed in the school program, where his work was on the fifth-grade level. After school hours he worked on the farm. With guidance and instruction from the farm supervisor, he learned to milk cows, drive a tractor, and perform other chores. Though Jerry has not returned to his own home, he is now living in a rural foster home where he is working as a hired hand. He has been praised for his knowledge of farming and has found a place for himself in the area in which he is living. Authorities at Arrowhead are confident that Jerry today is a much better citizen because of his experience at the ranch.

Approximately three hundred alienated boys—many like Jerry —have lived at Arrowhead. The staff and the board assert that most of these youngsters have been helped to develop socially acceptable behavior patterns.

CASE FOUR: *Santa Barbara, California*
Santa Barbara County High School Districts, Santa Barbara, California

WORK-EXPERIENCE
EDUCATION PROGRAM

A program in which six high schools co-operate
to provide an opportunity for their young people
to explore the world of work

The work-education program in the high schools of Santa Barbara
County is designed to give high school students enrolled in the
participating schools an opportunity to try out jobs. It is a distinc-
tive program—well organized and broad in scope—possessing
elements within its purposes and structure that are applicable to
work-study programs for alienated youth.

The Santa Barbara program was established in 1953 to meet
the need of the community's teen-agers for adult help in exploring
work as a part of the regular high school experience. A citizens
group took up their cause and convinced officials of a philanthropic
organization that money should be granted to the schools to experiment with work education.

A two-year pilot program was financed by the foundation.
Judged successful, it was later financed and expanded by the school

districts. Today the comprehensive program includes six high schools and a junior college.

Santa Barbara County, one of California's original twenty-seven counties, is located along the southern coast in a fertile section of land between the Santa Maria and the Santa Ynez rivers. Though the economy is diversified, agriculture, the original attraction of the area, still plays an important part in its many activities. Despite a 26 per cent population increase since 1950, the rich ranches, groves, and truck gardens continue to be important to the financial livelihood of thousands of residents. The agricultural base of the economy is supplemented by thriving stone, clay, glass, and food-processing industries. In addition, electrical equipment manufacturing plants, petroleum refineries, printing and publishing firms, and other industries offer regular sources of revenue to the area and provide a stable job structure for the citizens.

In this setting the city of Santa Barbara operates as the government seat, main tourist attraction, and commercial center for the county residents. Its schools also act as the co-ordinating centers for the work-education program, shared by five nearby high school districts.

The Santa Barbara work-education program was started in February 1953 to provide vocational counseling help, job placement, and work experience for the senior high school students in the co-operating schools. The needs of youth were studied by a citizens committee composed of school administrators, counselors, teachers, and private citizens. They concluded that schools should make curricular provisions to help students bridge the gap between school and work. Furthermore, they concluded that the transition of youngsters from school to work could be successful only with the co-operation of the schools, parents, students, and community residents.

The committee drafted a proposal for a work-education program and submitted it to the Rosenberg Foundation, a private philanthropic organization interested in community improvement projects. When the foundation approved the request and granted the group funds to finance a two-year pilot experiment, the committee reorganized itself from a fact-gathering organization into a functional group to serve as the policy-forming body in developing a program, dispensing funds, employing staff, and assisting in interpreting the program to the community.

A philosophy, developed by the committee to guide the establishment and development of the work-education program, stated the project's purpose: to give young people the opportunity to discover their vocational interests while doing actual work in business, industry, and the professions.

The program was also intended to help students to make better occupational choices, to gain the necessary preparation for their chosen work, to find placement on the job, and to adjust and grow on the job.[1]

Today the Santa Barbara Work-Experience Education Program, sponsored by the committee, is a well-integrated part of the five county high school districts: Carpinteria, Lompoc, Santa Barbara, Santa Maria, and Santa Ynez. The program, school-sponsored as part of the regular curriculum, has three distinct parts: exploratory work-experience education, general work-experience education, and vocational work-experience education.

The *exploratory work-experience education* phase includes work done on school time. The program is designed to offer high school students an introduction to the world of work, permitting them to explore their vocational interests and discover their aptitudes through a variety of part-time jobs in industry, business, or the professions. Students are supervised by school personnel and receive school credits toward graduation, though they do not receive any pay. (See Appendix D, Charts 1 and 2, for lists of jobs held by nonpaid students in the exploratory work-experiment education program in February 1955.)

The *general work-experience education phase* is intended to give students experience in bona fide work settings where they meet regular work standards. They work for pay and school credits, during or after school hours, on part-time jobs supervised by school authorities. Their job assignments, however, do not have to be related specifically to the careers for which they are preparing. (See Appendix D, Chart 1, for a list of jobs held by work-experience education students for pay and credit.)

The *vocational work-experience education* phase is set up to provide students paid jobs in the field directly related to the occupation they want to enter after they leave school. It is a laboratory experience for them while they are still enrolled in school.

Each student's assignment in the program is made on the basis of a number of criteria: the student's personal desire, the coordinator's evaluation of the appropriateness of a particular work station, the parents' approval, and state regulations. The number

---

1. Clarence Fielstra, *Work-Experience Education Program in Santa Barbara County High School Districts* (Santa Barbara: Rood Associates, 1961), p. 4.

of credits a student may earn toward graduation is limited by the California Administrative Code.[2]

> *School credit.* For the satisfactory completion of work-experience education, the district shall grant credit to a pupil in an amount not to exceed:
>
> *a) In high school,* a total of forty semester periods made up of one or a combination of two or more of the following types:
>
> (1) *Exploratory work-experience education:* Five semester periods for each semester, with a maximum of ten semester periods earned in two semesters.
>
> (2) *General work-experience education:* Ten semester periods for each semester, with a maximum of twenty semester periods.
>
> (3) *Vocational work-experience education:* Ten semester periods for each semester, with a maximum of forty semester periods.
>
> *b) In junior colleges,* a total of sixteen credit hours made up of one or a combination of two or more of the following types:
>
> (1) *Exploratory work-experience education:* Three credit hours per semester, with a maximum of one semester.
>
> (2) *General work-experience education:* Three credit hours per semester, with a maximum total of six credit hours.
>
> (3) *Vocational work-experience education:* Four credit hours per semester, with a maximum total of sixteen credit hours.

The communities in Santa Barbara County offer a wide variety of jobs to young people in the program. Just as the jobs vary, the kinds of business and industries co-operating in the program also exhibit a many-faceted picture of work experience. In 1961 there were one hundred employers. (See Appendix D, Chart 3, for a detailed list of the kinds and number of business and professional establishments employing students in the work-experience education program in Santa Barbara.)

As of August 1961, school officials estimated that approximately two thousand young people had participated in the program during the 1960-61 school year.[3]

The Santa Barbara school officials consider themselves to be successful because of the initial thought and planning put into the program by the citizens committee that instigated the project. They observe that the rapid expansion and acceptance of the program since 1953 can be explained through the relation of the

---

2. Art. 13.1, sec. 115.22, subchap. 1, chap. 1.

3. Secretary of Youth Conference Planning Committee, *Report of Santa Barbara Work-Education Program* (Sacramento, August 2, 1961).

program to those who participate in it as students, employers, or parents. They concluded that the program is valuable—

To the students. Working in the adult world has given students a new feeling of "belonging." Being given responsibilities has in turn made the student accept those responsibilities in a more mature way. The young person who has "tried out" in a variety of work situations is more able to choose the career for which he is best suited and in which he can contribute the most as a citizen. The work-education program has resulted in bringing youth and adults closely together in a way that has not been possible before.

To the community. This organized approach to work-education has been received with great favor by the citizens of Santa Barbara County. Young people have demonstrated that they can be relied upon for really important work. Giving them such meaningful activity as part of the community has meant that they are less likely to get into trouble. Testifying at the Santa Barbara Town Meeting on Juvenile Delinquency on March 20, 1956, several young people reported that youth's problems could be solved not by recreation, but by an extension of work opportunities such as those they had enjoyed.

To the schools. The close association of school and business that resulted from work-education—school supervision, conferences between school personnel and employers and between students and co-ordinators, and work evaluation—all help the schools become aware of needed changes in the curriculum to prepare young people for the demands of the working world. The work-education program is one of the best ways for the schools to learn about rapid changes and advances in work methods and to revise educational programs in accordance with these advances.

To the future of the country. The great scientific and technical advances in the United States today have brought about the age of automation—an age in which every worker must be a specialist. Young people who have been trained in work education during their high school days will be more able to make effective contributions to the adult world when their school days are over.[4]

The participants range from boys and girls of sixteen years of age to college students in their early twenties. The largest group includes high school juniors and seniors. The number of persons involved in a project of this kind is difficult to estimate. Including faculties, school staffs, employers, co-operating agencies, and almost five hundred adults, nearly two thousand persons participated during the 1960–61 school year.

An average of about 26 per cent of the graduates from 1955 to 1959 had participated in work-experience education for credit.

---

4. *Ibid.,* p. 14.

In most school districts, boys made up the bulk of the student population electing such courses. In Santa Barbara's program in 1955–56 only 35 per cent of the students participating in the various phases of the program were boys. In 1959 the percentage of boys in the program increased to 42 per cent. In 1960, 44 per cent of the participants were boys.

School officials reason that the program is more attractive to girls because—

> There are more suitable job opportunities for girls than for boys of high school age.
>
> At this age, girls are generally somewhat more mature than boys and can more readily see the benefits of taking part in the program.
>
> More boys than girls take highly academic college-preparatory courses, so that boys have less time for work-experience education.[5]

To be eligible for a work-education assignment a pupil must qualify under the California Administrative Code.[6] A pupil must meet the following requirements:

> Have attained junior standing in high school or sixteen years of age, except those with specific authorization by the principal. Pupils with exceptional need who are fifteen years of age may be enrolled.
>
> Be a full-time pupil. This means one of the following:
> (1) A legally indentured apprentice of a continuation pupil, regardless of the number of subjects or the secondary school in which he is enrolled.
> (2) A high school pupil enrolled in four or more subjects, including work-experience education as one of such subjects.
> (3) A junior college student enrolled in twelve or more credit hours including the credit hours for work experience.
>
> Have, if a high school pupil, parental or guardian approval.
>
> Have the approval of the school guidance service to enroll in the work-experience education chosen.
>
> Have a vocational or educational goal to which the work-experience education program chosen will, in the opinion of the district, contribute.

Interestingly, this program does not specify that pupils exhibit special characteristics other than those required by state mandate.

---

5. *Ibid.*, p. 18.
6. Art. 13.1, sec. 115.23, subchap. 1, chap. 1.

Over the years, the program has tended to become top-heavy with average and above-average students. This phenomenon may reflect the relatively small number of problem-prone youngsters in the Santa Barbara area. The population of alienated youth there is almost nil, according to statistics on juvenile offenses. As measured by police records, the county ranks among the lowest in the state of California in percentage of juvenile delinquents in the population.

Whether or not the work-education program in the schools contributes to the good record of the youth of Santa Barbara is undetermined. Any hypothesis about its positive correlation would have to be investigated before such a contention could be made in good faith. At any rate, whatever influence the program may have upon delinquency in the area, it certainly can be looked to as an example of a work-study program containing many elements applicable to school districts that possess a population of alienated youth. The program is adaptable in whole or in part to other schools in a variety of communities.

The administration of the program requires a close working relationship between school, state employment services, and employers. Each school district employs a co-ordinator, either full or part time, who oversees the placement of students, supervises them on their work assignments, co-ordinates their activities with their parents and employers, and reports to counselors and teachers on the progress of each student assigned to a work station. The number of staff personnel assigned to the program varies with each school. An example of the staffing of one program is the assignment of personnel in the largest district—Santa Barbara—containing two high schools and a junior college.

The Santa Barbara Staff

Co-ordinator (full-time)   His time is
                                  distributed as noted hereafter

SANTA BARBARA CITY COLLEGE
Secretary   Work-education program
                                  and student activities
                                  program

State Department of
Employment   Full time in program in
Youth Co-ordinator   all schools
Co-ordinator   2 hours a day

SANTA BARBARA HIGH SCHOOL

Four teachers	2 periods a day
State Department of Employment representative	4 hours a day
Co-ordinator	2 hours a day
Student secretaries	1 period a day each

SAN MARCOS HIGH SCHOOL

One teacher	6 periods a day
State Department of Employment representative	4 hours a day
Co-ordinator	2 hours a day
Student secretary	2 periods a day

Staff personnel are chosen because of their interest in the program and their ability to work with students, parents, and employers. Specific professional qualifications are not a requirement for appointment.

At all schools, monthly staff meetings are held to keep the personnel up to date on the progress of the total program. Individual co-ordinators from five participating districts hold frequent meetings to share information and to co-ordinate activities to insure a program of maximum flexibility.

The program has been evaluated thoroughly, under a grant from the Rosenberg Foundation to the Citizens Advisory Committee. The study during the 1959–60 school year was directed by Dr. Clarence Fielstra, on leave from his position as assistant dean of the school of education at the University of California at Los Angeles. The major purposes were:

To describe the nature of the Work-Experience Education Program in the five high school districts of Santa Barbara County.

To evaluate the purposes, procedures, and outcomes of the program.

To identify problems and issues, as well as strengths, in the program.

To recommend some basic principles that could provide guidance for the continuation of this program and the development of similar programs in other high school districts.[7]

7. Clarence Fielstra, *op. cit.*, p. iii.

The method of the research design included a questionnaire evaluation of the program and an experimental substudy to determine any differences between students who had participated in the program and those who had not. Extensive use was made of pupils' cumulative records. More than 1500 persons participated.

Here are conclusions and recommendations from the study:[8]

> The purposes of the study reported in this monograph were (1) to describe the nature of the Work Experience Education Program in the five high school districts of Santa Barbara County, (2) to evaluate the purposes, procedures, and outcomes of the program, (3) to identify problems and issues, as well as strengths, in the program, and (4) to recommend some basic principles which should provide guidance for the continuation of this program and the development of a similar program in other high school disttricts.
>
> Findings relative to the first three purposes of the study are reported in Chapters I through IX of this monograph, and the most pertinent of these findings are incorporated in this chapter as supporting evidence of the conclusions stated. Following the statements of conclusion, recommendations—related to the fourth purpose of the study—are presented.
>
> Some of the conclusions stated were based on the opinions expressed by the following groups in personal interviews or in response to questionnaires: principals of the five high schools offering the program, parents (N=123) whose sons or daughters had taken part in the program and had graduated from high school in 1959, teachers (N=130) who had completed at least one year of experience in the high schools of Santa Barbara County, employers (N=100) who had represented all of the communities of the county and who had employed students in the Work Experience Education Program, former students (N=146) who had taken part in the program and had graduated from high school in 1955 or 1956.
>
> Additional conclusions were based on the results of statistical tests of the tenability of null hypotheses which had been formulated with regard to differences between former student participants and nonparticipants in the program. In this part of the study 1,131 subjects were used; 320 had taken part in the program (for credit) while in high school, and 811 had not; 378 of the subjects had graduated from high school in 1955 or 1956, and 753 had graduated in 1959.
>
> The remainder of the conclusions were based on the observations and opinions of the research team members who carried on the study of the Work Experience Education Program.

---

8. Clarence Fielstra, *op. cit.*, pp. 69–81. (Because of the extent and depth of the evaluation, only the conclusions and recommendations of the study are reported here. Readers interested in the details of this fine piece of research are referred to the Santa Barbara Schools for the complete report.)

CONCLUSIONS

To the extent that the findings of this study are valid, the following conclusions seem to be justified:

1. *The Work Experience Education Program in the high school districts of Santa Barbara County is extensive, successful, and of much value.*

EXTENSIVENESS OF PROGRAM

During the years from 1953 to 1960 approximately one-fourth of all the graduates from the participating high schools located in Carpinteria, Lompoc, Santa Barbara, Santa Maria, and Santa Ynez high school districts of Santa Barbara County had taken part in the Work Experience Education Program for an average of about 10 semester periods of school credit while they were in the eleventh and twelfth grades.

The total number of students enrolled in the program for school credit during a given semester reached 325 in the Spring Semester of 1960 (not including 50 students enrolled in the program at San Marcos High school, a new school in the city of Santa Barbara). In addition to that number, 116 students were enrolled during the semester in the "non-credit" Work Experience Education Program of two of the five high schools. The latter group made up approximately 8 percent of the junior and senior classes in the two schools.

Many more girls than boys took part in the program for credit, the percentage of girls ranging from 65 percent in 1955–56 to 56 percent in 1960. In the non-credit program 50 percent of the participants were girls, and 50 percent were boys.

Two-thirds of the students who took part in the program for high school credit did not earn any monetary pay for their participation, but one-third of them gained credit *and* earned pay for their work in the program. The latter group worked twenty hours a week "on the job" to earn five semester periods of school credit, whereas the "non-pay" group worked ten hours a week "on the job" to earn five semester periods of credit. The average amount of credit earned by students through participation in the program was 11.58 semester periods for boys and 8.95 semester periods for girls.

The jobs held by students in the credit program ("pay" and "non-pay") ranged from assisting doctors, lawyers, teachers, and nurses to helping janitors and gasoline service station attendants. Most of the "non-pay" jobs (in Exploratory Work Experience Education) held by students were in professional fields; and most of the "pay" jobs (in General Work Experience Education) were in clerical, sales, or mechanical fields; but there were notable exceptions to these generalizations. "Non-pay" jobs were much more frequently held by girls than by boys, and "pay" jobs were much more frequently held by boys than by girls.

PURPOSES OF PROGRAM

Seventeen purposes were attributed to the Work Experience Education Program by the principals of the five high schools involved in this study. The purposes, ranging from the facilitation of vocational guidance and occupational exploration to the development of better personality and poise on the part of the student participants in the program, were the following—listed in rank order of ratings by the principals:

1.5 To gain knowledge and attitudes necessary for successful job performance

1.5 To explore the fields in which occupational interest lies and to determine suitability for those fields

4.5 To make wiser career choices

4.5 To make progress toward chosen occupational goals

4.5 To learn to assume greater responsibility

4.5 To develop more appreciation and understanding of the relationship between formal education and job success

7.5 To develop better understanding of the meaning of work

7.5 To broaden understanding of the occupational world and of working conditions in the world of work

10.0 To learn what employment entails

10.0 To learn how to get along with fellow workers and employers

10.0 To make better school adjustment and avoid drop-out

13.0 To develop better personality and more poise

13.0 To develop better understanding of the community

13.0 To make the transition from school to work

16.0 To acquire better work habits

16.0 To augment financial resources

16.0 To develop more appreciation of the value of wages

PLACE OF PROGRAM IN CURRICULUM

More than 95 percent of the parents, teachers, and students whose opinions were obtained considered the program to be of "much" or of "some" value; and an average of less than 2.5 percent of these groups of respondents believed that the program was of "little or no" value. Furthermore, great majorities of the respondents (98 percent of the parents, 83 percent of the teachers, 100 percent of the principals, and 90 percent of the employers) considered the program to be an "essential" or "useful" part of the total school curriculum.

It is quite probable that no other aspect of the total programs in these high schools—academic, non-academic, or extra-curricular—could have received such overwhelming and enthusiastic support from laymen, educators, and students as did the Work Experience Education Program in this evaluative study.

STUDENT BENEFITS FROM PROGRAM

Based on the opinions expressed by four groups of respondents—parents, teachers, employers, and students—the following purposes of the Work Experience Education Program were those which were most often achieved by student participants in the high school districts of Santa

Barbara County (listed in order of average rankings by the groups of respondents):

1. To learn what employment entails
2. To gain knowledge and attitudes necessary for successful job performance
3. To develop better understanding of the meaning of work
4. To learn to assume greater responsibility
5. To learn how to get along with fellow workers and employers
6. To explore the fields in which occupational interest lies and to determine suitability for those fields
7. To acquire better work habits
8. To make wiser career choice

SCHOOL BENEFITS FROM PROGRAM

All of the principals and more than half of the teachers whose opinions were obtained expressed the belief that the high schools of Santa Barbara County gained several benefits as a result of their having the Work Experience Education Program. Chief among those benefits were the following, listed in order of rankings by the teachers:

1. Provides assistance in occupational guidance
2. Develops good school-community relations
3. Acquaints employers with the work that young people trained in schools can perform
4. Utilizes many community facilities and resources for training purposes and thus makes it possible for the school to provide training in fields that the school program could otherwise not serve
5. Provides an opportunity for the school to relate academic training to job requirements
6. Provides a direct avenue through which the school can meet community needs
7. Increases the school's ability to hold students in school for a longer period of time

Although almost one-half of the teachers said that the Work Experience Education Program had "no effect" on their courses, 45 percent of them reported that the program had at least "some" effect. The effects on their courses most often noted by teachers were these:

1. Provides some topics or problems for discussion
2. Provides motivation for additional interest in my course (s)
3. Provides basis for more use of related community resources

EMPLOYER BENEFITS FROM PROGRAM

According to opinions expressed by employers with whom students in the Work Experience Education Program had been placed, the greatest benefits of the program to the employers themselves were those listed below, in order of rankings by the employers:

1. Helped train future full-time employees

2. Made available a valuable and carefully selected labor supply, and implemented recruitment from it

3. Improved public relations

4. Resulted in improved office procedures

5. Resulted in improved production methods

6.5 Reduced costs resulting from excessive turnover

6.5 Improved morale in the firm

In the attainment of these objectives through the employment of youth in the program, the employers reported that they had had complete support and cooperation from labor unions and governmental agencies.

NON-INTERFERENCE OF PROGRAM WITH
REGULAR SCHOOL WORK

More than four-fifths of the former participants in the Work Experience Education Program said that their participation had interfered neither with their other courses in high school nor with their extra-curricular activities; 11 percent said that extra-curricular activities were interfered with; and only 2.1 percent said that other school subjects suffered.

A study of students' cumulative records in the high schools revealed no differences which were significant at the 5 percent level between program participants and non-participants in the mean number of semester periods of either academic or non-academic subjects completed in high school. It was found, also, that even if the participants had not been given credit for work in the program, the males would have earned an average of 22.3 more semester periods of subject credit than are normally required for high school graduation, and the females would have earned an average of 29.8 more semester periods of credit than required.

These findings supported the participants' claim that work in the program was, on the average, not carried on at the expense of other subjects but that it was carried on over and above a normal load of regular course enrollment and activity. For some students, part of the time given to Work Experience Education was taken from "free" school periods; for some, part of the time was taken from extra-curricular activities; for some, part of the time was taken from elective non-academic subjects; but for very few was any time given to the program which otherwise would have been given to academic subjects.

FAVORABLE COMPARISON OF PARTICIPANTS
IN PROGRAM WITH NON-PARTICIPANTS

Based on a follow-up study of 1,131 graduates from the high schools of Santa Barbara County, of whom 320 had taken part in the Work Experience Education Program (for credit) while in high school and 811 had not, it was found that male participants in the program slightly excelled male non-participants in such factors as total semester periods of academic subjects completed in high school; semester periods of science, mathematics, business education, and shop completed in high school; socio-economic level; satisfaction with present job; weekly salaries earned in post-high school employment; grade-point averages earned in college; years of non-college post-high school training completed; agreement of high school interest-inventory scores with fields of occupational choice at time of high school graduation; agreement of interest-inventory scores with fields of occupations presently held; and in incidence of marriage within three or four years after graduation from high school. These differences, however, were not statistically significant at the 5 percent level of confidence.

It was found also that female participants in the program slightly excelled female non-participants in such factors as grade-point averages earned in high school; socio-economic level; semester periods of social studies, mathematics, English, and business education completed in high school; total semester periods of subjects completed in high school; satisfaction with job presently held; weekly salaries earned in post-high school employment; years of non-college post-high school training completed; agreement of interest-inventory scores with fields of occupational choice at time of high school graduation; and agreement of interest-inventory scores with fields of occupations presently held. These differences, however, were all found to be without statistical significance at the 5 percent level of confidence.

The only differences found to be statistically significant at the 1 percent to 5 percent level of confidence were between *female* participants and non-participants in the program. These differences were in the following factors:

1. Intelligence quotients (higher for participants)
2. Agreement of levels of occupational choices made at time of high school graduation with levels of occupations presently held (higher for participants)
3. Incidence of college-potential students who entered college (higher for non-participants)
4. Incidence of marriage within three to four years after graduation from high school (higher for non-participants)

Among the other differences found between former participants and non-participants in the program was the difference in percentages of the former students in both groups who reported receiving, while in high school, the kinds of help which were considered to be objectives of the Work Experience Education Program. Much higher percentages (by 20 percent or more) of participants than of non-participants said that they had received the following kinds of help:

1. To broaden understanding of the occupational world and of working conditions in the world of work
2. To make the transition from school to work
3. To learn what employment entails
4. To make progress toward chosen occupational goals
5. To explore the fields in which occupational interest lies and to determine suitability for those fields
6. To develop understanding of the meaning of work
7. To develop better personality and more poise

8. To augment financial resources

9. To develop understanding of the community

Another difference found between participants and non-participants was in the sources of the vocational guidance which they reported that they had received while they were in high school. Chief sources reported by participants were (1) Work Experience Education Program, (2) regular school subjects, and (3) parents and friends; and chief sources reported by non-participants were (1) parents and friends, (2) regular school subjects, and (3) part-time jobs—not related to the program.

OUTSTANDING STRENGTHS OF PROGRAM

The most outstanding strength of the program in Santa Barbara County, in the research staff's judgment, has been the high quality of its leadership—both lay and professional. The amount of time, effort, and wise counsel provided by lay members of the advisory committee has exemplified the very best kind of community interest in the education of its youth. The fact that the splendid services of these lay leaders were given without any remuneration whatsoever is particularly worthy of note. Without this kind of interest, support, and assistance, it is most unlikely that the program could have gained its amazing acceptance and approval by parents, business men, labor unions, professional groups, and other members of the community.

Most impressive also has been the kind of leadership given to the program by such educators as the county superintendent, the district superintendents, the high school principals, the guidance personnel, the consulting director of the project, and the program directors and coordinators. The dedicated efforts of a number of these leaders have been largely responsible for the development of a program which has earned the favorable attention of laymen and educators alike throughout the United States and many foreign countries.

Another outstanding strength of the program has been the extensiveness of its use of community resources. Banks, libraries, hospitals, medical offices, law offices, publishing offices, pharmacies, retail stores, automobile service shops, and literally hundreds of other community facilities have supplemented school classrooms as centers of some very important functions of education. Thus, millions of dollars worth of such facilities, plus the immeasurably valuable human resources afforded by the employers, have been made a part of the educational program of the Santa Barbara County High School districts. These excellent, up-to-date, varied facilities and resources could not be financed by means of school budgets; but even if they were, much would be lost in terms of the good school-community relations and understandings which have been resulting from the Work Experience Education Program.

A third great strength of the program has been its contribution to the dignifying of work. The cooperation of community and school leaders in the development of the program has provided students with assurance that education about work and experiences in work were considered important in the development of mature and effective citizenship. The granting of school credit for participation in the program has given them further evidence that well-selected, well-planned, and well-supervised experiences in real jobs were valued just as highly as educational experiences which are carried on exclusively within classrooms of a high school.

Furthermore, the initiation into the world of work has provided students with new insights regarding the nature of human relations on the adult level as well as regarding the nature of our economic system; and in many instances it has added to their sense of being an important part of their community with both the opportunity and responsibility for making their own best contributions to society whether it be on the professional or unskilled-labor level.

For the above reasons, and doubtless many other related ones, the Work Experience Education Program has apparently contributed a great deal to the "status" of work in the minds of students, and their general enthusiasm for the program has strongly reflected their "healthy" attitudes toward vocational aspects of life.

2. *There are some shortcomings or deficiencies in the present Work Experience Education Program.*

INSUFFICIENT CONFORMANCE WITH STATE
REQUIREMENTS AND RECOMMENDATIONS

It was found that although the program did generally comply with the requirements stipulated in the *California Administrative Code,* it was not in full compliance with its provisions for classification of students in the program and, in some schools, with provisions that credit must be given in each of these classifications. It also fell short of the "spirit" of the *Code* with regard to the amount of school supervision to be provided students.

Most of the recommendations made in Tyler's *Report of the Study of Work Experience Programs in California High Schools and Junior Colleges* (July, 1956) were found to be fully conformed with in the Santa Barbara County high school districts. In one or more of the high schools, however, the following recommendations were violated: that assignments to program coordinators should not exceed 50 students in the "exploratory" program or 72 students in the "general" work experience education program, that substantial amounts of well-qualified secretarial service—commensurate with the needed volume of work—should be provided program coordinators, that the program should consist of classroom activity and of part-time employment which is viewed as the laboratory portion of such school activity, and that the program should be administered through the guidance department of the school.

With regard to the evaluative questions raised in the California *Handbook on Work Experience Education* (May, 1959), it was found that most of them could be answered in the affirmative for the program in Santa Barbara County. Among the questions which had to be answered largely in the negative, however, were those which were concerned with the amount of on-the-job supervision by school personnel and with the adequacy of record keeping, evaluation, organization of students' learning experiences in the program, and correlation of the program with classroom instruction.

NEGATIVE CRITICISMS MADE OF PROGRAM
BY RESPONDENTS TO STUDY

Although overwhelming and enthusiastic support of the program was found on the part of the great majority of parents, teachers, employers, and students, a few "complaints" were voiced by some members of each group.

Fewer criticisms of the program were made by parents than by any of the other groups. A very small number of the parents, however, expressed their belief that some employers did not "live up to their promises" or that they "didn't pay high enough wages to the students working for them." An even smaller number thought that something was wrong with the school's management of the program because their children had not been placed in jobs even though such placement had been requested by both the children and their parents.

Almost no strong negative criticisms were made by school counselors, and few such criticisms were made by teachers of non-academic subjects; but a number of complaints came from teachers of academic subjects. Among their comments were those to the effect that the program "interferes with school work," that it leads to an over-interest in "getting a pay check now," that it has become "the tail that wags the dog" and controls the whole school schedule, that it permits some poor "placements" of pupils in jobs and thus contributes to undermining good public relations with employers (to the contrary, 77.6 percent of the teachers said that the program "develops good school-community relations," and 76 percent of the employers reported that the program "resulted in their better understanding of the school and closer relation with it"), and that in some instances it serves lazy students as an escape from good hard work in solid school subjects (however, 70 percent of the students reported that participation in the program required as much or more time and effort per semester period of credit than regular school subjects, and participants in the program were found to have taken no fewer "solid" subjects than non-participants did).

Few negative criticisms of the program were expressed by employers; and those which they did make were, without exception, directed against a small number of students whose attitudes or behaviors were considered to be less than desirable. They said that such students were interested overly much in the pay check, that they lacked sufficient responsibility, that they tried to avoid unpleasant aspects of their jobs, and that they lacked adaptability. Such criticisms were more frequently made of students who were in the program for "pay" than of those who were in it for credit only.

Critical comments made by students who had taken part in the program were almost invariably in the form of recommendations for its improvement. The few negative expressions which they did make were to the effect that "some kids goofed off" while in the program and, worse still, weren't "caught at it" and that in some instances the work experience was merely a "lark" permitting a waste of time and "rewarded with easy credit." There was also some "griping" by the students concerning the inappropriate nature of their job assignments and concerning the "difficult personalities" of their employers. Sharp criticism was also directed by them against certain teachers who "apparently failed to understand the values of the program and who seemed deliberately to interfere with its success."

CHIEF DEFICIENCIES IN PROGRAM

The deficiency in the present program most clearly identified by the research staff was in the amount of supervision provided by school representatives to students on their jobs. Although it was found that almost 20 percent of the student participants in the program reported being visited on the job by a school coordinator at least once each month, 43.8 percent of them said that they had no such on-the-job visits at all, and 13 percent stated that they had been visited on the job only at the time of their placement. To the extent that these reports were accurate, there have been serious violations of policies which earlier had been formulated with regard to the matter of on-the-job supervision by school personnel.

Further evidence that many students in the program were not given enough supervision by school representatives was found in the fact that 26 percent of the employers rated such supervision "inadequate" or "barely adequate." These low ratings were given in spite of the fact that the relatively rare on-the-job visits by coordinators had been supplemented by their telephone calls and personal discussions with the employers. Essential and useful as the latter procedures are, they could hardly be expected to completely supplant the visitation of students.

Reasons for the failure of program coordinators to pay at least two on-the-job supervisory visits per semester to each participant appeared most frequently to be lack of time on the part of the coordinator because of the heaviness of his load. In some instances, however, the problem was further complicated by the fact that the students worked on jobs during the evening or weekends when the coordinators were not "on duty."

The insufficiency of relationship between the job experiences and school experiences was also clearly recognized as a weakness in the program. It was found, for example, that 50 percent of the employers believed that closer relationships could exist between school courses and work experience jobs, and they recommended that either special classes for Work Experience Education Program students be organized or that present courses be modified to include material of greater value to these students.

Similarly, 85 percent of the students expressed the opinion that there should be greater correlation of the Work Experience Education Program with the remainder of the curriculum. Their chief proposals of means to accomplish this goal were that special classes be offered to students in the program, that "related units" be introduced in other subjects, and that clubs and conferences be organized for participants.

A third weakness in the program—the relatively small extent to which members of the guidance staff were involved in helping students make vocational choices—was especially evidenced in the finding that fewer than 25 percent of the students (both participants and non-participants in the program) reported the school counseling program to be a source of vocational guidance. It is rather generally recognized that guidance personnel have unreasonably heavy counseling assignments, and that may account for the apparent negligence in helping students make one of the basic choices of their lives—the choice of a career. Whatever may be the reasons for this shortcoming, it must be overcome if the Work Experience Education Program, as well as the total educational program, of the high schools is to be further improved.

The fourth marked weakness found in the program was the lack of clear distinction between participation in it for "pay" *and* "credit." Some students, for example, did not know whether or not they had been given school credit for their work experience. Also, a number of employers didn't know who of the students engaged by them got credit at school and who did not. This kind of confusion did not exist, of course, in school districts where only the Exploratory Work Experience Education Program (for which no pay but only credit was given) was offered.

There was even confusion as to who was in the program and who was not. It appeared that most students who had obtained part-time employment without any help from school personnel did not expect school credit for the experience and, therefore, did not request it; but some other students who had also obtained part-time jobs entirely on their own got school credit for it merely by reporting the employment (in a few instances even months after it was terminated) to the school officials.

It also appeared that some coordinators considered every student who had acquired a work permit to be in the Work Experience Education Program, and the policies governing the giving or withholding of credit to students with part-time jobs were not sharply drawn. These coordinators seemed not to have made a clear distinction between part-time "non-program" employment and participation in the General Work Experience Education Program (for pay and credit).

If credit is to be given for work experience in the same manner that it is given for other subjects in the curriculum, it would seem only reasonable that school personnel should be extensively involved in the planning, supervising, and evaluating of the experience. Conversely it would seem indefensible to give credit for any such experience when school personnel are not involved in its planning, supervision, and evaluation. It follows, then, that any confusion of credit and non-credit aspects of the program constitutes a serious weakness in the administration of the program.

3. *There is much similarity in the recommendations made by various*

groups for improving the Work Experience Education Program in Santa Barbara County high school districts.

Based on replies to specific questions, on "free-response" comments, and on results of personal interviews, it was found that parents, teachers, employers, and students had a number of recommendations to make for improving the Work Experience Education Program of the high schools in Santa Barbara County. There was considerable overlapping of the recommendations made by members of these four groups, and in no instance were the recommendations that were made by one group found to be in disagreement with the recommendations made by any other group.

PARENT RECOMMENDATIONS

The chief recommendations made by parents were the following:

a. Continue and, if possible, expand the program.

b. Increase the amount of supervision by school personnel.

c. Involve in the program only those employers who have a sincere and intelligent interest in its purposes.

TEACHER RECOMMENDATIONS

Recommendations most frequently made by teachers were these:

a. Continue and up-grade the program.

b. Coordinate the program more fully with the school guidance service and with the California Department of Employment service.

c. Correlate more fully the work done by students on the job with work they do in school.

d. Provide a greater amount of supervision by school personnel of students' work on-the-job.

e. Place the students in only those jobs in which they have an interest and from which they can gain planned learning experiences.

f. Provide program coordinators with more clerical assistants, office space, and transportation facilities; or reduce the number of students in the program for credit if such additions are not possible.

g. Arrange periodic (probably monthly) meetings of all students who are in the program for credit.

h. Provide students more and earlier orientation to the program, beginning no later than the first semester of the tenth grade.

i. Involve a representative of the teachers in local advisory committees for the program in each of the high schools.

j. Carry on a continuous program of informing parents, teachers, and employers about the program and its achievements through the use of periodic bulletins, special meetings, and other appropriate means.

EMPLOYER RECOMMENDATIONS

Employers of students in the program made the following recommendations most frequently:

a. Continue and expand the program.

b. Provide more supervision of student participants by school co-ordinators.

c. Screen students more effectively before placing them on jobs.

d. Keep employers better informed about the purposes and scope of the program and make certain that they know exactly what is expected of them.

e. Provide students more "school preparation" for "on-the-job" experiences, and place additional emphasis on the students' responsibilities to their employers.

f. Organize special classes or clubs at school for students who are participating in the program.

STUDENT RECOMMENDATIONS

Recommendations most frequently made by former students who had taken part in the program when they were in high school were these:

a. Continue and improve the program.

b. Begin the program earlier and provide orientation to it no later than at the beginning of the tenth grade.

c. Provide more school supervision and guidance of students in the program.

d. Arrange periodic group conferences and meetings of program participants.

e. Organize special classes or clubs (or both) for students who are in the program.

f. Develop better understanding and greater support of the program by faculty members.

4. *Although there is much agreement among members of the Advisory Committee regarding numerous "issues" involved in the program, several of the issues are still unresolved.*

General agreement was found among members of the Advisory Committee of the Work Experience Education Program concerning most issues which were identified in the course of the evaluative study. Such agreement was found, for example, with regard to the following points of view: that the program should continue to be open to both college-preparatory students and non-college-preparatory students; that the program should continue to serve the needs of all pupils—the dull or slow-learning, the average, and the gifted; that major purposes of the program should continue to include the enrichment of general education, the provision of occupational information and exploration, and the assistance of students in the choosing of a career; and that a regular high school course in occupational information should not supplant the Work Experience Education Program—even for college-preparatory students.

Some basic questions on which there was found to be considerable disagreement, however, among the Advisory Committee members were these:

a. Should high school credit only, monetary pay only, or both credit *and* pay be given students who take part in the program?

b. Should students who take part in the program for school credit be more carefully supervised than those who are in it for no credit?

c. Should more complete records be kept for students who take part in the program for credit than for those who are taking it for no credit?

d. Should program coordinators be required to hold the kinds of credentials already required for school counselors?

e. Which should receive the greater emphasis in the program—the objectives of general education or the objectives of vocational education?

f. Should the term "Work Experience Education" be used in reference to only that part of the program which involves high school credit or should it be used also in reference to non-credit aspects of the program?

g. Should students in rural areas, where long distances and transportation problems present difficulties, be permitted to be absent from school one entire day each week in order to participate in the Work Experience Education Program?

Opinions held by the evaluative study staff with regard to the above questions are indicated in the recommendations which follow.

RECOMMENDATIONS

Based on the conclusions reached in this evaluative study, the research staff recommends that the following principles be adhered to in the continuation of the Work Experience Education Program of the Santa Barbara County high school districts and in the initiation of such a program in other high school districts:

1. *Advisory committees should be organized in each high school district which has, or is initiating, a Work Experience Education Program.*

The membership of the district advisory committee should include both laymen and professional educators. The laymen should be community leaders who represent labor, business, industry, agriculture, and other similar groups. The professional educators should include the superintendent, principal, program coordinator, director of guidance, and at least one teacher. A representative of the State Department of Employment and the county school office should also be included on the committee.

The primary function of this committee should be the determination of the philosophy, objectives, and policies which govern the program. It should also serve as a liaison group between the school and the community. Continuous evaluation of the program should likewise be a concern of the committee.

Meetings of the local advisory committee should be held at least once each semester, and inactive members of the committee should be replaced whenever such inactivity appears likely to persist.

2. *The services of a county-wide advisory committee should be utilized.*

Whenever several high school districts within a county are carrying on a program, a county advisory committee should be organized to serve in the coordination of the programs of the various districts and to advise representatives of the districts with regard to matters of policy. Guidance should also be given by the county committee in evaluating and improving the programs of the local districts.

Membership on the county committee should include representative community leaders (as in local districts), the county superintendent of schools, superintendent of each participating school district, high school principals, directors of guidance, directors of the program, appropriate county school office personnel, a member of the State Department of Employment, and representative teachers selected from the district advisory committees.

At least one meeting of the county advisory committee should be held each semester, and members should be retained on the committee only as long as they are active.

The organization and operation of the Santa Barbara County Advisory Committee should serve as a pattern for other counties. As stated in the conclusions, this committee has provided outstanding leadership, counsel, and other service in the organization, development, evaluation and improvement of the Work Experience Education Program in the high school districts of this county.

3. *Program development and operation should be guided by code regulations and by recommendations based on careful study.*

State, federal, and local code regulations must, of course, be followed to the letter in any program, and adherence to the spirit of those regulations is equally important. In addition, recommendations based on extensive and careful study should serve as guides to the development and improvement of each program. It is the opinion of the research staff that the most comprehensive and useful source of such recommendations available at this time is the California *Handbook on Work Experience Education,* the preliminary edition of which was published by the California State Department of Education in May, 1959.

4. *The term "Work Experience Education" should be used only in reference to a program in which students participate for school credit or for school credit and pay.*

Non-curricular, non-credit work activities of students must not be considered a part of any Work Experience Education Program. In fact, the *California Administrative Code* (Article 13.1, Section 115.22) specifies that the school district *shall grant credit* for the satisfactory completion of work under each of the three classifications of the Work Experience Program— (a) Exploratory Work Experience Education, (b) General Work Experience Education, and (c) Vocational Work Experience Education.

Immediate steps should be taken in Santa Barbara County to discontinue the practice, now common in two high school districts, of considering some students who are engaged in non-credit work activity as being participants in the Work Experience Education Program. Such practice is clearly in violation of *Code* stipulations.

Although students who are served by the school only to the extent of being "placed" in a job or of being given some "follow-up" assistance while on a job cannot be considered a part of the Work Experience Education Program, such placement and follow-up service is a very valuable function of the school; and the time and effort given to it by school personnel should be fully recognized as a part of their professional load.

5. *Admission to the Work Experience Education Program should be limited to only those students for whom careful planning, supervision, and evaluation will be provided by school personnel and for whom the experience will have genuine educational value.*

As is true of other curricular experiences, the work education experience should be carefully *planned* to meet definite purposes, carefully *supervised* to assure best learning conditions and procedures, and carefully *evaluated* to assess results. This planning, supervising, and evaluating not only should involve the students, parents, and employers, but it also must extensively involve school personnel so that the work experience may qualify for curricular recognition along with other school subjects and so that the experience may be of greatest value in achieving educational objectives.

Any student who is not provided this comprehensive service by the school should not be considered a part of the Work Experience Education Program and should, of course, not be given school credit for his part-time employment. The giving of credit *ex post facto* for some employment experience a student may have had during his previous years in high school should not be practiced.

6. *Sound bases for the assignment of students to a given classification of Work Experience Education and for determining the ratio of on-the-job hours to semester periods of school credit which they may earn for participation in that classification must be developed and followed.*

Inasmuch as a secondary school student may take part in any one of the three classifications of Work Experience Education (*Code,* Article 13.1, Section 115.21) , it is essential that the reasons for assigning him to one rather than to another be well based. The chief factor to consider in this matter is the purpose which is to be served by the student's participation in the program.

If the chief purpose of his participation is that of getting vocational guidance through having "opportunities to observe and sample systematically a variety of conditions of work for the purpose of ascertaining his suitability for the occupation he is exploring" (*Code,* Article 13.1, Section 115.21,a) , he should be assigned to the Exploratory Work Experience Education classification. In that type of experience there should be no intent to teach production skills of any kind.

If the chief purpose of his participation is that of acquiring "desirable work habits and attitudes in real jobs" (*Code,* Article 13.1, Section 115.21,b), he should be assigned to the General Work Experience Education classification. The part-time job he holds in this classification need not be related to his occupational goal.

If the purpose of his participation is "the extension of vocational learning opportunities . . . through part-time employment in the occupation for which his course in school is preparing him" (*Code,* Article 115.21,c) , he should be assigned to the Vocational Work Experience Education classification.

It is clear that many students in the present Santa Barbara County program are incorrectly classified in terms of *Code* definitions. Many students, for example, who are participating in *one "real" job* for an entire semester (rather than observing and sampling many jobs) are now classified as Exploratory Work Experience Education students, but they should be classified as General Work Experience Education students. Some other students who should be classified as being in Vocational Work Experience Education are now erroneously classified as being in General Work Experience Education.

Two questionable practices in the Santa Barbara County program probably account for most of the current confusion in the classification of participants. One of them is the practice in some districts of considering all jobs for *pay and credit* as being a part of General Work Experience Education and all jobs for *credit only* (and no pay) as being a part of Exploratory Work Experience Education. The other practice is that of requiring 20 on-the-job hours of work for each 5 semester periods of credit in General Work Experience Education and 10 on-the-job hours of work for each 5 semester periods of credit in Exploratory Work Experience Education. This use of the factor of "pay" or "no pay" as a criterion for the student's classification and for determining the ratio of his on-the-job hours to the semester periods of credit he will receive does not appear to be justified and fails to take into consideration the basic criteria on which classification and credit should be based—namely, the criteria related to the purpose and nature of the work experience education in which the student is enrolled.

These questionable practices appear to be based on the un-supported belief that work for *pay and credit* is of less educational value than work for *credit only* and that therefore students earning both *pay and credit* should work twice as many hours as students who get *credit only* for the same amount of school credit. As previously stated, the practices are also based on the false assumption that all students now classified as being in Exploratory Work Experience Education are not engaged in *real jobs* for entire semesters.

In the course of this evaluative study it was very frequently impossible to distinguish any difference between the nature and purpose of jobs carried on by students in the General Work Experience Education classification and the nature and purpose of jobs carried on by students in the Exploratory Work Experience Education classification. Furthermore, no evidence was obtained that the *stated purposes* of the Work Experience Education Program were more fully achieved by students in the latter classification than by students in the former classification.

The fundamental questions, then, are not only those related to present classification procedures, but also those related to variations in the amount of on-the-job hours required per semester period of school credit given for participation in the classifications. Especially pertinent is the question as to why students who are paid are apparently arbitrarily required to work twice as many hours as students who are not paid in order to earn a given number of semester periods of credit. It may be argued, of course, that when an employer pays a student he will feel less obligation to supervise and to train him; but probably such an employer should not have students assigned to him in the first place. Moreover, it can also be argued that when an employer pays a student, the student's experience is likely to be more realistic and more related to the over-all purposes of the program than when no pay is given.

It is specifically recommended that in the Santa Barbara County Work Experience Education Program steps be taken to correct present classification procedures and that *Code* definitions of the classifications be used in determining the classification of each student who enrolls in the Work Experience Education Program. Re-classification of the student should be made whenever the purposes and nature of his work experience warrant doing so.

It is also recommended that in Santa Barbara County favorable consideration be given to eliminating entirely the factor of pay as a determinant of the ratio of work hours to semester periods of credit which are earned. If the paid experience is carefully planned, supervised, and evaluated (as prescribed in recommendation number 5), there is every reason to believe that the educational values received by the student will be just as great as those received in a non-paid experience which is similarly planned, supervised, and evaluated; and therefore equal credit should be given for both. It is suggested, accordingly, that for *every* classification of work experience education 5 semester periods of school credit be given for 10 hours of on-the-job work. Maximum semester periods of credit to be allowed in each classification of work experience must, of course, be in accord with *Code* stipulations, which state that in Exploratory Work Experience Education 5 semester periods of credit may be earned in one semester, with a maximum of 10 semester periods of credit in two semesters; that in General Work Experience Education 10 semester periods of credit may be earned in one semester, with a maximum of 20 semester periods of credit; and that in Vocational Work Experience Education 10 semester periods of credit may be earned in one semester, with a maximum of 40 semester periods of credit (*Code*, Article 13.1, Section 115.22,a-1,2,3).

The adopting of the above recommendation would not preclude a student's participation in the Work Experience Education Program—either in the Exploratory or the General Work Experience Education classifications—without pay. Indeed such a non-pay arrangement might be necessary for student jobs in schools, libraries, and hospitals; and it might be desirable in some other situations. Nor would the adopting of the recommendation preclude a student's working more hours for pay than he can earn credit for; additional non-credit work hours would be a matter of concern only to the student and his employer. But the adoption of the recommendation would result in classifying students according to the purpose of their participation as defined in the *Code*, and it would eliminate pay as a factor either in classification or in allowance of credit. Educational values in all classifications would be assured by the provision of adequate planning, supervision, and evaluation of the student's participation in the program.

7. Work Experience Education "agreement sheets" should be prepared and used for each kind of job open to students in the program.

Informal one-page agreement sheets should be written for each kind of job in the program. The agreement sheet should include, in outline form, statements describing the major work experiences which the student will have in the job, statements of the most important educational objectives to be sought in the job, and spaces for signatures of student, school representative, employer, and parent—indicating approval of the agreement by each.

These agreement sheets should be prepared cooperatively by the program coordinators and the employers, and their form and content should be approved by school administrators as well as by the program advisory committee. This practice would do much to clarify the nature and purposes of participation in the various kinds of jobs, and a file of these agreement sheets would be most useful to a student, his parents, and his school counselors in the selection of a job in the program. Every employer who was interviewed in Santa Barbara County stated that he would be willing to work with a school coordinator in the preparation of a description of the job in which he employed program participants, and most of them indicated a desire to know more specifically the purposes which they were expected by the school to help the student achieve. On the basis of these interviews, it would appear that school personnel would get much cooperation from employers in the development and use of the recommended agreement sheets.

8. The Work Experience Education Program should be closely related to school counseling services and to State employment office services.

Since a primary function of the program is one of vocational guidance, it should rely heavily on services of school counselors and State employment office personnel. Every student who is placed in the program should have had advice and clearance from the school's guidance office; and although any program coordinator or teacher should be free to suggest that a given student take part in the program, the responsibility for selection and screening of the participants should basically be that of guidance personnel.

The kind of cooperation which presently exists between the Santa Barbara County high schools and the California Department of Employment in the matter of placing students in jobs is outstanding and is most worthy of emulation elsewhere. It is recommended, however, that in Santa Barbara County the relationship between the schools and the Department of Employment become even closer. Specifically, it is recommended that every possible step be taken to arrange for the administration of the *General Aptitudes Test Battery* (now given to some students by the Department of Employment) to *all* high school students at the beginning of the tenth grade, that these tests be given at each of the high schools, and that results of the tests be carefully used by school counselors in the advisement of all students and especially in the advisement of potential participants in the Work Experience Education Program.

9. *The Work Experience Education Program should be coordinated with activities in the high school.*

Great care should be taken to avoid divorcing on-the-job experiences from in-school experiences on the part of participants in the Work Experience Education Program. Each of these kinds of experiences should supplement and enrich the other. When feasible (as for example in business education) and if the numbers of students in similar jobs warrant doing so, special classes for these participants should be organized in the high school. When this is not feasible, special job-related "units" should be offered in appropriate regular classes.

So that teachers may know what students are in the program and what their jobs are, at the beginning of each semester the program coordinator should send every teacher a list of these students and their assignments. In addition, copies of the students' work experience education agreement sheets, referred to in recommendation number 7, should be made available to the teachers who have program participants in their classes.

School clubs should also be organized specifically for students who are in the program. The clubs for future teachers as now organized in Santa Barbara County high schools provide an excellent example of the kind of organization desirable in the other occupational fields. These clubs should meet semi-monthly, providing opportunities for talks by employers, counselors, teachers, and others, and affording opportunities for the students to exchange ideas and discuss problems. Active membership in a work experience education club should be required of all students who are in the program.

10. *The Work Experience Education Program should be related to the objectives of both general education and vocational training.*

In every classification of work experience education emphasis should be placed on helping the student to assume responsibility, to develop mature self-concepts, to work effectively with others, and to achieve numerous other objectives commonly considered goals of general education. The achievement of objectives directly related to vocational education and training should also be emphasized in every classification. In the Exploratory classification the major vocational objectives to be achieved are those of acquiring occupational information and of determining suitability for the occupations explored, but the development of production skills should not be expected. In General Work Experience Education, however, the development of some basic vocational skills (as well as desirable work habits and attitudes) is to be expected, even though these skills need not necessarily be directly related to their future occupations. In Vocational Work Experience Education a marked emphasis should be placed on the development of specific vocational skills which are essential to the student's subsequent full-time employment as a competent worker in the occupation of his choice.

11. *Student orientation to the Work Experience Education Program should be provided in the tenth grade.*

Through the school's counseling program, students should be fully advised in the tenth grade about the opportunities afforded by the Work Experience Education Program. Furthermore, as is permitted by code regulations, some students should be allowed to enter the program while in the tenth grade (*Code*, Article 13.1, Section 115.23,a). This is especially the case for students who might thus be prevented from dropping out of school.

The program can have relatively little influence on the retention of students if they don't get into it or don't even hear about it until they are juniors. Moreover, the "exploratory" values of the program can have little influence on the remainder of a student's high school curriculum if he already is in his senior year when he enters it.

12. *Students in the Work Experience Education Program should be required to be in full attendance in all classes at the school in which they are concurrently enrolled.*

Even in rural areas where problems of distance and transportation exist, full attendance in classes at school for which they are receiving regular credit should be required of all students who are concurrently enrolled in the Work Experience Education Program. The excusing of these students one day a week to take part in the program cannot be justified. If these students were to be excused, there could be no good reason for not excusing the non-program students as well. If attendance four days a week is sufficient for one group, it should also be sufficient for another—especially when both groups are undifferentiated in terms of intelligence and ability.

The disruption of the teaching-learning procedures in classes as a result of having some students absent one day a week adversely affects not only the students who miss the classes but also the other students, whose progress is slowed down by the lagging effect of such students' behavior after they return from their absences.

The permitting of absences from classes for participation in the program also has a negative effect on teacher morale because it adds to their work and reduces their effectiveness. In turn, these teachers lose enthusiasm for the Work Experience Education Program and find it difficult to be at all supportive of it.

13. *Students in the Work Experience Education Program should be given on-the-job supervisory visits by school representatives at least once a month.*

Among the most important functions of a program coordinator is that of paying supervisory visits to students while they are on their jobs. Through such visits he can best become acquainted with the conditions under which the students are working, with the quality of the students' participation, and with their needs for related help at school. The visits also provide sound bases for conferences with employers, parents, and teachers, as well as with the students themselves.

Although highly consuming of coordinator time, these visits should be made to each student at least once a month. This means, of course, that coordinators should be available for visitation at all times the students are working. If, therefore, students are engaged in evening or week-end jobs, coordinators must also work during these hours.

14. *Written evaluations of students in the program should be made by employers at least twice each semester.*

In addition to mere attendance reports which employers should send to the school each week, evaluative reports should be prepared by employers at least twice a semester. These reports should be made on forms which incorporate many of the same items that appear on the work experience education agreement sheets referred to in recommendation number 7. The evaluation should be made in terms of the student's progress toward achievement of the goals agreed upon and in terms of his co-operation, responsibility, initiative, dependability, and similar personal qualities.

The specific nature of the report form used in various kinds of employment situations should be determined jointly by the program coordinator and the employer and should be subject to approval by the school administrator and by the advisory committee.

These evaluations by the employers should, of course, be supplemented by evaluations prepared by the coordinator and by teachers in charge of the special classes or clubs organized for participants in the program. The grade given to a student for his participation in the program should reflect each of these evaluations which apply to him.

15. *Adequate records regarding students' Work Experience Education should be retained in the permanent cumulative files of the high school.*

It is much more important to keep adequate records of student activity for which credit is given than of activity for which no credit is given. In science and mathematics, for example, better records must be kept of students' work than in some non-credit extra-curricular program. Accordingly, if the Work Experience Education Program is a credit program, the records kept of participants in the program must be as complete and accurate as it is feasible to make them.

The mere keeping of such records during the time of the student's participation in the program, however, is not enough; they should also be retained in permanent files for future study and reference. The retention of every item originally placed in the file would neither be possible nor desirable, but such scores as those made on interest-inventory, general aptitudes, and mental achievement tests should certainly be retained permanently. There should also be permanent retention of a summarized description and evaluation of the student's specific work experience.

These records will prove to be of much value to school personnel when in subsequent years prospective employers of graduates from the high school request information and recommendations regarding the former students. The records will also prove to be most useful in any evaluative study which is made of the Work Experience Education Program in a high school district. The dearth of such adequate permanent records was a serious obstacle in the conducting of this evaluative study in Santa Barbara County.

16. *The ratio of students enrolled in the Work Experience Education Program to school personnel who coordinate and supervise the program should be held to a level which will assure greatest effectiveness in terms of time and effort expended by the coordinators and educational values gained by students.*

The minimum daily time which should be allocated to a coordinator during the development of a new Work Experience Education Program is two class periods, and this amount of time should probably not have to be increased until as many as 20 students are enrolled in the program. It is recommended that three class periods be given a coordinator when from 20 to 32 students are enrolled; that four class periods be given when from 33 to 45 students are enrolled; and that full-time be given when from 46 to 60 students are enrolled.

Variations in local conditions and circumstances will affect the feasibility of implementing this suggestion, but it is most unlikely that the provision of less time for coordination than that recommended will result in a good program. It is especially unlikely that one full-time coordinator could do a good job with more than 60 students. For that number of students he would have to make at least 300 on-the-job supervisory visits per semester in addition to holding conferences with the students' employers, their teachers, their counselors, and, in many instances, their parents. Furthermore he would have innumerable conferences with the students at school; and he would supervise the keeping of all records regarding their work experience. He would also be expected to organize and even conduct, when appropriate, related classes or clubs at school. It is likely, too, that he would be called on to assist in placement and follow-up service of not only these students but also former students who had graduated from the high school.

All of the above activities would be carried on continuously in an established program. Along with them would be the need, especially in a new program, for the finding of employers to take part in the program and for acquainting these employers with what is to be expected of them.

The carrying on of this job in such a manner as to assure the highest quality of educational achievement by the participants can be expected only if the program coordinators' assignments and responsibilities are held to a reasonable level; and since the quality of the program must be considered much more important than its size, the number of students enrolled in it must be sufficiently restricted to allow essential coordinator services.

17. *Adequate clerical service, office facilities, and means of transportation should be provided personnel who direct and coordinate the Work Experience Education Program.*

The performance of a great deal of secretarial or clerical service by a program coordinator himself is a most uneconomical use of a professional person's time. Less costly personnel should be engaged to do such work so that the coordinator may be permitted to carry on the aspects of the work which only one of his qualifications is capable.

A considerable amount of the clerical work necessary in the operation of the program may well be done by business education students who enroll in the program for credit and spend two hours a day in the coordinator's office as their work experience education assignment. In a small program these students would work under the direct supervision of the coordinator, but in a larger program they would be supervised by a secretary who should be employed in the coordinator's office.

Sufficient office space for conducting conferences, for housing secretarial and clerical activities, and for storing record forms must be provided to permit effective and efficient handling of the program; and, of course, needed typewriters, files, and other necessary items of equipment and furniture must be furnished.

Transportation facilities must also be made available to coordinators for their use in visiting students, employers, and parents. A school-district-owned automobile may be provided for this purpose or the coordinator may be reimbursed on a mileage basis for the use of his own automobile.

18. *The responsibilities of Work Experience Education Program Coordinators should be clearly defined, and competencies to assume these responsibilities should be assured.*

Since the position of the Work Experience Education Program Coordinator is a relatively new one and since programs have varied somewhat from community to community, the responsibilities of the coordinator are as yet not precisely defined. It is good that precise definition of the job was not made during years when experimentation and flexibility in the position were essential. The time has now probably come, however, when such definition is not only possible but desirable—especially with regard to a full-time role in the position.

It is suggested that in Santa Barbara County a job analysis be made of the activities engaged in by the program coordinators and that an attempt be made to determine which activities are most pertinent to the achievement of the objectives of the program and what competencies on the part of the coordinators are most essential to the effective carrying on of these activities.

Competencies in pupil guidance and counseling are, in all probability, among the most important qualifications of a Work Experience Education Program coordinator. Competencies in teaching and administration are also likely to be of much value, as are competencies involved in various aspects of the business world. Fundamental to success in the coordinator's activities, moreover, are his dedication to the program objectives, his willingness to serve beyond the "normal call of duty," and his ability to work well with both youths and adults and with both laymen and educators.

A much sharper identification of just what competencies are needed in the successful performance of a coordinator's functions and of what background of experience and training are most likely to result in these competencies might be made in a research study, possibly by a candidate for an advanced degree at a university. The findings of the study could provide a basis, also, for determining what credential requirements should be met by a coordinator.

Particularly, in Santa Barbara County, should every effort be made to fill subsequent program coordinator positions with educators of such high qualifications—personally and professionally—as those held by men who have thus far served in this capacity.

19. *A continuous program of interpretation regarding the Work Experience Education Program should be carried on.*

Through the use of regular and special school bulletins, newspaper stories, periodical articles, school and community meetings, and other appropriate means, information about the program and interpretation of its purposes, achievements, and needs or problems should be systematically provided to school board members, teachers, employers, parents, and other laymen of the school district.

Only in this manner can intelligent and consistent support of the program be gained and maintained. Mere "enthusiasm" for the program, essential though such enthusiasm may be, is not enough; it must be based on an understanding of the program and on factual information about the "what," "why," and "how" of the program. Uninformed or unfounded enthusiasm can be quickly dissipated and may even "backfire" when a program is attacked by organized opposition to it. Criticism of the program should, of course, be welcomed and invited, and warranted changes in the program should be effected; but all actions taken should be based on *facts* which are clearly presented and widely disseminated.

20. *Periodic comprehensive evaluative studies should be made of a school district's Work Experience Education Program.*

Although program evaluation should be inherent in the very conduct of the program, comprehensive evaluative studies of its purposes, procedures, and outcomes should be made from time to time. As in Santa Barbara County, interested faculty members should be encouraged to relate their research for master's and doctor's degrees to various aspects of the program which are in particular need of investigation. Also, as in Santa Barbara County, studies of the kind reported in this monograph should desirably be carried on after a program has been in effect for a period of five or six years.

Since the program in Santa Barbara County is in many respects a pilot program, it is specifically recommended that in that county another study—patterned largely after this one—be made in 1965 or 1966 in order to assess the results of changes which are made in accordance with the present recommendations. It is confidently predicted by the research staff that such a study will produce findings which are appreciably more supportive of the program than are the present findings, which already reflect the existence of a successful and highly valuable program.

CASE FIVE: *Champaign, Illinois*
Champaign Community Schools, Champaign, Illinois

PREVOCATIONAL SERVICES
FOR HANDICAPPED YOUTH

An unusual example of the co-operative effort
of school personnel, community representatives
and state vocational rehabilitation counselors
in providing a school-work program designed
to help "handicapped" children from ten to
twenty make a successful transition from school
to full-time employment in three steps:
> In-school work experience
> Part-time community work experience
> Postschool job placement

Another phase of education of alienated youth includes programs
for those who are potentially maladjusted because of physical or
mental handicaps. A program for this type of youngster has flour-
ished in Champaign, where alienated youth are recognized as
"handicapped." In a complete special-education program within the
public schools, rehabilitation is accomplished through a prevocational curriculum designed to offer the educational, vocational, and
psychological support these boys and girls need to make a satisfactory transition from school to work.

Alienated youngsters are enrolled in small, special classes where
they are instructed by teachers trained to work with socially maladjusted children. In sheltered class environments, youngsters are
helped to understand themselves and their social responsibilities.

Those who make the social adjustment are placed on part-time work assignments in school and are supervised by school personnel. Work assignments and classwork are co-ordinated to help students appreciate the value of work and understand their obligations to others.

Children succeeding in the first stage are released from school for half-day job assignments in the community. Their adjustment is helped by co-ordinated efforts of employers, program supervisors, state rehabilitation counselors, school social workers, and special teachers.

Students who perform adequately on part-time jobs receive help from school personnel in finding regular employment when they leave school. Their successful transition from school to work is enhanced by regular follow-up studies.

Champaign, a community of approximately 50,000 persons, is located in one of the richest farm areas in the black loam prairie land of the nation. Together with Urbana, its sister city and home of the University of Illinois, it is the commercial center for a large rural population and the hub of activities associated with manufacturing in the area.

Champaign is progressive. The forging and casting works, the chemical plant, and the up-to-date farm machinery seen in the surrounding fields are tangible indices of its citizens' attitudes. The signs of material progress in Champaign, however, are not the best indications of the residents' concerns. The community's values are best reflected in its schools.

Champaign school personnel, under the school superintendent's leadership and with the community's support, have built a comprehensive program of basic education. An integral part is their recognition that many children classified as handicapped are unable to partake of a traditional curriculum. To provide for them, a work-study program of special education has been developed. The definition of the program:

> Special education refers to those provisions made available for children who deviate so markedly physically, intellectually, or emotionally from the normal that they need a special class organization, special curricular adjustments, special teaching techniques and materials of instruction, and/or special therapeutic and diagnostic services. Special education provides services for those children with individual differences which regular teachers are not usually trained to handle.[1]

1. Champaign Community Unit District No. 4, *The Special Education Program in the Champaign Community Schools* (September 1961), p. 1.

Though Champaign's special-education program has operated since 1934, when classes for children with partial sight functioned under the Illinois Society for the Prevention of Blindness, the program did not get well under way until 1945, when it was established under the Illinois Plan for Special Education of Exceptional Children. During 1945–46 the staff consisted of a social worker, a teacher of the homebound, a speech correctionist, and a psychologist. In September 1961 the staff of seventy-three persons offered:

Service to home and hospital cases

Service to crippled children attending school

Transportation service for children attending special classes and for those unable to walk to and from regular classes

Service to children with speech defects

Service to deaf children and those with impaired hearing

Service to blind children and those with impaired vision

Service to the multiple handicapped

Service to the mentally handicapped who are educable and trainable

Service to the gifted

Service to socially and emotionally handicapped children

Services of a prevocational counselor

Psychological services

In addition to providing for the city's children, the staff provides services to children attending schools within a radius of fifty miles of Champaign. In 1960–61, for instance, twenty-five communities sent handicapped children to classes in Champaign. Expenses are met through a cost-sharing plan between districts. Annually, almost twelve hundred handicapped children are served; of that number, approximately three hundred are secondary school students.

This abbreviated account of the special services program cannot describe the comprehensiveness of this part of the Champaign curriculum. The program is wide in scope, thorough in operation, and accurate in evaluation. This study's focus, however, necessitates attention to that part of the program applicable to work-study experiences designed for alienated young people.

Alienated children in Champaign schools are helped to adjust to society through prevocational services tailored to their needs. The premise on which the school personnel built the program mirrors the community's awareness of its responsibility to children. A study conducted in 1959 and supervised by the director of special services appraised the amount of aid the schools were offering handicapped youngsters. The researchers counted 103 adolescent handicapped children from thirteen to nineteen in various phases of the special-education program. The students' handicaps ranged from obvious physical disorders to subtle emotional or personal adjustment problems. A number of children were alienated; some of them were old enough to enter the adult world as individuals who should have been capable of providing for themselves and contributing to their society. Many, unfortunately, were not ready for the transition. Although the community had invested much money in establishing and maintaining an educational program for this segment of the school population, weaknesses in the program were detected and pointed out by the director and her staff. They contended that the schools were not effective. Handicapped persons in school became handicapped persons in the work force. On their own, most floundered. Who would employ a boy with a delinquency record? Who would hire a girl who read at the second-grade level? Many frustrated children reacted in an antisocial way in the grown-up world. Those not alienated exhibited a high probability of becoming so.

The study helped both the school staff and citizens realize that programs for alienated and handicapped youth were failing: the programs were not helping such youngsters acquire proper work habits or realistic attitudes toward themselves and others; curriculums did not offer worthwhile experiences to the handicapped youth; and the prevocational aspects were particularly weak. Summarizing findings, the special education staff determined the weaknesses in prevocational services to be:

An inadequate prevocational curriculum at the secondary level and lack of co-ordination of a prevocational program from the time a child entered school until he completed his schooling or dropped out prior to completion of the established curriculum.

Inadequate understanding, or misunderstanding, among school personnel of the prevocational needs of the handicapped. As a result, few opportunities were provided for the handicapped to engage in worthwhile in-school work experiences. This same lack of understanding, incidentally, militated against effective integration into regular classes in which the handicapped should have gained valuable prevocational experience.

No widespread community participation in a work-study program for handicapped youth: no program had been initiated or even encouraged. The reluctance of the community to participate in a work-study program had been fallaciously assumed.

Inadequacy of special-class teachers, because of lack of training in vocational counseling, to help secure jobs for the handicapped and to work with employers in the community. Not only were special teachers lacking in training, but time was also an inhibiting factor. Locating jobs for the handicapped had to be pursued after school hours.

Lack of adequate provisions for counseling the handicapped youth and their parents to help thém set realistic vocational goals and to formulate vocational plans.

Lack of adequate diagnosis of vocational aptitudes and interests of the handicapped; this weakness was further compounded by lack of personnel trained to translate findings into actual job situations.

Lack of sufficient services of social workers to help the handicapped overcome or modify social and emotional handicaps which might interfere with vocational adjustment.

Lack of community effort and full utilization of community resources in improving the prevocational curriculum.

Lack of a specialist on the special services staff with the training and time to co-ordinate the prevocational program in the school, to serve as a liaison person between the school and agencies in the community in placing the handicapped on jobs, and to formulate and conduct a follow-up program of the handicapped after they leave school.

Lack of a close working relationship with such agencies as the Division of Vocational Rehabilitation that can share the responsibility for planning of the handicapped youths' vocational training and subsequent job placement.[2]

The findings motivated the staff to call in representatives of the Division of Vocational ˙Rehabilitation, a state agency. With their help, the staff of the department of special education drafted a request for state financial support for an extended and improved prevocational program for the handicapped. It was submitted to the Division of Vocational Rehabilitation for an extension and improvement grant under Section 3 of the Vocational Rehabilitation Act of 1954.

The proposal received approval by state, regional, and federal divisions of vocational rehabilitation. Initiated in September 1960, the project also received professional support, and provides for:

Employment of a prevocational co-ordinator of the handicapped

2. *Ibid.*, p. 3.

Employment of a full-time secretary

Assignment of a full-time social worker to work with handicapped youth at the secondary level

Assignment of a full-time qualified psychologist to make
psychoeducational diagnostic studies of each handicapped
child at the secondary level, including the assessment of
vocational aptitudes and interests

Development of an efficient system of record keeping necessary for the orderly and effective operation of a continuing
project

Development of a resource library pertinent to promoting
greater understanding among personnel of the needs of the
handicapped

Organization of a council on prevocational education of
the handicapped

Organization of a community council on employment of
the handicapped

The Illinois Plan for Special Education of Exceptional Children encourages school systems to set up classes and services for
exceptional children by reimbursing the districts $3000 for each pro-
fessional working directly with such children. Additional funds reim-
burse districts up to $400 a year for the costs of transporting
children to special classes. Prevocational services under the department of special education are included for state aid purposes.
Thus, the prevocational services budget is provided by the Division of Vocational Rehabilitation and the local board of education.

Money for staff assignments and physical equipment gave im-
petus to the program's establishment. The special education staff
developed a philosophy of prevocational education, stated in the
introduction to one of their publications:

> All youth, regardless of their intellectual, physical, social, or emotional
> status, need the best possible prevocational education and services to
> assure adequate vocational adjustment. Even more careful planning
> must be carried on and more intensive services must be provided
> the handicapped to assist them in developing their potential and in
> making the transition from the school to full-time employment in the
> community. If the school does not accept its full share of the responsi-
> bility for helping the handicapped develop the attitudes, habits, and
> skills necessary for good vocational adjustment; modify problems that
> may interfere with adequate vocational adjustment of the handicapped;

and, if definite plans are not made and services not rendered to help the handicapped bridge the gap between school and full-time job placement, the handicapped are going to continue to drop out of school early and to be among the unemployed.

The unemployment of the handicapped is an intolerable waste of human resources; it contributes to a mounting financial burden to society; a fertile breeding ground for fostering the development of antisocial behavior may be the result. It is a part of our cultural heritage that persons must be gainfully employed to be accepted into our society.

Prevocational education of the handicapped becomes a responsibility of the schools the first day the child enrolls. We in the Champaign school system contend that it cannot be postponed until he reaches adolescence. Prevocational education involves all those experiences which foster the acquisition of desirable attitudes, habits, skills, and knowledge necessary for effective vocational adjustment. It is an extension of, as well as an integral part of, the special services program.[3]

From this philosophy the department of special education identified their initial objectives to be:

Development of policies and procedures to facilitate a close working relationship between the school and the Division of Vocational Rehabilitation to help handicapped pupils bridge the gap between the school and further training and/or full-time job placement in the community

Utilization of community resources that can contribute to the vocational development of the handicapped

Improvement of the prevocational curriculum for the handicapped

Formulation of a five-year plan for follow-up of handicapped youth after they leave school

Establishment of a committee to supervise the project, made up of representatives from the Illinois Division of Vocational Rehabilitation, the Champaign School Board, and the Champaign school staff[4]

To implement these objectives, the staff turned to the community for help. Thus the prevocational program evolved out of the co-operative work of school and community. Two committees were organized—the Council on Prevocational Education of the Handicapped and the Community Council on the Employment of the Handicapped. The former is within the school system. It consists of a chairman, the prevocational co-ordinator of the handicapped, the assistant superintendent of schools, the principal of

3. *Ibid.*, p. 5.
4. *Ibid.*

Champaign High School, the director of special services, the principals of the junior high schools, the chief psychologist, guidance counselors, the supervisor of social work, the director of industrial and vocational education, the director of athletics, the supervisor of speech and hearing, the administrative assistant in charge of business affairs, the director of food services, and the director of buildings and grounds. The council's purposes are:

> To promote a better understanding among school personnel of the vocational potentials of the various types of handicapped children enrolled in the school.

> To plan specific ways of improving the prevocational curriculum for handicapped youth (within the special class or resource room; in related areas such as homemaking, industrial arts, business education; in in-school work-experiences; and in work-study programs in which the handicapped are enrolled part time in schoolwork and also part time on a job).

> To evaluate the system of record keeping, which will include an evaluation of the prevocational experiences of the handicapped.

> To develop methods of communicating developments within the school in regard to extension and improvement of prevocational experiences of handicapped youth.

> To evaluate the current adequacy and effectiveness of prevocational education for the handicapped and to formulate future plans for the improvement and extension of services to the handicapped in the Champaign schools.[5]

The community council is composed of interested laymen, including representatives of business, industry, civic and professional clubs, community association leaders, clergymen, and spokesmen for veterans organizations. Members are chosen for their willingness to employ or seek employment for handicapped youngsters. Another important criterion is their demonstrated ability to interpret the program to others.

The major purposes of this council are to interest the public in the vocational potential of handicapped youth and adults and to help the community accept them. The council also serves as liaison between the handicapped and the community.

The co-operative efforts of both councils enabled them to establish a work-study program structured according to the philosophy of the department of special education within the Champaign schools. Their program is geared to provide individual attention

---

5. *Ibid.,* p. 25.

for each handicapped child. Its ultimate aim is to provide each handicapped youth with the experiences and the professional attention that will prepare him for his eventual successful vocational adjustment.

The Champaign system provides a developmental work-experience program in three categories: in-school work experience, part-time work in the community (the work-study program), and full-time employment.

In the primary grades, learning experiences in the special classes are designed to foster the development of socially acceptable personal habits, attitudes, skills, and work habits commensurate with the capabilities of each youngster. Typical goals are: perseverance until a task is completed, efficient use of time, ability to follow directions, and ability to work both independently and with a group.

As children progress through the special education curriculum, some become identified as needing professional help to ready themselves for employment. Others not in special classes may need similar services. All such pupils are referred to the prevocational co-ordinator or the vocational counselor. Any staff person may originate such a referral.

Any child identified by school authorities as handicapped is eligible for the work-study program. Once a child has been identified, the prevocational staff oversees his case. A conference is arranged to review the appropriateness of the referral and to determine the best way to help the child.

Pupils accepted in the program undergo complete diagnostic study including medical, psychological, educational, and social appraisal. Each child's characteristics are evaluated for his placement in the work-study program and for assignment of appropriate staff members to work with him.

Handicapped pupils who can profit from work experiences outside of the special classroom are to be considered for assignment to the in-school work program. Levels of maturity, specific vocational assets, and personal needs are the criteria used to determine a child's readiness for such a task. Age is not a primary consideration. Some children enter the program at the age of ten, whereas others may not be ready to participate until they are teen-agers. Flexibility is stressed, beginning with the child's first assignment.

Work experience gives handicapped pupils opportunity to transfer habits and attitudes acquired in special classes to extra-classroom work situations within the school setting. Exploratory work experiences—tasks performed near the students' special-class teachers—give handicapped pupils opportunities to expand their horizons and still maintain close ties with a person who can understand and help them. In this way pupils receive closer guidance and supervision than they would be likely to receive while employed on community jobs. In this phase the prevocational co-ordinator works closely with pupils and teachers to become well acquainted with each child, so that subsequent work experiences can be planned.

In-school work assignments include: cafeteria helper, one hour a day; vending machine maintenance, one hour a week; and custodian helper, one hour a day.

When a child is assigned a school task, the child becomes the responsibility of a school employee. This person is to provide a meaningful work experience for the pupil. The staff member plays an important role in helping handicapped youth develop behavior traits necessary for successful vocational adjustment. Stressed are traits such as punctuality, acceptance of authority, acceptable personal appearance, constructive use of time, proper use and care of tools, equipment, and materials, orderly completion of tasks, and an appreciation of the value of work. Work experiences of the child and procedures used in handling him are similar to the experiences and supervision he will encounter on a job in the community. Since the in-school work is a part of the total education of youngsters involved, children do not receive any pay, though school credit is granted.

In addition to his work with individual pupils, the co-ordinator meets with groups of handicapped children in weekly group guidance sessions. These conferences help the children gain better understanding of employers' expectations. Information is imparted through group discussions, role playing, and the use of audio-visual equipment.

School representatives meet periodically with the prevocational co-ordinator to discuss problems encountered in work with the handicapped youngsters. In the beginning stages of a pupil's in-school employment, the co-ordinator meets weekly with a school representative. Later the frequency of conferences is reduced. Handicapped children on jobs are seen by the prevocational co-ordinator on a scheduled basis, at least once a month.

A handicapped child's progress on an in-school job is evaluated systematically and continuously by the school employer, the special teacher, and the prevocational co-ordinator using written reports and test results. These evaluations are kept by the co-ordinator in the prevocational offices.

In-school work experience is an abbreviated work orientation differing from the next level—part-time work experience in the community—by the nature of the work, the length of time the student is involved, and the amount of supervision each child needs.

Pupils perform part-time work in the community under supervision of understanding employers. This entails considerable preparation by parents, pupils, and employers. The prevocational co-ordinator works closely with the vocational rehabilitation counselor in the placement of each handicapped child, aided by the Community Council on Employment of the Handicapped.

The child is prepared for his transfer to a part-time job from an in-school assignment by the co-ordinator and the vocational counselor. Assistance is offered in frequent counseling sessions with each handicapped youth. The pupil's interests and aspirations, and the counselor's understanding of the child, are the basis for selecting individual programs. Although the pupil's desires are an important consideration, the co-ordinator is responsible for final placement. He may assign youngsters to part-time jobs such as:

tray girl (hospital)	2 hours a day
housekeeper (private home)	½ day
Ditto machine operator (university)	2 hours a day
bus boy (hospital)	½ day
maintenance (private home)	½ day
sacker (grocery store)	2 hours a day
newspaper route	2 hours a day
usher (movie)	3 hours a day

Initial planning for placement of each pupil on a part-time community job is considered the most crucial element in the program. The co-ordinator counsels the employer, enabling him to acquire an accurate perception of the child he accepts as an employee.

The placement of children on community jobs does not reduce the co-ordinator's responsibilities. He holds frequent conferences with parents, teachers, and employers, the number depending on the child and on the problems arising in the child's adjustment to part-time work. Special services needed by a child at any time in his progress may be identified by anyone working with him and these services must be provided by the co-ordinator.

The co-ordinator also helps co-operating employers accord handicapped youngsters the same consideration given to any employee. Building respect for the individual does not mean preferential

handling of the children. Instead, the co-ordinator helps work supervisors understand that permitting handicapped youth to "get by"
either in performing a job or in behavior is not helpful. The success of subsequent full-time employment of these young people
depends on whether or not their tryout experience is successful.
Consequently, employers are accustomed to expect handicapped
children to comply with regular employee standards. The only aspect of the child's job experience that might set him apart from his
fellow employees is that the employer may understand him better
than the other workers.

Since handicapped youth on part-time jobs are paid by employers, overseers inform the co-ordinator when work fails to meet
expectations. The difficulties facing a child in adjusting to a work
situation structure the co-ordinator's action. A child may be counseled by the co-ordinator or the employer, referred to the vocational
rehabilitation counselor, transferred to another assignment, or returned to the special classroom. Since the start of the program, the
number of cases restudied as a result of errors in placement has
been negligible because of careful planning and thorough work
by the staff. During the 1960–61 school year, for instance, only one
placement was found inappropriate.

Another measure of the program's success is this partial list
of tasks that handicapped students performed satisfactorily during
the 1960–61 school year.

Private homes:
    baby sitter, maid (two educable handicapped senior high girls)
Printshop:
    Ditto machine operator (one deaf senior high boy)
University placement office:
    part-time helper in private homes (one educable mentally
    handicapped senior high boy)
Barbershop:
    porter, shoeshine boy (one educable mentally handicapped
    senior high boy)
Auto sales:
    new and used car cleanup (one educable mentally handicapped
    senior high boy)
Dry cleaners:
    presser (one educable mentally handicapped senior high girl)

Sporting goods store:
    stock boy (one educable mentally handicapped senior high
    boy)
Hospital:
    tray girl (one educable mentally handicapped senior high girl
    and one deaf senior high girl)
Bus company:
    bus maintenance (two educable mentally handicapped senior
    high boys)

Many of these youngsters had undesirable attitudes toward society before entering the prevocational program. All demonstrated acceptable patterns of social conduct, however, before they were deemed eligible for employment.

As in the in-school work-experience phase, continuous evaluation is made of pupil progress both in school and on the community job. Special evaluation forms are filed with the co-ordinator by teachers and employers. To complete records, the prevocational co-ordinator accumulates relevant information obtained from interviews with employers, school personnel, handicapped youth, and parents, and shares the information with the vocational rehabilitation counselor. When a child leaves school, either through graduation or as a dropout, the vocational rehabilitation counselor assumes responsibility for the vocational placement of the child.

Handicapped children who have progressed satisfactorily on community jobs are not abandoned when they leave school. Most of the pupils are helped to obtain full-time employment. Others benefit from a comprehensive evaluation by the vocational rehabilitation counselor as a final determination of their vocational potential. He reviews cases to evaluate students' in-school and part-time work achievement and may administer achievement and vocational aptitude tests. A number of handicapped pupils interested in further training are sent to trade schools. Others having the intellectual ability and the desire to continue academic study may be counseled toward college entrance. When youngsters attain this level, the Division of Vocational Rehabilitation handles their cases.

The Community Council on Employment of the Handicapped is most helpful when children are ready for full-time placement. Members identify employers and jobs for candidates, carrying out this task as another segment of their interpretation of the program to the community.

A systematic follow-up of handicapped youth is an integral part of the prevocational service and is a joint responsibility of the vocational rehabilitation counselor and the prevocational co-ordinator. They interview former pupils and their employers several times during the first year. Though the number of contacts depends on how well the former students adjust, a minimum of four contacts are made the first year and at least two are made annually for the next five years. The follow-up information available in the prevocational co-ordinator's office helps the staff evaluate the curriculum and improve the program.

Success of the prevocational service is apparent to persons visiting youngsters on the job. Consider one mentally retarded girl who was working as a full-time tray girl in a local hospital. She described her job this way: *I can't think of a place I'd rather be.*

Or consider Peter, a slim, seventeen-year-old Negro enrolled in the program for educable mentally handicapped youngsters. Pete and his twenty-two-year-old unemployed brother live with their grandparents. The grandfather was severely disabled in an accident and has been unable to work for several years. Pete's parents were declared unfit by a judge because of social irresponsibility.

Pete is rather shy, though he's co-operative and in good physical condition. He doesn't have any physical abnormalities severe enough to jeopardize his employability. His level of educational achievement is approximately fifth grade. He seems to be interested in repairing cars and engines.

In December 1960, Pete was referred for prevocational services. His special teachers contended that his vocational future would be bright if he could receive help in preparing for a vocation. During the initial interview the Champaign program was explained to him. On the Purdue Pegboard, an apparatus test of manipulative dexterity related to productivity in routine manual jobs, he scored in the 99th percentile for the right hand, 55th percentile for the left hand, and 25th percentile for assembly, comparable to scores of normal applicants for industrial jobs. Meanwhile, counseling sessions continued.

Ultimately an unskilled job was found for Peter. His direct supervisor was a capable, understanding person. In addition, the job provided the boy with two well-balanced meals a day, something he had not been getting at home. On this job as a dishwasher at a local hospital, he worked from 11 A.M. to 2 P.M. and from 3:30 P.M. to 6 P.M. He attended classes during off hours.

His adjustment to the job was excellent. Members of the project staff conferred with him at school and on the job every two weeks. In addition, his employer was contacted every two weeks. Each month the employer's written evaluation of the boy's work contained only kind words. The boy's future appeared brighter. The counselor in the Division of Vocational Rehabilitation interviewed him to determine his eligibility for services and concluded that Pete would make a desirable transition from school to adult employment.

Then, eight weeks after he had started his hospital job, he was arrested. For weeks, clusters of teen-agers had gathered on street corners as youngsters will. Occasionally stones and bottles had been thrown at passing cars, and irate motorists had complained to police. One night, the police told the gang to move along. The others ran but Peter, not fully understanding the seriousness of the situation, did not. He was arrested and charged with disorderly conduct.

When school officials discovered his predicament, they appeared in court on his behalf. They reasoned that Pete had not been involved in the vandalism but rather was the victim of a meager culture at home and of his low mental ability. The consequences were both good and bad. Pete was fined a few dollars and reprimanded in court. But because of the policy of the hospital he lost his job—a serious blow. This was turned into a genuine learning situation, however, for in the next few weeks he learned more about policemen and laws than he had ever learned before. The social workers in the prevocational service helped him, too, to better understand the turn of events.

The next step was to provide the boy with vocational counseling and to emphasize the importance of learning a trade. He was taken on a trip to eight different trade schools to give him a better understanding of the kinds of trades in which he might eventually be successful.

After further testing and interviews with trainers who thereby gained an understanding of his preferences, Pete was enrolled in Electric Motor Repair Trade School for a twelve-week evaluation period. More than four months had elapsed since his arrest. At the end of the period, trade school officials concluded that Pete was an excellent prospect and accepted him for further training. Monthly evaluation reports received by his counselor in the Division of Vocational Rehabilitation indicate he is doing above-average work in all aspects of his training.

Pete's story illustrates that through assistance in prevocational development, handicapped youth can become a valuable asset as members of the work force of the nation.

The case of Susan also illustrates how the Champaign program functions. Susan, an attractive, well-developed, eighteen-year-old girl, is enrolled in the program for educable mentally handicapped youngsters at a senior high school. She is the third of four children of parents of lower-middle socioeconomic status.

Susan was referred by her classroom teacher, who considered her a good candidate for prevocational rehabilitation services. In class Susan had shown signs of boredom and had stated that she felt there was not much use in continuing school. A review of her case indicated that emotional problems might have hindered her adjustment to school.

During the counseling process Susan was revealed as an oversensitive girl occasionally suspicious of others. She felt, for instance, that her schoolmates stared at her as they passed the classroom for the mentally handicapped. On another occasion—after she had entered the prevocational program—Susan was employed in the home of a school psychologist and complained that he was reading her mind. Her suspicion apparently stemmed from a feeling of basic insecurity about her ability and potential.

After she was referred for prevocational rehabilitation, Susan continued to receive the services of a social worker while working part time in the school program. In addition, she sought—and needed—a supportive form of counseling. The process began with referral statements as the main focus. These areas have been explored:

Peer relationships in the classroom and Susan's feelings about the special-education program

Evaluation of Susan's school experiences and achievements

Positive aspects of the school situation and of what Susan might gain by continuing in school

Future employment in regard to what Susan thought she might like

As a result, Susan was able to verbalize these points: She was not trained for any job; she did not have any vocational plans; she was seeing employment as an escape from school; by staying in school, she might develop some skills.

Through prevocational rehabilitation services, she was given a job in a nursing home and has done housework for several people. She has nevertheless requested continuation of school social work services. She seems to need to develop a realistic view of her employment potential and a concept of being satisfied with the attainable. She conceded that she was unhappy at the nursing home because both the suffering of the patients and a personal lack of freedom bothered her. She wanted to do more than be a baby sitter or a domestic. Since variety of work in the community is limited, however, she settled for housework.

At the latest report, Susan still was unhappy with housework but positive factors were being pointed out to her during counseling sessions:

She gets along well with children and adults.

She is able to accept criticism and to conform to the demands of her employers to be direct and honest about her work habits.

She is responsible, willing to work, and willing to learn new job skills.

Throughout the counseling interviews Susan has been talkative. She has become friendly with girls her own age at home and at school. She enjoys swimming, fishing, boating, dancing, and picnics. Ranking high on her list of leisure-time activities are movies and automobile rides. She's interested in boys, too, and frequently dates.

Because of her socialization skills, Susan is capable of being employed if she is adequately motivated. She can follow directions, is eager to please, and completes satisfactory work within her ability. Though she has developed insight into her feelings that others are talking about her, she will continue to need help and understanding in that area. But from the prognostic standpoint, Susan's chances for social and economic adequacy seem fairly good.

The foregoing cases illustrate how children in the program have been given the opportunity to assume work roles in their society—roles that are consistent with their physical, mental, and social capabilities.

The program of Champaign that has made this possible is well designed and well managed. No other program in this report has as complete job specifications as does Champaign. The service is a responsibility of the director of special education, whose duties necessitate broad supervisory responsibilities. The individual heading the prevocational service also has specific duties and responsibilities. As the key person in extending the help of the service, his task is broad. To accomplish it, he must possess unusual qualifications. Champaign's co-ordinator, an experienced teacher with a master's degree in industrial education, is also certified in special education. In addition, he has completed graduate work in vocational guidance and counseling and has held a variety of jobs in industry.

As a staff member of the department of special services, the co-ordinator reports to the director. He is under the general supervision of a joint committee composed of Champaign school administrators, board members, and representatives of the Division of Vocational Rehabilitation. He has responsibilities to four groups: teachers and administrators, individuals and groups of handicapped youths, parents of the handicapped, and personnel on the staff of the Division of Vocational Rehabilitation.

The rehabilitation counselor is an employee of the Division of Vocational Rehabilitation who is assigned to the Champaign schools. He is responsible to the local joint committees that oversee the prevocational program (the Council on Prevocational Education of the Handicapped and the Community Council on Employment of the Handicapped). His work at schools accounts for one-third of his schedule, although he usually contributes additional time to special problems when asked to do so by the prevocational co-ordinator.

The counselor is the person responsible for helping handicapped youth obtain full-time employment. Consequently, his work cannot be compartmentalized into any one category. He is responsible to school personnel, handicapped pupils enrolled in the school, and postschool handicapped youth.

Other school personnel included on the teams working with handicapped pupils are placement counselors, school social workers, school psychologists, the co-ordinator of vision and hearing screening, speech correctionists, and special teachers. These personnel staff cases of handicapped youth. Their services are requested by the co-ordinator, who keeps them informed about the progress of the children.

The department's continuous evaluation is an important stimulus to the development of the prevocational services program. Weekly and monthly staff meetings are climaxed by quarterly meetings when all department members review their work and establish the next quarter's goals. Consider the following remarks by the prevocational co-ordinator published in the *Third Quarterly Report of the Department of Special Services in the Champaign Schools.*

MAJOR ACCOMPLISHMENTS
DURING THE THIRD QUARTER OF THE PROJECT

Development of a Course of Study for the Educable Mentally Handicapped

One of the most outstanding accomplishments made this quarter is the plan for improving the prevocational curriculum for educable mentally handicapped youth. A course of study has been structured at the junior and senior high levels. Several resource units have been written and others are in the process. These resource units will serve as a guide to teachers in providing educational experiences that are more vocationally meaningful. The plans for next year include providing more field trips to business establishments in the community which offer job opportunities compatible with the vocational potentials of youth with limited intellectual ability. These firsthand experiences should be of value in helping these youth gain a better understanding of various types of work and should, as a result, be helpful to them in selecting a vocation. Employers who have an understanding of and experience with the intellectually limited youth will be asked to meet with the class and discuss various jobs and expectations of workers.

Increased Interest Among School Personnel in Employing the Handicapped

Although a relatively few children were placed on in-school jobs, there seems to definitely be a greater interest in and acceptance of employing these children on in-school jobs next year. Definite steps were recommended by the committee to improve the in-school work-study program. A proposed improved program of orientation of school employers has been prepared and is ready to submit to the school Council on Prevocational Education of the Handicapped for their approval.

This excerpt illustrates the advantages of ongoing evaluation of the prevocational work in Champaign's schools. Although the program is new, it is productive. Major outcomes are an increase in the number of employed handicapped young people in the community and a resulting reduction in the problems associated with unemployed youth. The program has hardly reached its full stature but evidence indicates it will continue to be successful.

SCHOOL-WORK PROGRAM
FOR SLOW LEARNERS

A three-year special-education program
designed to help slow learners
become employable, socially adapted adults

A work-oriented curriculum has been included in the special-education classes of the Rochester elementary schools for over fifty years. It was developed to provide a realistic study plan for mentally handicapped children who had little chance of progressing in school beyond the legal dropout age. The extension of this program for mentally retarded secondary school pupils started seventeen years ago. In addition, the thirty-two-year-old programs for elementary school slow learners were extended in 1958 to the secondary level. Two work-study phases were established according to mental ability for both groups of students aged fourteen to seventeen. Mentally retarded children with intelligence quotient scores between 50 and 75 are included in a three-year program known as Occupation-Education I, II, and III. Slow learners whose intelligence quotient scores range from 76 to 89 also participate in a three-year program known as School-Work I, II, III. In the latter program, school personnel are preventing students from becoming alienated youth.

Instructional experiences are alternated with jobs in and out of the school setting. The program is planned to help boys and girls develop appropriate self-understandings, appreciate their relationships to others, and become successful, socially adapted community workers.

The objectives are attained through a carefully constructed three-year curriculum. During the first year, in which classwork is stressed, teachers present practical reading, arithmetic, writing, spelling, and science experiences to enable pupils to improve their scholastic skills for the work experiences of the next phase. Second-year work combines a continued study of the academic courses started .the first year with daily experiences in industrial arts. In well-equipped and carefully supervised settings, students learn elementary skills associated with a variety of service and low-skilled occupations. Successful completion of this experience readies them for the third year, during which a half day is devoted to school-work and a half day to employment on paid community jobs. The program culminates in full-time employment on jobs suited to individual abilities and interests. Supervision by school authorities in all stages is systematic and thorough.

The school-work curriculum is one of many excellent components of the comprehensive educational program of the public schools of Rochester, a city that has built a reputation for good schools with diversified and progressive programs. Special education, in particular, is a well-developed area within which the School-Work Program for slow learners functions.

The Rochester School-Work Program was started, during the 1958–59 school year, to implement the findings of a committee appointed a year before by the school superintendent. The group evaluated offerings for slow learners in the one junior trade school in the system. After a few months of preliminary work, they extended their study to programs for slow learners in all the secondary schools.

The committee carefully analyzed the status of slow learners and determined that they came from a variety of backgrounds. Most entered high school from advanced, ungraded, elementary special-education classes. Others were overage for sixth- and seventh-grade classes and had never been identified officially as requiring ungraded class placements. A few were regular transfer pupils from the city's parochial schools. Finally, some had repeated the lowest level of junior high school nonregent classes.

At the beginning of the 1957–58 school year, 189 slow learners were enrolled in the four academic high schools and 227 in the trade school. In addition, 149 children were registered in the lowest nonregent classes; for classification purposes, they were included in the slow-learning category.[1] School offerings for children of poor scholastic potential varied widely. In two high schools, the instruction of this special group terminated in the so-called "overage seventh grade." In the other two, slow-learner facilities were provided for children through the "overage eighth grade." The choice of nonacademic electives available in all four schools was limited to traditional shop courses that were inappropriate for such pupils.

As would be expected, the youngsters' school progress was poor. In the period from 1952 to 1957, most slow learners terminated in the eighth or ninth grades. By then they had reached the age of sixteen and were eligible to leave school for full-time employment under the New York education code. Pointing up the plight of the youngsters, the committee reported that only seven out of the 109 children who entered high school in 1952 were still enrolled in what should have been their twelfth school year.

When the study was completed, the committee formulated a program appropriate for such children. Members concluded that the public schools were obligated to provide worthwhile educational experiences for post-elementary-school slow learners. Their recommendations to the superintendent stressed that slow learners needed a program to keep them in school for a longer time. Furthermore, they urged that a special program for these pupils be developed. They suggested that a curriculum be offered combining functional academic instruction and realistic shopwork in order to attain these objectives for the benefit of pupils, school, and community:

FOR THE PUPILS

An opportunity to achieve reasonable school success

An opportunity to explore their own occupational interests and aptitudes

---

1. Board of Education, "A Suggested Program for Slow Learners" (Report to the Superintendent, Rochester, N.Y., 1958), p. 5.

An opportunity to receive help and guidance in planning realistically for the future

An opportunity to prepare themselves to obtain and hold a worthwhile job

An opportunity to contribute to society

FOR THE SCHOOLS
A method of expanding facilities and curriculum offerings to meet the educational and occupational needs of this special population

A method of holding the bulk of slow learners in school beyond the usual age for school termination

FOR THE COMMUNITY
An opportunity to participate in a project intended to improve the lot of youth in this classification

An opportunity to reduce the social problems associated with retarded and slow youth not prepared to assume responsible roles in society[2]

The program established to meet these objectives is administered by the department of special education and is an integral part of the Rochester Board of Education's approved curriculums for secondary schools. Consequently, it is financed, staffed, and administered as a regular component of the Rochester school system and is offered in six of the city's eight comprehensive high schools.

The person administering the school-work program has the title of co-ordinator of instructional services. A department consultant supervises the program and links the department with co-ordinating teachers in participating schools. These teachers are assigned full-time supervising responsibilities and hold the status of department head in their schools. They serve as resource persons to the special-class teachers and assist the school principal and fellow staff members with—

Organization and supervision of the program

Counseling with pupils, parents, and teachers regarding total program

Investigation of matters of discipline, attendance, and contacts with community agencies

Selection of instructional materials and building of curriculum

Follow-up contacts with employers and pupils in co-operative work experience

2. *Ibid.*, p. 9.

Liaison responsibilities with the department of special education on total program development[3]

The central office personnel have definite responsibilities to the school personnel. They are to—

Place, transfer, and discharge pupils and maintain files and other records to insure adequate pupil control.

Assist in the selection, supervision, and in-service training of staff.

Plan curriculum, find work-experience opportunities, and assist in job placement.

Represent the Board of Education in all contacts with school and community groups as they relate to the total program for slow learners.[4]

The teachers in the program are selected with care. In addition to being certified, most of them hold New York special-education certificates. While certification in special education is not mandatory, personnel entering the program are encouraged to improve their understanding of slow learners by pursuing graduate work in special education. Many have also had non-school-connected business experience. Finally, they must have demonstrated ability as instructors and want to work with slow learners.

Rochester officials contend that instructors should also possess genuine warmth for and an understanding and appreciation of slow learners. These personal qualities, officials say, are as important as formal training.

Some school-work teachers are recruited from regular school faculties, where they demonstrated unusual teaching skills coupled with a natural ability to relate to and accept problem children and slow learners. No teacher is assigned, however, who does not request such an assignment.

Another successful facet of the procedure for selecting staff is the school's policy on recruitment of new teachers for the program. To encourage beginning teachers to consider professional careers teaching slow learners, cadet teachers are assigned to classes for slow learners whenever possible. A number, for instance, became interested in slow learners while still student teachers.

Slow learners are referred to the school-work program by clinical services personnel in the department of mental health, where each case is considered. School records, personal informa-

---

3. *Ibid.,* p. 11.
4. *Ibid.,* p. 10.

tion, family history, and other pertinent information are assembled and evaluated to avoid inappropriate placement of children who may possess average or low-average intellectual potential despite current cultural and educational deficiencies.

The criteria for the selection of children for the program are:

Intelligence: Dull-normal or low-average (approximately 76–89, D, D—).

Age: At least fourteen years of age as of September of the entering year. SW-III is a work-experience year, and the New York State Labor Department does not permit children under sixteen to participate in a co-operative job program. Children who will be under fourteen years of age in September should not be recommended. Fifteen- and sixteen-year-olds may be recommended for the second and third years of the program.

Sex: Both boys and girls are accepted.

Achievement: Two or more years retarded for grade level. (Fourteen-year-old pupils working at the sixth-grade level are less likely to be accepted than pupils of the same age working at the third-, fourth-, or fifth-grade level.)

Personality: Preference is given to candidates expressing a sincere interest in the three-year program. Those with a tendency to disrupt class routine receive less preference.[5]

In selecting students, the special-education staff strives to keep the school-work program from becoming a receiving ground for nonadjusted pupils of normal ability. In addition to the disadvantage incorrect placement would create for misplaced students, the number of bona fide slow learners makes careful screening imperative. In November 1961, for instance, 638 students were enrolled in Rochester's school-work classes.

To eliminate confusion with the traditional class sequence, the three years of the program are designated School-Work I, II, and III. Throughout the program, individual instruction and guidance are offered. Groups are limited to twenty-five youngsters, with an average class size of twenty. Traditional subject presen-

---

5. Rochester Public Schools, "Notice to Elementary and Secondary School Principals: Procedures for School-Work Program Referrals" (Rochester, N.Y., September 1961).

tations are de-emphasized in favor of integrated course work taught as a core program. The basic topics include personal and family living, community living, and working. Working on these units for three years insures continuous area development. The overall plan provides for gradual transition from core classroom experiences to community work experiences.

The first year—School-Work I—emphasizes practical work in reading, writing, arithmetic, citizenship education, science, and spelling, in units designed to capitalize on the children's interests. During this year of orientation children are helped to develop better self-understanding while working at improving academic skills. In general, they are prepared for the next two phases, when they are employed on jobs in the community.

School-Work II—the second year—is a continuation of the academic studies started during the introductory year. The Rochester Occupational Reading Series, written at three reading grade levels, is used with much success. Each unit has an occupational theme. These excellent instructional aids permit teachers to work with the entire class, since children of varying reading abilities and other academic skills use appropriate levels of occupational readers and workbooks.

In addition to their classwork, students are introduced to jobs by performing tasks in the schools where close supervision by teachers provides the security, support, and guidance needed during this transitional year. Each day the children spend a double period in school shops, where they learn how to care for and operate equipment.

The Rochester schools have five different shops used exclusively by slow learners in the School-Work II program. These complete shops—not superficial representations of commercial counterparts—offer instruction in food service (two schools), personal service, automobile service, home and building maintenance, and office practice.

The food service shop is an unusual, school-contained laboratory in a triple-sized classroom. It contains a study area, restaurant equipment including appliances for baking and meat cutting, and a dining area with tables and a short-order snack bar. Children are taught related academic subjects in a school atmosphere that can be turned into a food-service laboratory for the application of their knowledge in a cafeteria setting. Each school day they plan a menu, determine their work assignments, and prepare lunch. The faculty is invited to use the dining room to give the children experience operating their restaurant snack bar. Prices for the food are on a par with those charged at regular cafeterias. In such a situation, children develop a realistic appreciation of people, work, and efficient use of facilities.

In another school the personal service shop closely parallels the food laboratory. In this one a dry-cleaning plant and shoe repair shop are operated by the students. Students and teachers in the school are encouraged to use the facility. Nominal charges supplement the plant's operating budget, which is administered by the students.

The automobile service center offers a variety of practical learning situations for boys. Washing, waxing, greasing, changing oil, repairing tires, tuning motors, and balancing and aligning wheels are a few of the operations. In accomplishing all the tasks of a typical neighborhood service station, the boys keep their accounts and order supplies, utilizing most of their school-learned skills.

Boys working in the home and building maintenance shop learn to use hand tools and power equipment for painting, laying floors, installing tile, and making plumbing and electrical repairs. Instruction relates academic knowledge to the functional use of skills associated with building maintenance.

The office practice workshop introduces slow learners to fundamental clerical and commercial concepts. Students develop skill in operating simple office equipment. The curricular material is presented to each student on an individual basis, with methods of instruction depending to a great extent on the child's experience. The implications of this, both here and in the other shops, are limitless. Bona fide school-work experiences co-ordinated with instruction create the element crucial to the success of any work-study program: realism.

The third year—School-Work III—consists of a half day of study and a half day of on-the-job work experience. Students either attend morning classes and work afternoons on jobs in the community, or the reverse. Instruction continues in the areas studied during the preceding two years. In addition, students are permitted to elect a number of nonacademic classes in the regular school program.

The youngsters' job assignments are located by the consultant in the co-operative training program and are then referred to the co-ordinating teacher of special education in the school. The consultant and teacher work closely with representatives of the Rochester Industrial Management Council, the U.S. Department of Labor, and New York State Employment Service. Jobs representative of almost all the unskilled tasks have been held by students in Rochester. The scope of the school-work program is indicated by Table 1, a tabulation of students who held jobs in the program during 1958–60.

Table 1

SUMMARY OF JOBS HELD IN FOUR AREAS BY SPECIAL EDUCATION PUPILS[6]

TIME RANGE	FOOD	CLOTHING	AUTO	BUILDING
Sept. 5, 1958–June 1, 1959	63	20	7	20
Sept. 1, 1959–June 1, 1960	64	16	6	21
Summer and after school	39	6	4	9
Full-time jobs	41	27	50	40
TOTAL	207	69	67	90

Satisfactory performance in the three-year program entitles students to receive certificates of completion. School-work pupils can qualify for a high school diploma by returning to regular classes and completing requirements for graduation. Some, however, complete their diploma work by attending evening classes.

Evaluation of the Rochester program has taken two forms. Periodically, the curriculum is studied by committees of teachers and administrators in the program. Their findings are translated into improvement of courses and revision of teaching units. Officials also survey graduates. The co-operative training office of the central administration conducts studies to determine the number of former students employed. Survey results indicate that more than half of the program's graduates are gainfully employed. The most recent study was conducted in 1960 to determine the reasons why certain youngsters did not complete the full course. Findings are reported in Table 2.

The Rochester program has demonstrated its holding power. This criterion of success corroborates the staff's subjective evaluation of the program's worth. Staff members are confident it has

6. "Special Education Department Report" (Rochester, N.Y., January 16. 1960).

prevented many slow learners from becoming alienated. Their prognosis is that the program will continue to be successful.

Table 2

REVIEW OF AGE LEVELS AND REASONS FOR LEAVING THE SW III PROGRAM

	AGE AT LEAVING FOR FULL-TIME WORK	AGE AT LEAVING FOR OTHER REASONS*	
		VOLUNTARY	INVOLUNTARY
SCHOOL A	16- 0—2	16-7—1 SS	16- 1—1 J
	16- 5—3	17-1—1 SS	16- 2—1 HP
	16- 6—1	17-1—1 MS	16- 4—1 HM
	16- 7—1	17-3—1 SS	16-10—1 D
	16- 8—1	18-1—1 SS	16-11—1 D
	16-10—2		17- 3—1 J
	16-11—1		
	17- 6—1		
	TOTALS 12	5	6
SCHOOL B	16- 5—1	16-5—1 NR	16- 2—1 HM
	16- 6—1	17-3—1 TT	16- 3—1 HM
	17- 3—1		16- 6—6 HM
	17- 4—1		
	17-11—2		
	TOTALS 6	2	8
SCHOOL C	16- 4—1	16-7—1 PS	15-10—1 HM
	16- 8—1	18-1—1 MS	16- 3—1 T
	16- 9—1		16-11—2 HM
	17- 1—1		
	17- 2—1		
	TOTALS 5	2	4
SCHOOL D	16- 3—1	16-0—1 NR	16-11—1 J
	16- 5—1		
	16- 7—1		
	16- 8—1		
	16- 9—2		
	17- 2—1		
	TOTALS 7	1	1
	TOTAL 30	10	19

*CODE AND SUMMARY

VOLUNTARY LEAVERS			INVOLUNTARY LEAVERS		
SS	sick of school	4	HP	health physical	1
MS	military service	2	HM	health mental	12
NR	transfer to NR	2	D	disciplinary	2
TT	trade training N.Y.S.E.S.	1	T	transfer out of district	1
PS	parochial school	1	J	incarcerated	3

Fall semester attendance data indicates that pupils leaving school from SW III classes do not terminate directly on their 16th or 17th birthdays.

The average age of SW III school leavers for the fall semester is 16-10. Approximately 20 per cent of those SW III pupils remaining in the program on January 25, 1960, have passed the dates of their 17th birthdays.

An examination of the record clearly indicates that the age factor plays a relatively minor role in determining when pupils may leave the program prior to graduation.

CO-OPERATIVE SCHOOL-HOSPITAL
EDUCATION PROGRAM

A work-study program designed to orient students
to hospital-related vocations

Cranston High School's Co-operative School-Hospital Education
Program prepares non-college-bound girls for post-high-school employment as nurse's aides, ward secretaries, and medical secretaries. This is an excellent example of how a school can utilize a
community resource to offer some of its young people a work-study
program. The program's typical yearly enrollment is twenty to
twenty-five students, senior girls exploring and learning nonpro-
fessional-level vocations in hospital settings. Some are good students
with definite vocational goals. Others use their experiences to explore medical vocations. Still others are potential dropouts who see
the worth of continued education in a practical work-study curriculum. Some of these girls are alienated. They are helped to explore the adult vocational world while learning acceptable work
habits and an appreciation of their civic responsibilities.

In the one-year program, students alternate two-week periods of class attendance with two-week periods of work in local hospitals. Each girl receives a certificate and a diploma when she completes the program.

In the four years that Cranston High School has experimented with this venture, more than 120 girls have completed the program and only three have dropped out.

Cranston is a city of 65,000, similar to many of the other suburbs of Providence. Many residents do not work in Cranston, commuting instead to jobs in Providence, Fall River (Mass.), and other nearby communities. Cranston does not have any large industries but it does have a few small clothing factories, a costume jewelry firm, and a valve manufacturing plant.

In this community, like many others lacking new, growing industries, young people have trouble preparing themselves for immediate post-high-school employment. Of the high school's annual enrollment of two thousand, about one thousand elect traditional college-preparatory courses. Less than half that number enter four-year colleges.

During the 1957 recession Cranston's school personnel became concerned about students' vocational opportunities. Graduates not planning on advanced education found job hunting extremely difficult. In addition, the perennial dropout problem remained. Many children, dissatisfied with the usual school offerings, left school when no longer required to attend by compulsory attendance laws. These dropouts, more hampered than their fellows with diplomas, had little chance of competing for jobs. Their presence in the community troubled school people, who were aware of the danger of such young persons becoming delinquent as a reaction to idleness and to the adult world not admitting them to jobs.

The situation caused the staff at Cranston High School to consider their responsibilities to students facing this problem. In the spring of 1957 they acted. The principal suggested establishing a school-work program in conjunction with the four local hospitals. He broached the subject to the teacher who functions as the coordinator of the Co-operative Employment Program, who agreed with the idea. With the principal's help, the co-ordinator developed a work-study plan that permits students to attend school part time and work part time. The plan was envisioned as a regular school program leading to graduation. The co-ordinator agreed to add it to his other supervisory responsibilities. Until then he had taught classes and administered the fourteen-year-old co-operative retailing course, a noncredit, after-school experience.

After developing their preliminary plans, the staff invited personnel officials and administrators of the local hospitals to a conference at which the school's idea was presented and discussed. Representatives of two hospitals—one large and one small—were particularly enthusiastic. They noted many advantages in permitting young people to receive vocational experience while still in school, as well as benefits for the hospitals in training future workers who would be ready to assume full employment responsibilities immediately after completing high school. Personnel turnover, the time spent orienting new workers, and the increasing demand for hospital personnel made the proposal attractive to them, so they decided to participate.

School and hospital representatives planned a definite program built on the philosophy of using job assignments in hospitals to provide boys and girls with an opportunity to experience responsibilities of work. The job assignments were arranged to permit young people to explore hospital-related vocations while studying appropriate school subjects. These objectives were determined:

To introduce students to jobs related to medicine.

To help students gain a better appreciation of the functions of hospitals and of the way in which they might contribute their individual skills to institutions performing these functions.

To prepare and encourage students to enter hospital-related vocations after high school graduation by teaching them the practical skills necessary for particular occupations in the hospital.

To provide a school curriculum closely related to the work the students would be performing in the hospitals.

The program provides students with an overall orientation to vocations associated with hospitals and specific training for three jobs: nurse's aide, ward secretary, and medical secretary.

Senior students interested in vocational opportunities in hospital work and having at least 57 points toward graduation are eligible to participate after obtaining parental consent. Although boys have not taken advantage of the program, they are eligible. Though the maximum enrollment is forty, usually twenty to twenty-five girls participate each year. During the 1961–62 school year, twenty-two girls were enrolled.

Student applications are reviewed by the co-ordinator or assistant co-ordinator, who appraises school records and confers with teachers and parents to determine whether hospital work is an appropriate experience for the interested students. College-bound pupils are discouraged from entering the program unless they have established definite vocational objectives that would be furthered by the course content.

The class is divided into two sections to permit rotation of students in the work-study plan. While one group works in the hospitals, the other group attends classes for school credit. Academic work is in four areas: English, science, home economics, and social studies.

The English course, taught in a double period, includes the regular senior-year material and units designed especially for work-study students. Medical terminology, report writing, and vocabulary development are stressed. Material is introduced as an integral part of the work experience. The sequence of subject presentation parallels the girls' work progress.

Science includes units on arithmetic review, the metric system, principles of first aid, common diseases, fundamentals of physiology, and an introduction to basic pharmacology.

Home economics covers these units: grooming, health and personality, patients' needs, medical records and charts, food and nutrition, mental health, principles of art, expenses of illness, spiritual needs of patients, and the nurse as a person.

The social studies course deals with the fundamental concepts and skills, attitudes and resultant ideals, and appreciations that all citizens of a democracy should acquire. Besides regular classroom work and discussions, teachers and students take field trips. To round out the program, various speakers address the class on religious dietary laws, the clergy's visits to hospitals, ethics of the nurse, community services, and juvenile delinquency.

Girls working as nurse's aides wear a uniform with a circular patch on the left shoulder identifying them as program participants. Each fall, when a new group of girls begin their hospital training, a special school assembly is held to recognize their entrance into the program. At this time each pupil receives her patch in a ceremony not unlike the traditional capping of beginning student nurses in many hospital training programs. The uniforms worn by the girls are provided by the hospitals, but each youngster must provide her own hospital-type shoes and a wrist watch with a sweep second hand similar to those worn by registered nurses. Girls working in hospital offices wear regular clothing.

While the girls are on their jobs, they receive a weekly stipend from the hospital. At the large hospital, each student receives $15 a week. At the small one, girls receive $12.50 a week and their lunches.

On completion of the senior year, girls who have earned sufficient credits for graduation receive a regular high school diploma. In addition, they are granted a certificate identifying the work-study program completed. The certificate carries the course title, since the school also offers a retailing work-study program and an experimental co-operative business education program.

The courses in the program are taught by the regular school faculty. Since the girls are grouped into two sections, the regular school curriculum is not disrupted. The supervisor co-ordinates job assignments and schoolwork, informing teachers of the students' experiences on their job assignments and informing hospital authorities of the girls' class activities.

The students' hospital training is supervised by registered nurses or hospital personnel officers, depending on whether the youngsters are assigned as aides or as office workers. While in the hospital phase, students are introduced by supervisors to all the job opportunities available in the institution. In addition, a supervisor oversees each student's work to assure acquisition of skills necessary to perform a particular task. A student on a work assignment is required to complete a program identical with the one expected of an adult trained by the hospital personnel. At both participating hospitals, for example, nurse's aides receive twelve weeks of varied work experience. Cranston students' hospital work assignments are for a twenty-week period.

The co-ordinator visits the hospitals frequently to confer with staff members regarding the students' progress. Meetings are regularly held throughout the school year.

Evaluation of the Cranston program consists of annual follow-ups of graduates. Two students, for instance, entered a school of practical nursing, one of whom received the highest mark in her class. The other planned to work in a hospital as a licensed practical nurse and stated that the Cranston program had helped her find a field in which she could offer the most service.

Another girl was seeking admission both to schools for laboratory technicians and to schools of nursing. She was taking college chemistry courses during the summer. Still another reported that she was working as a licensed practical nurse in a hospital.

Since the program is relatively new, however, insufficient information is available for a thorough appraisal of its impact. Trends have appeared, nevertheless, in responses such as those cited. Many other girls have entered work directly related to the program. The enthusiasm of both graduates and girls enrolled is high. School officials and hospital supervisory personnel are also pleased with the results.

One indication of the confidence school officials have in the success of the hospital education and the retailing and business cooperative programs is their recent proposal to create a technical institute. On the basis of the worth of the existing offerings, they hope to establish an afternoon-evening program which would provide work experience and classroom instruction for out-of-school youth, adults, and secondary-school dropouts. This ambitious plan to extend work-study experiences to out-of-school youth is tangible evidence of the feeling of confidence the faculty of Cranston High School has in its program.

CASE EIGHT: *New York City*
Board of Education of the City of New York

WORK-EXPERIENCE PROGRAM
FOR POTENTIAL DROPOUTS

A work-experience program initiated in 1955
as part of the Ten Priority Program,
designed to prevent juvenile delinquency
in New York City

New York City school officials, responsible for overseeing the world's largest public school system, cannot help being statistics minded. One trend under their constant scrutiny is the schools' holding power. Their concern for increasing the number of children who remain in school until they complete programs causes them to offer innumerable courses of study. The Work-Experience Program for Potential Dropouts is the one they use to reach and help alienated youth.

The program, initiated in 1955 in the city's senior high schools, is part of the Ten Priority Program adopted by New York to combat juvenile delinquency. This phase provides realistic school experiences for students unable to adjust to traditional curriculums. The youngsters are alienated, incapable of getting along in school, home, or community. Some have police records.

Only boys participate in the program. During the morning they attend school. Afternoons, on official school time, they work in private industry. Pupils are supervised by teacher co-ordinators who teach the academic part of the course in the morning session and locate student work stations and visit boys on jobs in the afternoon. Class activities and work assignments are co-ordinated to motivate students to learn and to develop new appreciations of themselves, of work, and of society.

The program is not isolated from other school offerings. Alienated youth are expected to remain in special class situations for just one year. The course is designed for rehabilitation. Consequently, youngsters are expected to return to regular school "streams" when they can profit from conventional instruction. To foster this objective, boys are required to elect two courses in the regular program each semester. This procedure, officials contend, enables alienated youngsters to identify with classmates and eases their transition back to routine curriculums.

To date, results have been encouraging. From September 1959 to June 1960 more than 30 per cent of the alienated boys enrolled in the program returned to regular courses of study. Another 30 per cent remained in the program for an additional year. Approximately 24 per cent entered full-time employment or the armed forces. The remainder dropped out of school. Those not continuing in school exhibited enough positive behavior change to cause the staff to believe instruction and guidance had benefited them. Their attitudes toward school, work, and society had improved, in sharp contrast to those of similar youngsters not included in the special work-study program.[1]

New York's program for alienated children was developed out of an evaluation of the system's power to hold students until graduation. Awareness of the need for such a curriculum can be traced back to a study that school researchers conducted during the 1950's. A follow-up study of members of the 1951 class revealed that the number of students who had been graduated varied from 37.59 per cent (vocational high schools) to 62.40 per cent (academic high schools).[2] The results created genuine concern on the part of the administrative staff. Evidence based on research in schools indicated that delinquency was most prevalent among juveniles who failed to complete formal school programs. Personnel were also aware that in New York, as in other cities, many young workers face a society that requires more education and training of each new generation. They therefore assumed the task of design-

---

1. Board of Education of the City of New York, *Work-Experience Program for Potential Dropouts* (mimeographed report, September 22, 1961), p. 1.

2. *Ibid.*, p. 2.

ing an educational plan to provide for pupils headed for early termination of school. They knew this population contained many obviously alienated young persons and many more children heading toward a socially unacceptable way of life. Finally, they knew from the study that the dropout pattern started in the tenth grade when most youngsters are legally qualified by age to work.

The high school division was given the responsibility for creating a plan to retain potential dropouts. There were other related programs such as intensive four-week employment courses for students in continuation schools and career guidance programs in junior high schools. These offerings help reduce the number of early school leavers, but they are not designed specifically for such a purpose. The present work-experience program is the first school project intended to hold problem youngsters in school.

In attacking their task, division personnel held to a general theory. They believed severe youth problems resulted from students lacking a life purpose. In addition, they recognized the frustrations and resulting idleness experienced by youngsters attempting to assume adult roles. Their awareness of problem children helped them formulate this philosophy:

> Boys will respond to the personal guidance provided by a teacher co-ordinator who supervises their studies and work experience.
>
> A sympathetic and imaginative teacher can provide effective guidance and instruction for these boys when he works with them in a small group, not to exceed twenty or, in the extreme, twenty-five pupils.
>
> Paid supervised employment in part-time jobs will give the boys a sense of status, provide insight into the value of learning, motivate efforts to improve performance in school, and inculcate attitudes necessary for success in full-time employment.
>
> A course of study that meets the pupils on their own level, that meets their immediate needs and concerns, and that emphasizes pre-employment training and adult responsibilities will, in conjunction with work experience, engage the interest of the pupils, remedy weaknesses in fundamental skills, and provide the educational background for full employment.[3] The total effect of the program will be to give the pupils a sense of direction and responsibility and lead them to formulate realistic goals and ambitions.
>
> The way must be kept open, for pupils who are motivated to do so by the program, to resume full-time studies leading to high school graduation.[4]

---

3. *Ibid.*, p. 3.

4. Board of Education of the City of New York, *Youth Achievement Program* (mimeographed report, September 8, 1961), p. 1.

The two objectives that emerge from the philosophy are to lower the dropout rate through school retention beyond sixteen years of age, and to provide those students who leave school at sixteen with a terminal education that will prepare them to assume adult roles in their work and in their community.[5]

The program that implements these objectives is for teen-age boys identified as early school leavers whose school records reveal scholastic failure, truancy, and behavior problems. For boys in such a category the program provides school preparation and work experience to prepare them for employment or to rekindle their desire to resume traditional school studies. Either objective satisfies school personnel. They believe both avenues lead boys to responsible adulthood.

During its first three years the program was experimental and restricted to two senior high schools. The success in these years resulted in the program's expansion. In 1959-60 it was extended to five schools, and in 1960-61 a sixth school offered work experience. At present more than eight schools in the city's five boroughs have the program.

The program's basic design organizes subject matter along functional lines. Emphasis is on job orientation and mastery of school skills, such as communications, reading, and arithmetic, necessary for success on jobs. Class size is restricted to a maximum of twenty-five boys fifteen to seventeen years old.

The co-ordinator is the program's focal point for the boys. He acts as their homeroom teacher and instructs them in some of their course work. In four schools, co-ordinators teach English and social studies. One co-ordinator offers an integrated course of applied physics and machine shop. Another teaches business practice. Regardless of subject area, however, emphasis in class instruction is on orienting boys to the world of work.

Much work has been done to develop a curriculum best suited to the objectives. A committee composed of central administrative officials and curriculum specialists worked with teacher co-ordinators developing units of study. They produced an experimental teacher guide, *Curriculum Materials To Meet School Retention and Pre-employment Needs,* published by the Board of Education in February 1962. This guide contains study units appropriate to the needs of pupils not expected to remain in school until graduation. Although designed for students enrolled in courses other than

---

5. *Ibid.*

those offering work experience, the difficulty level of the units and the practical subject presentation are relevant to pupils in the special work-education curriculum. In fact, as part of the preliminary work necessary in validating the course, some work-education students were taught from the tentative experimental units. Another reason the guide is appropriate for work-education students is that the majority of them have lower levels of intelligence, according to the system's testing program. Even those of average native intelligence and the few receiving high scores on intelligence tests are considered slow learners in an operative sense. They have, as a group, failed school and are retarded in learning situations. Moreover, since their immediate plans involve leaving school for employment, job-centered units in the new teacher guide are especially applicable.

In the development of the units, much thought went into the procedures and techniques to make them useful with slow learners. The principles the committee determined to be applicable to the guide's organization and format were:

Job orientation; preparation for work and on-the-job guidance

Improvement in basic skills, especially reading

Opportunities for enrichment

Integration in subject matter among the units

Guidance emphasis; adjustments and responsibilities in living as part of a group

Provisions for individualization

Articulation between school and out-of-school environment

The units included in this bulletin are:

Our American Heritage	Your Use of Leisure Time
Language Arts	Your License as a Future Driver
You as a Consumer	Personal Mathematics
You and Success on the Job	Using Mathematics as a Worker
You as a Worker in Industry	and Citizen
How Our Government Works	Science in Daily Living
Your Family Membership	Salable Skills[6]

Methods and materials were adapted from those proven useful

---

6. Board of Education, *Work-Experience Program*, p. 3.

with slow learners. The difficulty levels of the lessons are kept low, but suggested additional work with each unit permits teachers to vary instruction and level where student effort can be expected. Integration of the instructional material with students' work experience is emphasized.

Besides studying the core program under their particular co-ordinator, the youngsters also participate in physical education classes of the regular program. Finally, except in one school, they attend at least one other class outside of work education.

Afternoons are set aside for the program's work aspects. After lunch each boy reports to a work station. The majority of the assignments are in clerical, merchandising, and service fields located in private establishments in the neighborhoods of the schools offering the program. Most jobs are obtained by the co-ordinators. Many times they locate work stations with the help of the New York State Employment Service. The agency has co-operated with the schools since the program began. Occasionally boys obtain their own jobs. In such cases co-ordinators must approve the assignment before a boy offers it as the work experience. Boys not capable of employment because of behavior or lack of a community job are assigned tasks in school.

While on jobs, boys are paid by employers at the same rates as those paid regular employees. Though the schools do not contribute toward the boys' salaries, credit is granted for satisfactory completion of work assignments. The Carnegie unit granted counts toward the total number of graduation requirements. Still, the program is not a regular course of study leading to a high school diploma.

Students participating in the program are identified by the school's guidance staff, dean of boys, and class co-ordinator. Youngsters needing part-time work are not included unless they exhibit antisocial tendencies or other behavior symptomatic of potential dropouts. Just as the program is not intended for nonalienated pupils, neither is it open to seriously disturbed youngsters and hard-core delinquents. Such children receive intensive clinical aid through the school's psychological services. The work-experience program is reserved for alienated youngsters who can be rehabilitated through such a program.

Although planned as a one-year course of study, the program may be entered by students at any time. Acceptance is contingent on the appropriateness of the curriculum for them. In some cases placement of youngsters in the course also depends on the existence of vacancies, since the number in a class is limited. Boys also may leave the program at any time during the school year to return to regular courses.

Some students remain in the program for more than a year. They are the ones identified by the staff as not yet capable of resuming regular studies. Flexibility of instruction and work stations enables such students to benefit from an additional year. In some special cases students have remained in the program until graduation. These boys entered near the end of their schoolwork and had accumulated enough course credits to permit them to complete requirements for diplomas while enrolled in work-experience classes.

One other criterion must be met by boys prior to acceptance: they must be employable. Finding work stations for them is sometimes an exceedingly difficult problem. Many industrial organizations have rigid employment policies that forbid the employment of any youth below the age of eighteen. Also, state employment codes restrict the kinds of jobs boys fifteen and sixteen may accept. Co-ordinators keep on the alert for possible student job opportunities. They seek work stations primarily in the neighborhood of the local school. For the most part, their efforts have been productive. The program's registration and employment summary of October 1960 is typical of the usual number of youngsters employed.

PROGRAM REGISTRATION
AND EMPLOYMENT SUMMARY
October 1960 [7]

High School	Registration	Number Employed
DeWitt Clinton	21	15
Haaren	24	22
Jamaica	14	8
John Jay	19	14
Port Richmond	19	18
Westinghouse Vocational	11	6
TOTALS	108	83

The problem of employment is a troublesome one. School officials have considered establishing a central employment agency of some kind to act as a job clearinghouse for all the program's students. Such an office, they reason, might relieve co-ordinators of the burdens associated with their present individual responsibil-

7. *Ibid.*

ities for locating work stations. In any event, the primary responsibility for job placement will remain with the local school.

While the job is the most important element from the motivational aspect, the co-ordinator is most important from the operational standpoint. He has multiple functions as an effective teacher, counselor, vocational adviser, and placement officer. All roles are considered of equal worth in the fulfillment of the program's objectives. Teachers in the program and those to be included as the program expands have been and will be selected because they exhibit certain personal traits. To date, both men and women have been selected to oversee the program. Co-ordinators' personal characteristics are considered more important than their competence in particular teaching fields.

Each year a follow-up study is made to determine what has become of each student. In addition, a study of 51 students who had resumed a regular school program in September 1960 revealed the following: 34 were discharged from school (31 to full-time employment; 3 to the armed services), 10 are continuing a regular school program, 6 have been graduated, and 1 transferred to another New York City high school.

The statistics indicate the program has been a success—if disposition of cases is a method of evaluation. Specific examples are equally encouraging.

Consider the case of Bill. He was placed in the work-experience program for the usual reasons. He was a truant; he had a record of almost total academic failure; he was no stranger in the dean's office. Bill was severely retarded in reading and his spelling was weirdly arbitrary. In the work-experience program, he was placed in an afternoon job as a stock boy for a small distributing company. Soon he was asking the program co-ordinator for special help in reading and spelling because he had found himself handicapped on the job for lack of facility in the basic skills. Just before summer vacation, he told the co-ordinator that his employer had offered him a chance to become an inventory clerk the following September if he continued to improve his writing skill. Bill pleaded for reading materials and spelling lists that he could work with during the summer. He copied each word on the spelling lists on index cards and carried these cards wherever he went, so that he could study them in spare moments. He spent many hours, too, reading materials that he had been given. When the first week of the autumn term arrived, the co-ordinator tested Bill on spelling and reading. The results of the tests indicated that the boy was up to normal grade level. He has earned—and he received—his promotion to inventory clerk.

Another example is Frank, a likable but undisciplined boy. His parents had little education and approved Frank's intention to leave school at the earliest legal moment. Despite his native ability, he suffered from the handicaps of a disadvantaged home and neighborhood. His attendance in school, where he was a chronic failure, was spotty. Frank was selected for the work-experience program and placed in a job with a local clothing store. The work seemed to interest him and the weekly wage provided him with a sense of status. He responded, too, to the interest in him shown by the co-ordinator and his employer. Both his work in school and his attendance record improved. At the end of the school year his employer encouraged him to plan a course of study for the following year that would earn a diploma. In turn, the employer offered to pay Frank's college tuition if the boy was actually graduated from high school. In the meantime Frank was permitted to hold a part-time job in the store. Today Frank is within a few credits of a high school diploma. He is still employed by the store—and he's looking forward to a college education culminating in a degree in business administration.

Fred's case is different. His widowed mother was unable to control him and at sixteen he was leader of a neighborhood gang. On those irregular occasions when he did attend school, he disrupted classes. Soon after he had his first brush with the law, the school guidance department suggested that he be placed in the work-experience program. The prospect of regular income from an afternoon job in a small food market persuaded the boy to attend classes. He discovered for himself that the double class period taught by the co-ordinator dealt with practical problems related to employment. He also discovered that the co-ordinator could speak and listen to his language. At the food market Fred worked in close contact with his employer, who repeatedly stressed the need for a boy who wants to get on in the world to get an education. After six months in the program, the boy confided to the co-ordinator that he wanted to remain in school to obtain a diploma. He still belonged to the gang, he admitted. But he added that he did not have much time for it any longer, since his day was taken up with school and work and he had to do homework at night.

These cases are just a few illustrations of what New York's program is accomplishing. To make the outcomes more meaningful and to measure them more objectively, the program's supervisory personnel have set up an experimental evaluation study that includes three of the eight schools.

The study design includes control and experimental groups in the three schools. The control group is composed of boys, not in work education, similar to boys who are in the work-education program. The subjects have been matched on variables such as intelligence quotients, attendance records, and educational achievement. The hypothesis is that boys in the program will exhibit significant improvement over a year as compared with the boys not participating in the program. The criteria for measuring progress toward improved behavior include school attendance, educational achievement, attitudes toward work, realistic occupational goals, job turnover, and school behavior.

Pending results of the experiment, school officials contend they have enough evidence available to convince them that the program is worthwhile. They have found uniform results in all the schools. Attendance records of most boys in the program improve, with a corresponding sharp decrease in the incidence of misbehavior in school. Although the boys' educational achievement has not improved to the same extent as has their attendance and behavior, most boys exhibit upward trends in grades and in progress reports of teachers. The close contacts of the co-ordinators with employers and with parents have had a positive effect on school relations with the community and the home. The support of the program by local employers has been invaluable. The consensus of the staff is that their program is successful. Their final evaluation is reserved, though, until results of the experiment are available.

CASE NINE: *Kansas City, Missouri*

Kansas City Public Schools, Kansas City, Missouri

WORK-STUDY PROGRAM
TO PREVENT
JUVENILE DELINQUENCY

An experimental school-work program
designed specifically for alienated youth

The Kansas City work-study program differs somewhat from the
other cases in this report. It is unique because it is an experimental
project designed specifically for children fitting the definition of
alienated youth.

The program was started in September 1961 after two years of
preliminary planning by a committee composed of Kansas City
school personnel, civic leaders, representatives of a mental health
foundation, and the consultant, Dr. Robert J. Havighurst. Interest in the experiment has been nationwide. Representatives of
school work-study programs from many parts of the country contributed ideas to the committee and participated in a related workshop conducted by the Kansas City schools in August 1961. The
interest of nonschool groups is evidenced by the financial support
granted the experiment by the Ford Foundation. This philanthropic organization is sharing the cost of the project with the
Kansas City Board of Education.

Two hundred boys were selected for the experiment from the 1960-61 seventh-grade classes of the four junior high schools participating in the program. They were chosen because they had exhibited the behavior characteristics of alienated youth. Two hundred more were selected in 1961–62, making a total of four hundred boys, which was split into an experimental group and a control group. Half of the boys in the former category started the school-work program in September 1961. Those in the control group were not removed from the regular educational program. As the experiment progresses, the boys in both groups will be studied and their progress contrasted to determine the influence of the main variable in their school experience—the work-study program—and the behavior of the experimental boys compared with the behavior of the boys in the control group.

The program for the experimental group has three stages. The first is a general orientation period consisting of half-day classes and half-day group work assignments. At this level most boys are in the thirteen-to-fifteen age range. After they complete the first or second year, according to age, they enter stage two. In this stage they continue school studies on a half-day basis and spend the other half of each school day working as part-time paid employees in the community. When they attain the age of seventeen or eighteen and have completed the first two stages, they will begin stage three—full-time employment on regular community jobs. While on such assignments, boys are to receive regular school supervision from personnel who have worked with them during the preceding four years.

Throughout all stages of the program, continual evaluation is to be carried on by the researchers. Yearly reports will keep supervisory personnel informed of the progress of the youngsters in both groups. A final follow-up evaluation will be made when the boys attain young adulthood. At that time the entire experiment is to be reviewed to determine its worth as a vehicle for reducing juvenile delinquency in a population of young boys.

The experiment was developed after intensive research by a committee which reviewed the experience of schools offering work-study curriculums. The committee incorporated this review and the latest research findings on juvenile delinquents in its report. It concluded that delinquency could be prevented in two ways. One is through the community organization, based on the assumption that strengthening youth-serving institutions such as the home, the school, and the church results in corresponding improvement in adolescents' social development. The other is through work roles. The premise of the latter approach is that modern society lacks work for youngsters, and that an increasing number of children consequently manifest unacceptable behavior as a reaction to an unaccepting world.

Consideration of both approaches resulted in the committee's decision to use elements from each to provide for alienated youngsters. The major purpose was to create a new school-work experience for alienated youth that would offer boys a realistic and worthwhile avenue to adulthood. The objective was:

> To reduce the amount of juvenile delinquency by providing boys who are vulnerable to delinquency with a better opportunity for growth into adulthood through combining school with work experience.[1]

The experiment was designed to test the following hypothesis:

> Boys vulnerable to delinquency will become less delinquent if they are given a systematic work experience commencing as early as age thirteen or fourteen and continuing until they reach age seventeen or eighteen.[2]

The design includes contrasting the progress of two groups of boys:

Experimental Group	*Control Groups*
200 boys, about evenly divided between white and Negro	A. 200 boys, matched with the experimental group
	B. Possibly 30 boys whose parents refuse to have them in in the experimental group

The experimental group participates in the following program:

Work-Study Stage I. This first stage, for boys aged thirteen to fifteen, consists of two parts. They perform socially useful work in and around the school for half of each day. Groups are limited to twenty-five boys and are under the supervision of a skilled worker. During the other half of the day they study an academic program geared to their level and interests.[3]

---

1. School District of Kansas City, "A Work-Study Program To Reduce Juvenile Delinquency" (December 12, 1960), p. 1.

2. *Ibid.*

3. The curriculum objectives and sample units designed to prepare them for assuming responsible roles as citizens and workers are included in Appendix C.

Work-Study Stage II. The second stage is for boys from fifteen to seventeen years of age who have completed the first stage. Youngsters are placed on community jobs for half of each school day. Cooperating employers and the school employment co-ordinator supervise them on their jobs. Students continue academic classroom work during the other half of the school day. At this level the committee expects boys to drop from school. Some will terminate because they will have reached legal school-leaving age. While efforts will be made to keep them in the program, restrictions will be few and will be kept flexible. Other boys may transfer to a regular course of study. Those desiring to do so will be encouraged to make the transition, though it is not anticipated that many boys will fall into this category. For the most part, pupils in the school-work program at this level will be boys expected to drop out of traditional curriculums.

Work-Study Stage III. Boys are eligible for this stage if they are between the ages of sixteen and eighteen and have completed stage two successfully. The employment co-ordinator-supervisor will help them find full-time employment. When they are on jobs, he will oversee their satisfactory adjustment from school to work. In accomplishing his task, the co-ordinator will check each student's progress through personal contact and through employers' evaluations. Boys officially complete the program when they reach the age of eighteen and when the supervisor has completed a final comprehensive evaluation of their competence. This step is the final one in the experiment.

Throughout all phases of the program, individual help and counseling are offered each boy by academic teachers, school counselors, and the supervisor. Youngsters also receive attention from community agencies such as the YMCA and Boys Clubs. Thus community participation is a part of each child's experience. The project director communicates with representatives of groups such as the Central Labor Council, Chamber of Commerce, Urban League, and Rotary Club, and agencies such as the YMCA, Boys Clubs, and Juvenile Court. The initial involvement of representatives of these organizations led the way to the formation of a related community committee. Such a group interprets the program to the community, solicits citizens' aid and co-operation in understanding alienated youth, and locates jobs for the boys in the rehabilitative process.

Since the experiment began slowly, any early mistake could be identified and corrected before the later groups joined the early ones. The boys selected so far had to—

> Possess an intelligence quotient score between 80 and 104.
>
> Exhibit characteristics of aggressive maladjustment as determined by their performance on two instruments: the *Who Are They Inventory* (a sociometric device) and the *Behavior Description Chart* (a teacher-rated form).
>
> Have a grade point average below 2.9.
>
> Come from a family group not rated as "cohesive" in the judgment of a family interviewer.
>
> Have parent's consent to participate in the experiment.[4]

In addition, each pupil's cumulative record is used to evaluate his school achievement and behavior and attendance records.

The boys are placed in the experimental and control groups on the basis of intelligence, race, school achievement, home background, and socioeconomic status. In matching the youngsters, care is taken to maintain the experiment's scientific structure.

The work-study experiment is an integral part of the Kansas City schools. The work-education section of the project, together with the selection and preparation of the four work supervisors, the four assistant work supervisors, the employment supervisor, and the three employment co-ordinators, is the responsibility of the practical arts division under the assistant superintendent in charge of instruction. The experiment best fits into this division, which includes industrial arts, vocational education, co-operative occupational education, joint apprenticeship, and trade extension programs, and consequently possesses the leadership and staff required to initiate and carry out such an experiment.

The academic curriculum and counseling services associated with the first two stages are the responsibility of the instructional division. The division personnel selects the four academic instructors assigned to the project and prepares the course of study. The guidance and counseling services received by the boys are the responsibility of the counselors in the schools housing the program. Special counselors do not work exclusively with the alienated youth.

Since research is one of the project's prime objectives, one research associate from each district department works closely with the research associate assigned to the program. The department

---

4. School District of Kansas City, *op. cit.*, p. 5.

representative's major responsibility is to accumulate and analyze data in the pupils' school records. His report is to complete the project's final evaluation.

The senior research associate, a person competent in the design of statistical research and in the techniques of social investigation, is attached to Community Studies, Incorporated, a private organization. He has the major responsibility of carrying out continuous evaluation of the project's results. His duties include the analysis of data from out-of-school sources to measure the subjects' adjustment patterns. He works with community organizations and agencies such as the YMCA, police department, juvenile court, and churches, as well as with employers. He co-ordinates his findings with those of the school research associate to evaluate the worth of the total program.

Both researchers are key personnel during the experiment. Although no one period of time can be identified as the one in which they will make their greatest contributions, the first two years are considered crucial. During this period they are adhering to a rigid program of ongoing evaluation paced with the project's first phase. They are responsible for insuring the operation's success by constant scrutiny of results to permit readjustment of the experiment at any time when findings indicate that errors have been incorporated into the design. The schedule of major research concerns during the first two years is included in Appendix D.

Both research associates will be fairly busy for the 1963–65 period. After that, Associate B, based in the school, might go on a part-time assignment, unless he were to work more closely with Associate A on extraschool studies.

In summary, the total program's staff will consist of:[5]

Director	1
Academic instructors	4
Work supervisors	4
Assistant work supervisors	4
Employment co-ordinators	3
Research associates	2

BUDGET

The budget for the project may be divided conveniently into three categories of expenses as follows:

---

5. *Ibid.*, pp. 26–27.

Ordinary operating expense. This covers the cost of instruction of the experimental group, which will be carried by the Kansas City Public Schools as part of the regular school budget. This is the equivalent of about $400 per pupil per year.

Extraordinary operating expense. This will include the cost of administration of the project and of additional service (during the summer) of school personnel assigned to the project; also the cost of transporting pupils to work sites during the first phase of the project, and the cost of the payment to these pupils in case such payment is made part of the project. These expenses appear to be a reasonable charge against the experiment.

Research expense. The costs of selecting the boys for the project, studying them and the control group, recording the details of the project, evaluating the results of the experiment, analyzing data, and preparing a written report on the experiment are included.

The project, which started in September 1961, is expected to last a minimum of six years. By that time the boys who were thirteen or fourteen when they began the program will have left school and made their initial adult adjustment. While the participants will be studied throughout the entire experiment, the program's final evaluation will be impossible until all the boys terminate their schooling. Consequently, the planning team anticipates retaining the research staff until 1968 or possibly 1969. During the final period, findings will be accumulated and conclusions summarized in reportable form. (See Appendix D, Example 3.)

The project's evaluation will consist of testing the major hypothesis that there will be less delinquency in the experimental group of boys than in the control group. To do this, relevant data contributing to the researcher's knowledge of the boys' development will have to be collected. The major comparisons to be made regarding the youngsters' adult adjustment will be in the following eight areas:

Regularity of school attendance

Conditions associated with school dropout: to take a job or with nothing in view, attitude toward school at the time, relations with school personnel at the time

Reading, arithmetic, and general knowledge, as measured by achievement test scores

Personal adjustment, as measured by objective and projective techniques

Social adjustment, as measured by a sociometric instrument and by teacher ratings

Attitudes toward school

Self-concept and vocational aspiration

Job adjustment and work competence at the end of the experiment[6]

The timetable for the total experiment's evaluation completes the description of this experiment, which is sure to have far-reaching implications for the nation's schools.

TIME SCHEDULE OF ACTIVITIES[7]
January 1961–August 1969

TERMINOLOGY

X_1 = 1st Experimental Group (100 eighth-graders in '61–'62)

X_2 = 2nd Experimental Group (100 eighth-graders in '62–'63)

STAGE I = Stage of Work in Groups (ages 13–15)

STAGE II = Stage of Individual Part-Time Employment (ages 15–17)

STAGE III = Stage of Full-Time Employment (ages 16+)

Note that the stages are overlapping in age. Boys will move from one stage to the next when they are ready and when appropriate employment is available to them. The experiment officially terminates for a boy when he reaches age 19, although he will not be actively involved in the project after about age 17. After age 17, his progress will be noted and a small amount of service may be given to him.

January 1961–August 1961

Selection, organization, and training of operation staff

Selection of research staff

Selection of boys for experimental and control groups

Interviews with parents of boys in X_1 group

September 1961–August 1962

Operation started with X_1 group (ages 13–14)

Selection of X_2 group

Organization of base-line data on X_1 and X_2 groups and on control groups

September 1962–August 1963

X_2 group starts operation.

X_1 group begins to terminate Stage I. A few X_1 boys move into Stage II (age 15).

---

6. *Ibid.*, p. 13.

7. *Ibid.*, pp. 23–24.

Employment co-ordinator-supervisor starts work, January 1963.

Research staff collects data systematically on work experience and on academic achievement in State II. Research staff collects data on community relations of X_1 and X_2 and control groups.

September 1963–August 1964

X_1 group completes transition to Stage II (ages 15–16).

X_2 group begins transition to Stage II.

Work-supervisor staff reduced in number.

Employment co-ordinator-supervisors increased in number.

Research staff collects data by interview on school dropouts in X and control groups. Research staff organizes testing for personal-social adjustment of group approaching age 16—this to be completed on the rest of the group next year. Research staff organizes for data collection on employment experience of X and control group members.

September 1964–August 1965

X_1 group commences transition to Stage III (ages 16–17).

X_2 group completes transition to Stage II.

This is the period of most rapid school dropout rate.

Research staff busy with dropout interviews.

Research staff continues data collecting on employment experiences of X and control group members.

Operation entirely in hands of employment co-ordinators-supervisors.

September 1965–August 1966

X_1 group all in Stage III (ages 17–18).

X_2 group commences transition to Stage III.

Research staff commences final data collection on boys as they pass 18th birthday. Data on delinquency, on community relations and activities, and other data necessary for a measurement of initial adult adjustment.

September 1966–August 1967

X_1 group is terminated (ages 18–19).

X_2 group all in Stage III.

Operations staff reduced to one employment co-ordinator-supervisor and the director. Research staff commences organizing and analyzing data.

September 1967–August 1968

X_2 group is terminated.

Research staff finishes data collection. Spends most of its time on data analysis.

September 1968–August 1969

Period of final write-up of experiment.

Staff consists of one or two research associates plus assistants and typists.

The Challenge

The reported cases have important implications for school personnel who are establishing or reviewing work-study programs for youth. Educators, moreover, are not the only ones who can find a use for these examples. Alienated young people are the responsibility of the total community. Thus, their rehabilitation should challenge both the school and the community.

The establishment of school-sponsored work-study programs for maladjusted boys and girls is not any one group's prerogative. The Cranston case pointed up the competency of certain school people in starting and operating a program with the co-operation of two institutions but little or no supplementary community counsel. Their approach can be contrasted with a program being developed in Grand Rapids, Michigan. This city, a recipient of *Look* magazine's All American City Award, is planning a comprehensive curriculum for its young, alienated population. The idea originated with local industrial representatives.

While existing programs are helpful examples, they must be used with caution. Work-study situations cannot be duplicated outside their environment. Elements are transferable; total structures are not. School-related work-study programs must evolve within the community in which they will function. All the cases share this characteristic of indigenous development. Consequently, models such as the nine described can aid only insofar as they provide a common structure translatable into other specific situations. A review reveals certain common characteristics inherent within their development, organization, and administration. Some of these programs have implications for other communities, either in their creative adaptability to beginning programs or in their evaluative applicability to established curriculums.

SCHOOL-COMMUNITY PLANNING

Careful thought must precede the initiation of work-study programs for alienated youth. Planning has to start with the initial suggestion and continue throughout the program's existence. Regardless of the source—whether an educator or a community agent—school personnel should lead the development of the proposal. They should begin by forming a committee composed of educators and laymen. The latter group might include representatives of local industries, businesses, churches, social agencies, and service organizations. School members should be the superintendent, an administrator, a guidance worker, one or more teachers, and supervisors of appropriate district departments, such as a director of special education.

The committee should emulate the Moline fact-finders in studying schools and the community. The committee's task is to determine whether the number of alienated youth is appreciable and whether a school-sponsored work-study program is an appropriate method of rehabilitating such children. In fulfilling the first part of this task, the group might enlist the help of local authorities on children to view youth in the light of recent findings relating to identification of delinquency-prone children. The investigators' second consideration—determining a rehabilitative plan for alienated youngsters—also requires the aid of community agencies. School and community resources must be evaluated to determine whether existing social service facilities need to be bolstered by work-study curriculums.

If research identifies a need for work-study offerings, the committee should transform itself into an advisory group to oversee development of the program. The committee's primary function, therefore, changes to that of establishing philosophy, objectives, and operational procedures. Pursuit of such purposes carries with it a number of obligations. First, the overseers must survey school-community resources pertinent to work-study programs. Primary considerations involve studying the curriculum and evaluating the potential of community part-time jobs. As exemplified in Champaign, laymen should play a responsible role in this task. Second, the committee should review other schools' programs to glean from them appropriate ideas and procedures. Some of these findings may be incorporated with little change; other aspects may require modification prior to adoption. At this stage it may be advisable to obtain the consultative services of authorities on education, delinquency, and youth. Also, benefits of conferences such as the Kansas City workshop should be considered.

Third, while accomplishing their purposes, the advisers must not disregard the structure of their own group. The group's organization, work schedule, and delegation of responsibilities must allow for maximum efforts toward establishing a workable program. Therefore, administrative trivia and tangential activities should be minimized. In addition, procedures must be designed to perpetuate the committee by establishing methods of replacing inactive members or those whose association has been terminated.

Fourth, a primary committee function is to establish program philosophy and objectives. These must evolve from the local educators' and the community's basic beliefs. The philosophy should provide the basis for the objectives. The objectives, in turn, should identify program goals specifically and direct efforts toward their achievement. The formulation of philosophy and objectives are the committee's most important tasks.

PROGRAM

After the completion of the preceding steps, a curriculum based on the objectives should be designed. Its preparation may be delegated to school representatives. This group's guiding principle must be the integration of students' classroom and work experience. The resultant comprehensive program has to maintain a close relation between study and work throughout all phases and levels. Co-ordinated development promotes curriculum flexibility and ultimate program success. Careful adherence to objectives must be stressed. The care with which Cranston's school and hospital work is co-ordinated illustrates this tenet.

A program's academic phase should include class instruction in English, reading, mathematics, science, and social studies. These subjects need modification to the grade level, interests, and peculiar needs of the participating alienated children. Core presentation, as practiced in the New York City program, is the preferable instructional method. Focus upon children's classroom and work experience must be maintained. It is recommended that classes have not more than twenty students studying with one teacher. Elective, nonacademic courses from the regular school curriculum should be offered alienated youngsters. Involvement with their better-adjusted peers counterbalances their semi-isolated state in the school.

Work experience, the other program phase, must also follow objectives closely. Offerings should consist of work orientation and part- and full-time school and community job assignments providing realistic work situations. Steplike experiences such as the in-school, out-of-school work stations of the Mount Diablo program might be considered. The assignments may be located in the school or community, depending on the program's philosophy and resources. Rewards should be offered for work, in the form of either school credit or money, or both.

Regardless of the emphasis, pupils' work assignments require supervision by competent teachers or co-operative laymen to tie in practical learnings with classroom instruction. Constant program supervision is necessary, too, to insure compliance with state and local school and work regulations. The Fielstra recommendations to the Santa Barbara schools regarding their compliance with state law emphasize the importance of this suggestion.

Throughout a program's operation, students and their special curriculum should be integrated with the regular school routine. Rochester's use of full-time co-ordinators helps that program achieve this objective. To promote this goal further, teachers and counselors from outside the curriculum should be involved with the participating students. Also, continuous interpretation of the program to the community by staff and committee members is mandatory. Eventual acceptance of the work-study program as a regular segment of the school offerings should be a constant objective.

STUDENTS

Students to be included in work-study education programs must be selected carefully. A case approach is the most valid method. As in the Kansas City experiment, definite selection criteria can be formulated. Data on age, grade level, school attendance and truancy record, academic achievement, performance on standardized tests, behavior patterns in school and in the community, as well as information from teachers' anecdotal records, home environment, psychological evaluations, and children's and parents' expressed desires, should guide selectors. Early identification of alienated youth is particularly desirable. Rochester's program emphasizes that care must be taken to avoid incorrect placement of pupils who could not benefit from work-study. For example, slow learners and psychologically maladjusted boys and girls requiring intensive remedial or therapeutic aid should not be included in the program. Finally, alienated children should be maintained in work-study education until they are prepared to return to traditional curriculums or are ready to enter the adult world as responsible citizens. This emphasis is necessary for an effective program; evidence of it in New York City's stated objectives reveals the importance placed on this goal by that city.

STAFF

Educators and laymen associated with work-study programs for alienated youth must possess special qualifications. Administrators and supervisors need, in addition to organizational and leadership abilities, an awareness of alienated children's characteristics and of their personal, social, educational, and vocational needs. The success of the Champaign program, for example, is certainly a reflection of the staff's unusual professional capabilities. To perform their role adequately, officials should have experience as teachers of maladjusted children. Strong leadership is needed for organization, development, and evaluation of a program.

Teachers should be chosen on the basis of their professional preparation, teaching ability, and personal qualities. The latter consideration overshadows all other qualifications. Men and women should be selected who are sensitive to alienated children and able to accept them, relate to them, and support them in their school and work experiences. Moline's staff illustrates this suggestion. In all the cases described, the children's progress depended most on their teachers' unique ability to work with them. While certification, professional preparation, and experience contributed to effectiveness of individual teachers, the empathic traits noted were crucial to program success.

Nonschool people involved in work-study programs need the qualifications suitable for their particular roles. In addition, they must be helped to appreciate the contributions they can make to the program. Champaign's orientation of employers is an example of the way laymen can be helped to prepare themselves to be effective participants. Committee members' responsibility for program policy and public relations requires the special qualities that enable them to perform their roles adequately. Likewise, employers charged with supervision of alienated youngsters on part-time jobs must possess the vocational skills and personality traits suitable to their tasks. Exact guides cannot be established for the selection of lay personnel, other than to emphasize that any individual working directly with alienated children must have sufficient empathy to be able to relate to them.

EVALUATION

A process of evaluation must be inherent in work-study programs if accomplishment of objectives is desired. Appraisal procedures should be built into program design in the planning stage. While methods of measuring progress toward objectives vary, experimental approaches as exemplified in the Kansas City project are the best. Such techniques best lend themselves to continuous checks on program direction and effectiveness. Knowledge gained from frequent evaluation can be used to modify procedures to insure attainment of the desired objectives.

Final comprehensive evaluation determines whether the program is a success in that it measures the degree to which program goals are attained. Qualitative or quantitative devices for evaluation may be utilized. No matter which kind of device is used, evaluation must be a constant element of work-study programs for alienated youth.

These suggestions merely provide a partial picture of the characteristics of a work-study program. The recommendations are not all-inclusive. They are not meant to be complete. Rigid rules for development eliminate the unique qualities that programs can achieve through the personal involvement and efforts of their creators. Successful work-study plans need to differ from each other as radically as individuals set themselves apart from their fellows. New work-study programs, in particular, must include facets not yet even dreamed of.

Without projecting far into the future, the need for new approaches to combating juvenile delinquency is apparent. The country's work force as one barometer of the approaching problem already points up the situation's seriousness. During this decade, the U.S. Department of Labor predicts, 26 million young job seekers will enter the labor market. Of that number 7.5 million will not have graduated from high school. Another 2.5 million will not have completed eighth grade.[1] Statistics such as these are warnings of

---

1. Science Research Associates, *Research Report,* September 1961.

social as well as economic problems for the nation. School dropouts invariably experience difficulty locating jobs; approximately 30 per cent of them are not even employable. The social implications are frightening. Add to the economic causes of delinquency the many other sources of maladjustment in children, and the problem is further compounded.

This nation must face the problem of juvenile delinquency, investigate all avenues of prevention and rehabilitation, and act with little or no lost effort. In the accomplishment of such goals, work-study education requires serious consideration. The method combines educators' and laymen's efforts in a common purpose. The objective—help for alienated youth—is the schools' and the community's challenge.

Appendix A

A STATEMENT OF NATIONAL POLICY
FOR ALIENATED YOUTH[1]

A statement prepared by Robert J. Havighurst
and Lindley J. Stiles for the Commission
on the Role of the School in the Prevention
of Juvenile Delinquency as recommended policy
for Phi Delta Kappa

If citizens of all occupational, political, and religious affiliations
were asked the question, "What should this country do for its young
people?" the answer would be unanimous that the United States
should give its boys and girls a good chance to grow into productive workers, successful parents, law-abiding citizens, and happy
persons—in effect, help them become *competent adults.*

There would of course be some differences of opinion as to
how society should provide opportunities suited to the accomplishment of this goal. In addition, disagreement might prevail as to
which tasks are appropriate for the schools to do, which are best
left to the family, and what contributions should be made by
churches and other agencies. Further, there might be some differ-

---

1. Reprinted from the April 1961 issue of *Phi Delta Kappan.* © 1961, Phi Delta
Kappa, Inc.

ences of opinion as to the kinds of opportunities that are appropriate for girls as compared with boys, for Negroes in contrast to white youth, or for the mentally dull as compared with the gifted.

General agreement would probably prevail, however, that opportunity is relative. One boy's chance would be another's burden. The circumstances that spell opportunity to a boy or girl depend on the youth's abilities, on what he has been brought up to want from life, and on which openings or positions in the adult society are likely to be available to him.

Thus young people with below average abilities whose family backgrounds have given them limited contact with books and ideas will more likely experience satisfactory growth if they get stable semiskilled or unskilled jobs, make stable marriages, and get an income that provides reasonably adequate housing and the standard of living they have learned to want. Nobody can rightly say that they lack opportunity if they drop out of school at age 16 and find a stable job.

On the other hand, many children from culturally inadequate homes do much better in life than their parents did, mainly through using educational and economic opportunity. One should not, therefore, force the children of poor parents into rigid educational or occupational molds that prevent them from showing potential abilities. This premise is generally accepted and followed. The United States has reason to be proud of practices in its schools and industries which challenge young people to find, develop and use hidden powers in themselves.

It is generally agreed that the great majority of young people in this country will profit from the educational opportunities afforded by the high school, and that the upper third to half of them will profit from a college education.

Satisfactory growth depends upon appropriate opportunity, while appropriate opportunity depends upon the abilities and the personality of the individual.

HOW WELL IS OUR GOAL FOR YOUTH ACHIEVED?

Opportunity for satisfactory growth is provided to a fairly adequate degree for the great majority of young people. To evaluate a community's performance in this respect it is useful to think about four classifications of youth, each of which has a particular pattern of opportunity, advantages, and disadvantages.

A. The Academically Superior

The Conant report on the American high school[2] speaks of the 15 per cent of boys and girls who are academically superior. Such young people have IQ's generally above 115 and are good "college material"; it is generally agreed that they should be encouraged to achieve well in high school academic courses and to go on to college.

Academically superior students have been the center of attention in the decade just past. Most of the recent improvements in secondary school programs have been aimed at them. They have been able to profit from the new science and mathematics curricula, from more intensive foreign language teaching, and from college level courses taught in high school or from early admission to college.

Because of the shortage of young adults due to the low birth rates of the 1930's these young people have been regarded as a precious resource which must be cared for and cultivated to the fullest.

B. The Middle Two-Thirds

In addition to the 15 per cent just mentioned, some two-thirds of young people get along reasonably well under present educational and social conditions. Most of them graduate from high school and some of them go to college. A quarter of this middle two-thirds, or 15 to 20 per cent of the age group, do not graduate from high school, but they manage to get jobs at the age of 16 or 17, or to marry at those ages, and to grow up to adulthood in a fairly acceptable manner.

These young people were the focal point of discussion immediately following World War II before public attention shifted to the gifted in the early 1950's. They are assumed to be able to adapt themselves to school and to the society, and actually most have done so reasonably well. When a multi-track system has been introduced in high school, this group occupies the middle one or two tracks. Some of them do fairly well in college. Most of them have found the labor market of the 1950's to be hospitable.

C. The Handicapped

Two or three per cent of boys and girls have serious mental or

---

2. James B. Conant, *The American High School Today*. New York: McGraw-Hill, 1959.

physical handicaps which obviously interfere with their progress to competent adulthood. Some of them are slow to learn, with IQ's below 75 or 80 that place them in the group defined as the "educable mentally handicapped." Others are deaf, or blind, or crippled, or afflicted with cerebral palsy. While it is next to impossible to provide opportunities that will equate their chances for satisfactory growth with those enjoyed by the "normal" youngster, society has made substantial effort in this direction.

Special provision has been made in most states for the education of those children at a greater-than-average expense. Their teachers obtain special training and are usually paid higher salaries than teachers of normal pupils receive.

D. The Alienated Group

Some 15 per cent of young people do not grow up in a satisfactory way. This group has been identified in several studies. It has been called by various names—the uneducables, the nonlearners, the hard-to-reach, the alienated. The "alienated" is an appropriate name for this group, because it expresses the fact that they are somehow alien to the larger society in which they live. Such youth have been unsuccessful in meeting the standards set by the society for them—standards of behavior, of learning in school, of performance on a job. By the time they reach adolescence these boys and girls are visible as the misfits in school. Either they are hostile and unruly, or passive and apathetic. They have quit learning and have dropped out of school psychologically two or three years before they can drop out physically.

Most alienated youth come from low income homes; most of them fall in the IQ range 75-90; almost all drop out of school at age 16 or before; they tend to come from broken homes, or homes which are inadequate emotionally and culturally. Yet this is not simply a group low in economic status and IQ; two-thirds of working-class children do satisfactory work in school, as do two-thirds of children with below average IQ's. This is a group whose start in life has been poor because of the disadvantages its members face. Their families have been inadequate. Often their physical health has been poor. Their intellectual skills are usually too marginal to compensate for other deficiencies.

It should be emphasized that alienated youth can be found in all IQ ranges and from middle and upper class homes, although the percentages are higher in the 75-90 IQ bracket and among groups which are culturally and economically disadvantaged. Any child who lacks recognition at home or in school, or who is emotionally insecure, can become alienated.

Within this alienated group are found the majority of juvenile delinquents. Among the girls of this group are found the majority of 16- and 17-year-old brides.

We call them "alienated" because they do not accept the ways of living and achieving that are standard in our society. As younger children they probably accepted the standard ideas of right and wrong, complied with school regulations and tried to succeed, but the combined and repeated frustrations of failure in school and mistreatment at home have turned them either into members of delinquent sub-groups or into defeated, apathetic individuals. The 15 per cent about whom we speak are found in a community which has a normal cross-section of American youth. But in the slum area of a big city the proportion may be doubled. As many as 30 or 40 per cent of the eighth and ninth graders in some of our city schools are alienated youth. On the other hand, this group comprises only a small percentage of youth in the upper middle class suburbs of a metropolitan area.

Members of underprivileged racial or immigrant minorities are likely to be found in the alienated group. Thus Negroes, Mexicans, and Puerto Ricans make up a large proportion of alienated youth in the industrial cities of today, whereas thirty or forty years ago this group would have been composed largely of children of European immigrants. On the other hand, many boys and girls from racial and immigrant minorities are growing up successfully, and these numbers are increasing.

The alienated group seems to be a product of society, its size the resultant of combinations of socio-economic factors, and its particular composition determined by the presence of one or another social group at the bottom of the social scale. Thus in a Midwestern city of 45,000 this group was found to be present to the extent of about 15 per cent; there were no Mexicans or Puerto Ricans in the community, and few Negroes. The boys and girls in the alienated group carried names that reflected English, Scotch, Irish, or German origin. Their families occupied low status in that particular community.

The alienation of a youth in this community may be illustrated by the case of a boy whose nickname was Duke. He was the older of two boys born to his mother when she was living with her second husband. This man deserted her when the boys were young.

She supported them by working and from help provided by the government aid for dependent children program. Duke's IQ was about average as measured by an intelligence test, yet he did poor work in school and was required to repeat the sixth grade. He was regarded by his agemates and by his teacher as a highly aggressive boy. His sixth grade teacher checked the following adjectives as descriptive of him: aggressive, alert, boastful, bossy, cruel, depressed, honest, loyal, revengeful, show-off, tease, touchy, vindictive.

As Duke grew older he became more actively aggressive in school, until in the ninth grade, the record shows, he was frequently "sent out" of his classes by his teachers. Finally, shortly after he reached his sixteenth birthday, he decided to quit school. One of his best friends had just been expelled and another had dropped out.

When asked by an interviewer how it seemed to him after he had been out of school several months, Duke said: "I'd rather be in. But when I quit I had a feeling that they were going to kick me out anyway. It was quit or get kicked out because of my bad behavior. I couldn't mind my teachers or they couldn't mind me; I don't know which. Anyway, I had mostly study halls when I quit. They kicked me out of science and social studies and algebra."

Duke's first brush with the law had come when he was 10 years old. On this occasion he was brought before the police matron with some other boys for putting their footprints in some freshly-laid cement. By the time he was sixteen he had accumulated an assortment of misbehaviors on the record, including stealing, fighting, and sexual offenses.

From the time he quit school at 16 and until he was 17 Duke loafed around town with cronies, working at unskilled jobs periodically for a few weeks at a time, and getting into various kinds of trouble. Finally he enlisted in the Navy.

Here we see a boy whose pattern of failing to grow up according to society's expectations became clear to him and to others by the time he was 10 or 11 years old. He reacted to this failure by becoming aggressive, tough, masculine, and boastful. Since he could not hold jobs for any length of time, he stole in order to get money. Within his delinquent gang he was accepted as a leader, and thus he earned his nickname. His enlistment in the Navy marked another effort to grow up by doing something active. This did not work out, however, since he lacked the stability and the affirmative attitude required by the military service; he was soon discharged back into his home community, where he resumed his delinquent ways. Not until he reached the age of 19 did he seem to be stabilizing somewhat. At this time he married and became a steadier and more dependable person.

NEED FOR AN ALTERNATIVE PATHWAY TO ADULTHOOD

The essential problem of the alienated group is that they have not found a satisfactory avenue or channel of growth toward adult competence. Since they are failing in school, they cannot grow up by means of the school. They need an alternative pathway to that offered by the school as we now know it.

These boys want the same things in life that are achieved by boys who are growing up successfully. They would like to have money, a job, and as they grow older they want the use of an automobile. They want girl friends, and eventually desire to have a wife and children. Unlike the majority of boys, however, they do not have the combination of family assistance, the intelligence, the social skills, and the good study and work habits necessary to achieve their goal legitimately. Nevertheless, they want to grow up and to have the symbols of manhood, and they become discontented when they do not succeed.

Alienated boys, thwarted in the normal channels, seek illegitimate means to achieve the symbols of manhood. They may turn to the delinquent gang for "moral support" and for instruction in ways to get money, excitement, power, and the feeling of masculinity. These boys, frustrated by the adult society around them, may become hostile and aggressive toward that society. Often they may vent their hostility through such activities as destroying property, burning school buildings, and attacking law-abiding people.

Forty years ago there were many boys who could not grow up through the school system. But at that time there was a clear alternative road to adulthood—the road of work. A boy could quit school at age 14, 15, or 16 and get work on a farm or in a business. In fact, more than half of all boys in 1920 did drop out before graduating from high school; nevertheless, they found work and grew up along the pathway provided by a series of jobs with increasing pay and increasing responsibility. Census records show that in 1920 somewhat more than 50 per cent of boys aged 14 through 17 were employed full-time or part-time. The proportion of 14-year-olds who were out of school and employed full-time was low, but more than half of all boys were out of school by age seventeen and at work. At that time a boy could easily follow a well-traveled highway of work from early adolescence to adulthood.

During the past forty years the number of jobs open to juveniles has been decreasing. Jobs as telegraph messengers, delivery boys, office boys, elevator boys, etc., have grown scarce. The farm population has been reduced greatly and with it the farm as a place where a nonacademic boy could be doing a man's work by the age of 16. The proportion of unskilled and semiskilled jobs in the labor force has also decreased. Employers, faced with an oversupply of adult labor during much of this period, have adopted as a standard for employment the minimum age of 18, or high-school graduation. The 1960 census will show that fewer than 35 per cent of boys aged 14 through 17 were employed at that time, and a large proportion of them have only part-time jobs. The unemployment rate is at least twice as high among boys between 14 and 17 as it is among older boys who are in the labor market. During the latter part of the 1950's, while the overall rate of unemployment in the United States was about 5 per cent, the teen-agers' unemployment rate was 10 per cent, while 16- and 17-year-olds who had dropped out of school had an unemployment rate of 20 per cent.

The employment situation for teen-agers is not likely to improve during the 1960's, for the high birth rate of 1947 and later years will cause the numbers of 16- and 17-year-olds to increase by 1963 to a figure 40 per cent above the numbers in this age bracket in the 1950's.

Thus there is a strong prospect that the road to adulthood through juvenile work which has been narrowing since 1920 will become even more constricted during the coming decade. This road will remain in existence, however. It is being followed with fair success by about half of the 35 to 40 per cent of boys who now drop out of school before finishing a high-school course.

What our society must do is to widen this narrow road once more, through finding or creating more juvenile jobs. With work experience, there is a good chance of bringing many alienated boys back into the mainstream of American youth, where they can grow up with confidence in themselves and in the society.

Since jobs in the American economy, as we now define jobs, are not likely to increase in numbers for boys, it becomes necessary to find ways to provide boys with the *moral equivalent of work,* a kind of work experience that has the growth value of a job, though it is not a job in the narrow sense of the word.

IMPORTANCE OF WORK IN THE GROWING UP PROCESS

The idea that work experience should be provided for boys outside of the labor market, if the labor market as then constituted could not accommodate them, was generally accepted during the depression of the 1930's. By 1933 the mounting wave of unemployment had engulfed hundreds of thousands of families. Fathers were unemployed, and adolescent boys could not find work. Boys took to the road, partly in the hope of finding jobs elsewhere, and partly to take some of the burden of feeding a family off their fathers' shoulders. Soon a quarter of a million homeless boys were riding freight trains and hitchhiking toward places where work was rumored to be, or where they might at least find a change from the grim conditions at home.

This situation was soon recognized as an emergency, and was treated as such by President Roosevelt. The Civilian Conservation Corps was established to place boys over 16 in resident camps under a semi-military regime. In this program boys learned to do socially useful work, under supervision, and were paid a small sum of money, most of which was allotted to the assistance of their families. The program was not related to schools; indeed, school administrators were excluded from its policy making bodies and top leadership because they were believed by President Roosevelt to be unsympathetic to work experience. This program worked well, but it was limited to boys who had already dropped out of school; it was also rather expensive. In some situations the lack of cooperation between schools and the Civilian Conservation Corps Program tended to hinder the full development of youth who needed and desired both work experience, by which some income could be derived, and academic training. Groping for a type of work experience that would have school-relatedness and which would be available to youth of both sexes, the federal government next created the National Youth Administration plan, which provided for part-time work with pay for students of high-school and college age. The work projects in the NYA program were developed mainly by schools and colleges; the funds for the payment of salaries were provided by the federal government. Program regulations specified that work provided could not compete with ordinary business and industry. The objective was to provide supervised work experience which would have educational value and promote an allegiance to society while permitting young people to continue their schooling.

This experiment in providing youth with jobs continued until the entry of the United States into World War II, when the armed services and war industry quickly absorbed all available youth.

During the late 1930's the American Youth Commission, a group of citizens appointed by the American Council on Education to study the problems of youth in the depression years, made studies of the Civilian Conservation Corps and the National Youth Administration work program. They drew the following conclusions:

> Every young person who does not desire to continue in school after 16, and who cannot get a job in private enterprise, should be provided under public auspices with employment in some form of service. . . .
>
> The Commission is impressed with the success of experiments that have been made with combinations of part-time schooling and part-time employment. . . .
>
> Public work for young people should be planned with special regard to its educational quality. It should be superintended by persons who are competent to train young people in good work habits as well as in specific skills. It should be carried on in a spirit that will give to the young worker a sense of being valued by and valuable to his country. Finally it should provide an opportunity to try various kinds of work, so that the young person may find his own aptitudes and abilities and may be given some guidance in preparing for private employment in a field where he can be most useful and successful. . . .
>
> The Commission recommends, therefore, that in the formulation of public policy at all levels, explicit recognition be given to the social responsibility of seeing to it that all young people are constructively occupied up to some appropriate age. The Commission believes that 21 is the age which ought to be recognized for this purpose. Insofar as any specific age can do so, it corresponds to a real point in the process of maturation for a very large number of individuals, and it has been imbedded in law and custom by centuries.[3]

A NEW NATIONAL EMERGENCY

While we are not in a severe economic depression, and we do not have a quarter of a million homeless boys on the road, we do have almost a quarter of a million alienated boys in each annual cohort—a quarter of a million reaching their fourteenth birthday this year, another quarter of a million becoming 15, and so on. Consequently, alienated youth might be considered a national emergency equal to or worse than that of the 1930's.

---

3. *Youth and the Future.* Washington, D.C.: American Council on Education, 1942.

Dramatic testimony on the need and desire for work experience for youth was presented last year by Congressman Frank Bow of Ohio, in the following letter, published on September 12, 1960, with his own statement:

I have an anonymous letter, postmarked Louisville, that reads in part as follows:

"As future taxpayers and voters, my buddies and myself, all teen-agers, are writing this to tell how we feel about the unemployment and juvenile delinquents.

"Our opinion is [that] if most boys 17, 18, and 19 who quit or finish high school could find work to get them off the streets and supply them with some money, they won't have to steal or rob for it.

"All teen-agers are not delinquents. We looked hard for work of any kind and found very little. If someone took time to do something for us, they would be doing a favor for all.

"Older people said 'look harder' or 'write your Congressman,' so we are. Ohio streets are bad, the parks are not clean. Why not hire teen-agers to do some of this work?"

If I could reply, the first thing I would tell the anonymous teen-ager is that youngsters of his generation should not quit high school, and should make every effort while in high school to equip themselves for productive work in our era. There will not be much future in the "Space Age" for a teen-ager who lacks even the preparation of a high-school education.

I would try to resist a lecture on whether anyone should think for a moment that he must "steal or rob."

But most important, I would ask the community to act on this young man's suggestion. Why not a community project to use the talents and energies of such boys? Encourage them to set up their own central agency for job information. Make a real effort to find work that will help them to keep their self-respect.

CURRENT PROGRAMS AND PROPOSALS

The fact that work experience is important in the process of growing up has not escaped the attention of educators. For a long time, vocational education has contained work experience as an integral part in many courses. What has been called "cooperative education," which combines a job with study, has been practiced in some engineering schools and technical institutes, as well as in some high schools, for more than thirty years. In 1928 there were seventy-eight cities with 5,682 pupils enrolled in cooperative courses under the Smith-Hughes Act. The government-aided diversified occupations work-study program was started in 1933. Since World War II there has been a substantial growth of work experience programs in schools. In a survey of work experience education programs published by the U. S. Office of Education in 1957, 145 items in the working bibliography of 276 items were produced after 1950. More than 200 articles, books, and research reports on work experience education have been published since 1941.

The following types of work experience are now found in secondary schools:[4]

1. *In-school, nonremunerative general education work experience programs.*

Experience is provided in the school for students as typists, clerks, parking lot attendants, messengers, multigraph operators, library assistants, motion picture machine operators, locker maintenance workers. Students are not paid except for after-school work. In some cases, credit is given toward graduation.

2. *Out-of-school, nonremunerative general education work experience programs.*

    a. Community service work in noncommercial organizations: libraries, parks, social agencies, elementary schools.

    b. Student-learner assignments in physicians' or dentists' offices, architects' studios, hospitals, city or county offices.

3. *Remunerative general education work experience programs at the junior high-school level.*

This is for youth who are likely to drop out of school at age 16. It is usually provided for 15-year-olds. School credit and "going wages" are given. Typical jobs are as bus boys, messengers, waitresses, car washers, printers' helpers, sales clerks.

4. *Remunerative general education work experience for pupils in senior high school.*

This type of program is for youth in senior high school who will profit personally and economically from work experience in such a way as to make their schooling more attractive and more successful. Scholastic credit is generally given for work which is coordinated with school studies.

5. *Remunerative vocational work experience in senior high schools not subsidized by federal vocational education funds.*

A "diversified occupations" type of course is offered, mainly to high-school juniors and seniors over 16 years of age who have

---

4. DeWitt Hunt, *Work Experience Education Programs in American Secondary Schools.* Washington, D.C.: Department of Health, Education, and Welfare, U. S. Office of Education, Bulletin No. 5, 1957, p. 13.

good records. Often the course is set up in schools or communities too small to qualify for the federal subsidy. Some of these students will get work experience in selling jobs, some in office assignments, and some in factories. An effort is made to place the student in the field where he is likely to work as an adult.

6. *Remunerative vocational work experience programs in high schools subsidized from federal vocational educational funds.*

Commencing in 1917 with the Smith-Hughes Act (which was amplified in 1946 by the George-Barden Act), a cooperative part-time education and employment program is available to high-school juniors and seniors. Jobs are in the trades, industrial occupations, and distributive occupations. This is the most highly selective program; it is seldom available to a student who has done poor work in school.

NEEDED: PROGRAMS FOR ALIENATED YOUTH

The most widespread programs are for senior high-school pupils, age 16 or over, who have a good school record. Thus they are not open to alienated youth. They are useful programs; but something more is needed.

The kind of work experience program that will be most useful to alienated youth will have the following characteristics:

1. It will commence at age 13 or 14, and continue to age 18, though many boys will graduate from it a year or two before age 18.

2. It will attempt to teach boys elementary work disciplines: punctuality, ability to take orders from a boss, ability to work cooperatively with others in a team, responsibility on the job.

3. It will lead directly into stable adult jobs.

4. It will be a part of the public school program, with the curriculum adapted to the intellectual level, the interest in practical endeavors, and the work-experience program of alienated youth.

A preventive program of this type must of course rest upon a procedure for identifying the future alienated youth at least by the age of 13 or 14. This can be done and has been done in several researches. The identification process consists of finding those boys who show a combination of aggressive maladjustment with failure in school, plus checking in marginal cases by visiting the home and evaluating the nature of family discipline and help given to the boy.

A work experience program will need to be organized in stages which reflect the boys' level of maturity and responsibility, and which at the same time are geared to prevailing child labor legislation. Probably three stages are indicated.

A. The first stage should be work in groups, under school supervision, completely or partially outside of the labor market. For example, boys might work in groups on parks, school grounds, alleys, beaches, thus contributing to community housekeeping. Alternatively, boys might work in a "sheltered workshop" in the school which would contract for jobs with local business and industry. The workshop might take contracts for stuffing envelopes with advertising matter; simple assembly jobs, such as collecting nuts and bolts into packages for sale; processing material with a simple machine. The difficulty with the sheltered workshop idea for boys is that similar facilities are badly needed for handicapped adults and for old people who need employment.

B. A second stage should be part-time work on an individual basis with employers in private or public business or industry. Here the boy would be more nearly "on his own" in the labor market, but he would still work under close supervision by the school.

C. The final stage would be full-time employment in a stable job, aided by some guidance and supervision on the part of school or employment service personnel.

RESPONSIBILITY OF SOCIETY AS A WHOLE

The corollary school program provided for alienated youth would need to be adapted in content, methods of instruction, and learning materials to the ability and orientation of youth involved. The content would need to be appropriate to the goals of instruction and to the age level of the pupils. At the same time, it would, in most cases, need to be presented in textbook and other learning materials at a lower reading level, and with less abstractness, than is common for high-school courses. Instruction would need to be characterized by practical approaches to problems, shop or laboratory experiences, and an extensive use of audio-visual aids. A close relationship between the program of the school and work experiences would be desirable.

A program of the type just outlined cannot be lodged in the labor force as it is now constituted. There are not nearly enough juvenile jobs, and the trend is toward reduction of juvenile jobs and unskilled jobs. Private business is not in a position to provide all the jobs needed, nor is organized labor in a position to cooperate in a program that might reduce the number of adult jobs in the economy.

Nevertheless, there seems to be good reason for adopting a social policy which guarantees work experience as a part of education to every boy who needs it, just as instruction in mathematics or science or foreign language is guaranteed to youth who need that kind of education. And the society should bear the cost of one kind of education just as it bears the cost of the other kind.

If the provision of juvenile jobs becomes a part of social policy, there are two presently expanding areas of the economy in which jobs for boys may be created fairly easily. One of these areas is that of conservation of natural resources, and the other is that of public service. Assuming that federal, state, and local government funds will be used increasingly on projects for soil and water conservation, and on the maintenance of parks, parkways, highways, beaches, and forest preserves, the respective government agencies might deliberately design work projects in such a way that substantial numbers of boys could be employed on work crews.

A PROGRAM SUPPORTED BY FEDERAL GOVERNMENT

Recently Senator Hubert Humphrey introduced a bill in Congress to set up a Youth Conservation Corps. His proposal was incorporated into the platform of the Democratic Party in 1960. This idea has much in its favor. It might well be developed for boys 16 and over, but if it were limited to work camps, it would not be applicable to boys under 16, where the need is especially great.

Possibly the plan might be developed into a more general Youth Development Program, for boys aged 13 to 20. The program might provide for locally-based work projects in the earlier stages, so that the boys could live at home and go to their regular schools while taking part in a work-study project.

Federal grants might be made to the states for the support of work experience programs meeting certain criteria. The state which received the grant might develop a program with three elements:

1. A program for the big cities, based on elementary or junior high-school units, with a job-creating and job-finding program supported by city-wide civic, business, and labor organizations.

2. A program for the community of 20,000 to 100,000 people, based on a particular junior high school or several elementary schools, and backed by a community commission of business and labor leaders.

3. A program for rural counties and rural sections of urban counties, based on elementary schools or consolidated schools, and developed in collaboration with the county agricultural agent and local community business leaders.

WHAT A WORK-EXPERIENCE PROGRAM WOULD NOT DO

The work experience program suggested in these pages is not a panacea for all youth problems. It is merely one element (but a highly important one) in a complex of arrangements which our society should make in order to reduce the number of alienated youth.

Such a program might be expected to cut down juvenile delinquency by as much as 50 per cent. It could not reduce juvenile delinquency more than this, because a substantial proportion of juvenile delinquency is committed by boys who are not aggressive or are not failing in school, and such boys would not be in the program.

A work-study program needs to be supplemented by community agencies, such as Boys Clubs, Settlement Houses, YMCA, CYO, and other organizations that give boys a chance for wholesome recreation and social life.

Furthermore, a work-study program for adolescent boys may not be needed as much in the future as it is right now. It is likely that the number of boys who fail in school and who become socially maladjusted can be reduced materially by preventive measures taken earlier, when the boys are in kindergarten and first grade.

More work and more effective work needs to be done with these boys and their families when they are five or six years old. A more successful program at this age might cut the numbers of teen-age alienated youth in half, and thus reduce the size of a work-study program.

SUGGESTED STRATEGY FOR COMMUNITIES

Thus the strategy of attack on the problem of alienated youth appears to have the following phases:

1. Development of a work-study program for alienated 13-and 14-year-old boys.

2. Supplementation of the work-study program by social agencies and community organizations which create and maintain a wholesome social situation for alienated youth.

3. Preventive programs for work with young children in the primary grades and their families to help them make more satisfactory progress in school and thus to reduce the future numbers of alienated youth for whom a work-study program is needed.

This country should be doing all three of these things. If we do, we can look ahead with some confidence to a time, ten or twenty years from now, when the unhappiness and frustration of young people and the danger to society of having a large group of alienated youth will be reduced to less than half their present proportions.

Appendix B

SELECTED FORMS USED
IN WORK-STUDY PROGRAMS

1 JOB SPECIFICATION FORM
Champaign Community Schools

2 STUDENT PREVOCATIONAL SKILLS SCREEN-
ING FORM
Champaign Community Schools

3 STUDENT REQUEST FOR JOB-COUNSELING
APPOINTMENT
Mount Diablo Unified School District

4 STUDENT APPLICATION FOR INSIDE WORK
EXPERIENCE
Mount Diablo Unified School District

5 STUDENT REQUEST FOR JOB-COUNSELING
APPOINTMENT
Santa Barbara High School

6 STUDENT REFERRAL FORM
Champaign Community Schools

7 STUDENT REFERRAL FORM
City School District, Rochester

8 WORK ASSIGNMENT PLACEMENT FORM
City School District, Rochester

9 PERSONAL AND FAMILY INFORMATION FORM
Mount Diablo Unified School District

10 STUDENT-EMPLOYER AGREEMENT FORM
Champaign Community Schools

11 STUDENT WORK-EXPERIENCE RECORD
Mount Diablo Unified School District

12 STUDENT WORK-EXPERIENCE RECORD
Champaign Community Schools

13 EMPLOYER RATING SHEET
Santa Barbara High School

14 EMPLOYER RATING SHEET
City School District, Rochester

15 STUDENT MERIT RATING SHEET
Mount Diablo Unified School District

16 EMPLOYER RATING SHEET
Cranston High School

17 STUDENT PLACEMENT FOLLOW-UP
Champaign Community Schools

Example 1

JOB SPECIFICATION FORM
Champaign Community Schools

Office of Special Services
Champaign Public Schools
Prevocational Education

JOB SPECIFICATION   Administrator _____

Name of Job _____

Place of Job _____

Hours Spent on Job _____

Brief Description of Duties _____

_____

_____

_____

Job Requirements:

Academic -   Mathematics - Grade Level   _____

              English - Grade Level   _____

              Typing Speed   _____

              Penmanship - Above Average ____ Average ____ Not Essential ____

Physical Ability To:

              Sit _____ Walk _____ Reach with One Arm _____

              Stand _____ Stoop _____ Reach with Both Arms _____

              Lift: Light _____ Heavy _____

                     One Hand _____ Both Hands _____

              Carry: Light _____ Heavy _____

                     One Hand _____ Both Hands _____

Additional Requirements: Ability to Use Telephone _____

              Vision - Normal _____ Part. Sighted _____ Blind _____

              Hearing - Normal _____ Hard of Hearing _____ Deaf _____

              Communication with Outsiders: Yes _____ No _____

Please note any specific requirements necessary for this job: _____

_____

_____

APPENDIX B

Example 2

STUDENT PREVOCATIONAL SKILLS SCREENING FORM
Champaign Community Schools

SPECIAL EDUCATION DEPARTMENT
CHAMPAIGN COMMUNITY SCHOOLS

SIGNIFICANT PREVOCATIONAL SKILLS

Name _____   Date _____

School _____   Teacher _____

1. Ability to accept authority   Ex.____ Good _____ Fair____Poor_____

2. Ability to accept criticism   Ex.____ Good _____ Fair____Poor_____

3. Behavior

    (a) Cunning ____; deceitful ____; underhanded ____

    (b) Boisterous ____; loud ____; ill mannered____

    (c) Quiet____; well mannered ____; cooperative ____; respectful ____

    (d) Dependable ____; trustworthy ____

4. Work Habits

    (a) Careless ____; poor in application ____

    (b) Steady ____; needs direction ____; persistent in application ____

    (c) Industrious ____; little direction needed ____; completes tasks
                                                assigned _____

5. Sociability

    (a) Withdraws ____; distant ____; self centered ____

    (b) Amiable ____; reserved ____; slow to make friends _____

    (c) Quiet ____; respectful ____; cooperative ____

6. Personal grooming habits   Ex. ____ Good _____ Fair ____ Poor____

7. Physical

    (a) Sound ____; not sound ____ (enumerate)

8. Speech: adequate ____   voice quality ____

           articulation ____   projection ____

           stutter ____   other ____

9. Hearing

    (a) Normal _____   Mild loss _____
    (b) Medically significant loss _____ Moderate Loss _____
                                Severe loss _____

10. Motor coordination   Large Muscle   Ex.____ Good ____ Fair ____ Poor ____
                               Small Muscle   Ex.____ Good ____ Fair ____ Poor ____

Example 3

STUDENT REQUEST FOR JOB-COUNSELING APPOINTMENT
Mount Diablo Unified School District

Date_____   #_____

REQUEST FOR JOB COUNSELING APPOINTMENT
To: Mr. Wight, Work Experience Co-ordinator
From: _____
            (Print your name legibly)

Front

Reason: (Circle one)
   1. Outside Work Exp.   5. After School
   2. Christmas Work   6. Summer Work
   3. Full-time Work   7. Baby Sitter
   4. Volunteer Work

Comments: _____
_____
_____

Homeroom Teacher: _____

Birthdate: _____

Counselor: _____

Place this request slip in Mr. Wight's box in
the main office. An application will be sent
to you and an interview will be scheduled.
Please fill in both sides completely.

Address: _____

Period	Subject	Teacher	Room
A			
1			
2			
3			
4			
5			
6			
7			

Back

Telephone Number: _____

Semester I, II

Example 4

STUDENT APPLICATION FOR INSIDE WORK EXPERIENCE
Mount Diablo Unified School District

```
                        MT. DIABLO UNIFIED SCHOOL DISTRICT          #_____
I.W.E.                        Concord, California

              Application for Inside Work Experience Education Program

STUDENT SECTION  (After you have completed this section, have your parents sign this
                  application, then return the application to your counselor or the
                  I.W.E. Co-ordinator.)

     Name_____ Grade_____ School MDHS  PHHS  PHS  CVHS  CPHS
           (Last)      (First)       (10,11,12)               (Circle one)
     Male___ Female___  Height___ Weight___  Birthdate_____  Age in years_____
                                             (Mo. Day Year)
     Previous I.W.E. experience: Job Supervisor_____  Job Title_____
                                 Job Supervisor_____  Job Title_____
     What do you expect to gain from an I.W.E. assignment?_____

     In which office would you like to work?    1st choice       2nd choice
                           Job Supervisor:_____     _____
                           Job Title:
     When are you available for an I.W.E. assignment?
                           Semester:  (Circle one)    I      II      Both Semesters
                           Period:    (Circle one)  A 1 2 3 4 5 6 7 8
                           Student's Signature_____     _____
PARENT SECTION                                                         Date
     I give my consent for my son/daughter to work in a school office one period a day for
     Work Experience Education credit.
                           Parent's Signature_____     _____
                                                                      Date
COUNSELOR SECTION  (Send this application to the I.W.E. Co-ordinator when completed)
     Work experience education credit completed to date:
          I.W.E. Exploratory:  5 semester hours___; 10 semester hours___  (first year)
          I.W.E. General:      5 semester hours___; 10 semester hours___  (second year)
     Number of days absent last semester___; This semester to date__; Citizenship_____
     Recommended job station:
          Job supervisor:_____      Job title:_____
          Semester I__ II__ both__; Period(s) preferred: A 1 2 3 4 5 6 7 8

                        Counselor's Signature:_____     _____
I.W.E. CO-ORDINATOR SECTION                                           Date
     Tentative assignment:  Job Supervisor_____  Semester: I II Both
                            Job Title_____       Period: A 1 2 3 4 5 6 7 8
                            Job number_____  I.W.E. Classification: Expl.___ Gen'l___
                            Room/bldg number_____
                            I.W.E. Co-ordinator's Signature_____     _____
                                                                             Date
JOB SUPERVISOR SECTION  (Return this application to the I.W.E. Co-ordinator when completed)
     Applicant interviewed_____    Approved   Not Approved   Uncertain
                            Date                     (Circle one)

                        Job Supervisor's Signature_____     _____
-- # -- # -- # -- # -- # -- # -- # -- # -- # -- # -- # -- # -- # --    Date
I.W.E. OFFICE SECTION
     Assignment notice sent to Counselor:_____(date)
     Assignment posted on Work Experience master chart:_____(date)
     Student rating sheet to job supervisor: I Sent_____(date) Returned_____(date)
                                            II Sent_____(date) Returned_____(date)
```

Example 5

STUDENT REQUEST FOR JOB-COUNSELING APPOINTMENT
Santa Barbara High School

Last Name _____

Year of Graduation _____

First Name _____   Middle Name _____

Date of Birth _____   Height _____   Weight _____

TYPE OF WORK DESIRED:
1 _____
2 _____
3 _____
4 _____
5 _____
6 _____

EXPERIENCE
Months   Type of Work

CLASS SCHEDULE
(In PENCIL Only)
Per Room   Class

1 _____
2 _____
3 _____
4 _____
5 _____
6 _____
7 _____

What is your ultimate vocational goal? _____
Do you have a driver's license? _____
Car available for transportation? _____

DO NOT WRITE BELOW DOUBLE LINE

Typing Test _____   Shorthand _____

x
sa
rs
gd
sb
cm
dl
tp
ss
bk
gc

Example 6

STUDENT REFERRAL FORM
Champaign Community Schools

OFFICE OF SPECIAL SERVICES
CHAMPAIGN PUBLIC SCHOOLS
PREVOCATIONAL EDUCATION

Referral for Prevocational Services

Name _____ Sex _____ Age _____ Date _____

Birthdate _____ School _____ Grade _____

Handicap _____

Address _____ Person Initiating Referral _____

Name of Father _____ Occupation _____

Name of Mother _____ Occupation _____

Record of School Achievement:

    Mathematics _____   _____

    English _____   _____

    _____   _____

    _____   _____

    _____   _____

Type of Service Requested:

    Prevocational Counseling _____   Teacher Conference _____

    Parent Conference _____   Employment Follow-Up _____

Specific Needs of Pupil: _____

_____

_____

_____

_____

Background Information Relative to Need of Service: _____

_____

_____

_____

_____

Example 7

STUDENT REFERRAL FORM
City School District, Rochester

CITY SCHOOL DISTRICT
Rochester, New York

Special Education Department

Pupil Referral for Placement in the School-Work Program

From School _____ Principal _____ Psychologist _____ Date _____

Grade	Name	Address Parent	Birth Sept. Age	Mental Test Date Test	I.Q.	Reading Date Test	Net.	Gr. Trt. Est.	Arithmetic Date Test	Net.	Gr. Trs. Est.	Emotional or Physical Prob.
6	Bently Jane	11 Winslow George	1/4/45 11-8	2/58 1/59	S.B. 85 O. 78	10/58	5.4	4.8	10/58	4.8	5.0	

Note: If an agency outside the school system is currently active with a child, indicate the name of such agency and the contact person under section entitled "Emotional Problems". Use additional paper if necessary.

APPENDIX B

Example 8

WORK ASSIGNMENT PLACEMENT FORM
City School District, Rochester

```
                                                    Front
SCHOOLS' COPY
                    SCHOOL PLEASE FILL OUT BELOW AND RETURN TO
                          WORK PLACEMENT OFFICE
Pupil's Name _____ School _____ OE III _____
                                                                 or
Pupil's Address _____ HOME ROOM GROUP _____ SW III _____
Pupil's Home Phone _____ Teacher _____
Registered Last Year        Birth-        Letter      Reading      Arith.
At _____ School   date _____   Rating ____Level _____Level _____
Parent _____ or Guardian _____
Teacher Comment _____
         - PLACEMENT OFFICE AT BOARD OF EDUCATION WILL FILL OUT BELOW -
Social Security No. _____ Work Permit No._____ Soc.Agency
                                                             Clearance_____
JOB PLACEMENT:

Date          Employed By:        Job Supervisor      Comment
_____
_____
_____
_____
_____
_____
_____

                                            Back
PREVIOUS JOB EXPERIENCES, HOBBIES, PREFERENCES, ETC.: _____
_____
_____
_____

SPECIAL INFORMATION - HEALTH, FAMILY, SOCIAL AGENCIES, COMMUNITY GROUP, ETC.___
_____
_____
_____

INTERVIEWS:
   Dates              (Purpose or Occasion of Interviews, Impressions,Plans,etc.
_____
_____
_____
_____
_____
_____
```

Example 9

PERSONAL AND FAMILY INFORMATION FORM
Mount Diablo Unified School District

MT. DIABLO UNIFIED SCHOOL DISTRICT
Concord, California

PERSONAL AND FAMILY INFORMATION
(A student-kept record)

M. Wight
10-7-60

Name_____Birthdate_____Birthplace_____
      Last   First   Mo/day/year   City and State

Street Address_____City_____

Father's name_____Father's occupation_____

Mother's name_____Mother's occupation_____

If you are staying with adults other than your parents, please give the following information:

Name_____Relationship_____Occupation_____

Names of brothers and sisters   Birthdate   Occupation, if employed

_____   _____   _____

_____   _____   _____

_____   _____   _____

HEALTH RECORD

List serious illnesses, injuries and operations you have had. Give dates_____

_____

Last immunization dates: Smallpox_____Diptheria_____Tetanus_____
                   Polio Vaccination: (1)_____(2)_____(3)_____

	9th Grade	10th Grade	11th Grade	12th Grade
Your height	_____	_____	_____	_____
Your weight	_____	_____	_____	_____

Do you have any physical limitations or disabilities?_____

ATTENDANCE RECORD

Grade	Report Period	Semester I — Major reasons for absences	Days Absent	Report Period	Semester II — Major reason for absences	Days Absent
9th	1	_____	___	3	_____	___
	2	_____	___	4	_____	___
10th	1	_____	___	3	_____	___
	2	_____	___	4	_____	___
11th	1	_____	___	3	_____	___
	2	_____	___	4	_____	___
12th	1	_____	___	3	_____	___
	2	_____	___	4	_____	___

Example 10

STUDENT-EMPLOYER AGREEMENT FORM
Champaign Community Schools

OFFICE OF SPECIAL SERVICES
CHAMPAIGN COMMUNITY SCHOOLS
CHAMPAIGN, ILLINOIS

Prevocational Education

Prevocational Coordinator
of the Handicapped
Guy R. Jones
705 S. New
Champaign, Ill.
FLeetwood 9-1723

Employer's Name _____

Company _____ Telephone _____

Address _____

In cooperation with the Prevocational Education Program of the Special Education Department, I, _____, as a student-learner trainer agree to abide by the following rules:

1. I will make no change in the agreed upon wage of $_____ per hour without first consulting the Prevocational Coordinator.

2. I will make no major change in jobs without first consulting the Prevocational Coordinator.

3. I will make no change in working hours without first consulting the Prevocational Coordinator.

4. I will make no severe reprimands without first consulting the Prevocational Coordinator.

5. I will make no change in the direct supervisory personnel without first consulting the Prevocational Coordinator.

Employees Name _____ Telephone _____

Address _____

As a student-learner in the Prevocational Program of the Special Education Department, I _____ agree to work for the _____ _____ and abide by the following rules:

1. I agree to work from _____ to _____ on the following days each week. S M T W T F S

2. I agree to work at a job best described as _____ _____

3. I agree to attend school from _____ to _____ each school day.

4. I agree to work for the wage of $_____ per hour.

5. I will not quit without first consulting the Prevocational Coordinator.

6. I will contact the Prevocational Coordinator concerning any difficulties I have on the job.

Example 11

STUDENT WORK-EXPERIENCE RECORD
Mount Diablo Unified School District

MT. DIABLO UNIFIED SCHOOL DISTRICT
Concord, California
WORK EXPERIENCE RECORD
(A student-kept record)

Social Security Number

Student's name:

School:

Name of Employer and Job Supervisor	Inclusive dates of employment Began Left	What was your rate of pay?	What were your major responsibilities?

If you belong to a labor union give the name _____ Local # _____

Example 12

STUDENT WORK-EXPERIENCE RECORD
Champaign Community Schools

PREVOCATIONAL EDUCATION
SPECIAL EDUCATION DEPARTMENT
CHAMPAIGN COMMUNITY SCHOOLS
Champaign, Illinois

WORK RECORD

NAME _____ School _____ Birthdate _____

Incidental Work Record: Mow Lawns ____ Shovel Snow ____ Paper Route ____ Other ____

Type of Work _____

Employed By _____

Hours: _____ Date of Employment _____

Reason for Termination: Quit _____ Promoted _____ Fired _____ Released _____

Placed By _____ Wages _____

Student Comment _____

_____

Counselor Comments _____

_____

Employer Comments _____

_____

Incidental Work Record: Mow Lawns ____ Shovel Snow ____ Paper Route ____ Other _____

Type of Work _____

Employed By _____

Hours: _____ Date of Employment _____

Reason for Termination: Quit _____ Promoted _____ Fired _____ Released _____

Placed By _____ Wages _____

Student Comment _____

_____

Counselor Comments _____

_____

Employer Comments _____

Example 13

EMPLOYER RATING SHEET
Santa Barbara High School

SANTA BARBARA CITY SCHOOLS WORK EXPERIENCE EDUCATION PROGRAM
Report on Student Worker by Person Who Knows His Work Best

Name of Student .... Date..

Name of Employer .... Address ....

Name of Person Filling Out This Form ....

Position ....

Date Employment Began .... Schedule of Hours: From.............. to ....

Check the Phrase Which Is Most Descriptive of the Employee's Performance

1 CONSIDER THIS EMPLOYEE'S DEPENDABILITY IN ASSUMING AND FULFILLING JOB ASSIGNMENTS.   REMARKS:

☐ COMPLETELY RELIABLE REQUIRES MINIMUM DIRECTION   ☐ REQUIRES NORMAL SUPERVISION   ☐ REQUIRES CLOSE SUPERVISION   ☐ ONLY OCCASIONAL INSTRUCTIONS AND CHECKING REQUIRED   ☐ NEEDS DIRECTION AND FREQUENT CHECKING

2. CONSIDER THIS EMPLOYEE'S KNOWLEDGE OF HIS PRESENT JOB.

☐ UNDERSTANDING OF JOB LIMITED IN SOME AREAS   ☐ SATISFACTORY KNOWLEDGE OF JOB   ☐ VERY WELL INFORMED ON ALL PHASES OF WORK   ☐ SOUND WORKING KNOWLEDGE OF MOST PHASES OF WORK   ☐ DEFINITE WEAKNESSES IN KNOWLEDGE OF MAJOR ITEMS

3. CONSIDER THIS EMPLOYEE'S JUDGMENT.

☐ FREQUENTLY MAKES INCORRECT DECISIONS   ☐ GENERALLY MAKES SOUND DECISIONS IN ANY SITUATION   ☐ CONSISTENTLY MAKES SOUND DECISIONS   ☐ JUDGMENT SOUND UNDER NORMAL CIRCUMSTANCES   ☐ OCCASIONALLY MAKES INCORRECT DECISIONS

4. CONSIDER THIS EMPLOYEE'S ATTITUDE TOWARD JOB, SUPERVISION, OTHER EMPLOYEES AND COMPANY.

☐ INDIFFERENT AND UNCOOPERATIVE AT TIMES   ☐ DEFINITELY INTERESTED AND COOPERATES WELL   ☐ GENERALLY INTERESTED AND COOPERATIVE   ☐ EXCEPTIONALLY ENTHUSIASTIC AND COOPERATIVE   ☐ OFTEN DISINTERESTED AND UNCOOPERATIVE

5. CONSIDER THE AMOUNT OF EFFORT THIS EMPLOYEE APPLIES TO THE JOB.

☐ STEADY WORKER   ☐ FREQUENTLY WASTES TIME   ☐ HARD WORKER   ☐ OCCASIONALLY WASTES TIME   ☐ EXTREMELY INDUSTRIOUS

6. CONSIDER THE EFFECT THIS EMPLOYEE HAS ON OTHERS.

☐ CREATES EXCELLENT IMPRESSION   ☐ SOMETIMES CREATES AN UNFAVORABLE IMPRESSION   ☐ FREQUENTLY IMPRESSES PEOPLE UNFAVORABLY   ☐ IMPRESSES PEOPLE FAVORABLY   ☐ GENERALLY CREATES A SATISFACTORY IMPRESSION

7. CONSIDER THIS EMPLOYEE'S ABILITY TO LEARN.

☐ ADEQUATE LEARNING ABILITY   ☐ EXCEPTIONALLY FAST TO LEARN   ☐ HAS FREQUENT DIFFICULTY IN LEARNING   ☐ LEARNS RAPIDLY   ☐ HAS SOME DIFFICULTY IN LEARNING

8. CONSIDER QUANTITY OF ACCEPTABLE WORK PRODUCED BY EMPLOYEE.

☐ OUTPUT CONSISTENTLY ABOVE REQUIREMENTS OF JOB   ☐ OUTPUT OCCASIONALLY ABOVE THE REQUIREMENTS OF JOB   ☐ MEETS NORMAL PRODUCTION REQUIREMENTS OF JOB   ☐ OUTPUT OCCASIONALLY BELOW THE REQUIREMENTS OF JOB   ☐ PRODUCTION FREQUENTLY BELOW JOB REQUIREMENTS

Example 14

EMPLOYER RATING SHEET
City School District, Rochester

EMPLOYER RATING SHEET

PUPIL_____SCHOOL_____

JOB TITLE _____

REQUIREMENTS OF JOB _____

Please indicate your estimate of this worker by placing a check mark in the
proper column. Specific comments or suggestions may be made in the last
column. Please return to coordinating teacher by _____. A stamp-
ed self-addressed envelope is enclosed for your convenience.

JOB PERFORMANCE	Excellent	Good	Accept-able	Poor	Comment
1. Punctuality in arriving for work					
2. Regular daily attendance					
3. Ability to follow instructions					
4. Quality of work					
5. Judgement					
6. Ability to work with others					
ATTITUDES ON THE JOB					
1. Interest in work					
2. Courtesy					
3. Ability to accept criticism					
4. Cooperation with company rules					
PERSONAL APPEARANCE					
1. Appropriate dress					
2. Cleanliness					
3. Neatness					

                    Date_____   Supervisor's Signature_____

This form is made out by the employers of the third year students several
times a year. They are included in the pupil's cumulative record.

Example 15

STUDENT MERIT RATING SHEET
Mount Diablo Unified School District

MT. DIABLO UNIFIED SCHOOL DISTRICT
Concord, California

WORK EXPERIENCE STUDENT MERIT RATING

Name _____ Employer _____ Job _____ School _____

INSTRUCTIONS TO RATERS: Rate the individual only in accordance with the description of the qualification as given below and in comparison to others doing the same kind of work. Decide where on the scale the man best fits, and there is one of the blocks, place a check (X) mark. Use other side for comments.

QUALIFICATIONS	POOR	BELOW AVERAGE	AVERAGE	ABOVE AVERAGE	EXCELLENT	SCORE
JOB PERFORMANCE: Consider the quality, waste, number of errors and overall efficiency of his work. Use company standards and comparison with others as a basis of rating.	Unsatisfactory. — 9 18 27 36 45	Barely acceptable. — 54 63 72 81 90	Generally satisfactory. Meets standards. — 99 108 117 126 135	Does good work. Fast and efficient. Betters standards. — 144 153 162 171 180	Exceptional work. Rapid, accurate and complete. — 189 198 207 216 225	
OVERALL KNOWLEDGE OF JOB: Consider how much he knows about his present job and other closely related jobs. Consider his past experience, and how much he needs to know.	Inadequate. Knows little about job. — 3 6 9 12 15	Knows routine only. Needs considerable coaching. — 18 21 24 27 30	Fair and working knowledge of his job. — 33 36 39 42 45	Understands his job. Good background of experience. — 48 51 54 57 60	An expert on his job and knows related work. Wide experience. — 63 66 69 72 75	
INDUSTRY AND DEPENDABILITY: Consider the effort he puts forth during working hours. Consider his application to his job, his attendance and punctuality. Can he be relied on? Is he dependable?	Lazy. A leader. Late starter—early quitter. Unnecessary absences. Undependable. — 3 6 9 12 15	Takes it easy. Clock watcher. Requires close supervision. Not very reliable. — 18 21 24 27 30	Works steadily. With some supervision will do a fair day's work. Usually reliable. — 33 36 39 42 45	Willing worker. Gives a full day's work. Consistent and dependable. — 48 51 54 57 60	100% on the job. Does more than required. Conscientious and very dependable. — 63 66 69 72 75	
APTITUDE AND ABILITY TO LEARN: Consider his ability in doing jobs both foreign and related to his own. Consider how quickly he learns, grasps new ideas and retains information.	Dull. Poor memory. One-job man. — 3 6 9 12 15	Learns slowly. Requires excessive instruction. — 18 21 24 27 30	With average instruction, can do related work satisfactorily. — 33 36 39 42 45	Can do a turn at most jobs in his line of work. — 48 51 54 57 60	All-around-man. Can do many high-type jobs. Learns rapidly. — 63 66 69 72 75	
INITIATIVE: Consider his ingenuity— self reliance and resourcefulness in thinking, planning and carrying out his job.	Always waits to be shown and told what to do. — 3 6 9 12 15	Relies heavily on others. A follower. — 18 21 24 27 30	Fairly aggressive. Starts some things. — 33 36 39 42 45	Resourceful. Develops assignments ably. — 48 51 54 57 60	A self-starter. Sees things to be done and does them. — 63 66 69 72 75	
JUDGMENT: Consider the intelligence, logic and thought he uses in arriving at decisions, suggestions and conclusions as related to his job.	Has a poor sense of values. — 3 6 9 12 15	Jumps at conclusions. — 18 21 24 27 30	Tries to reason things out intelligently. — 33 36 39 42 45	Uses good common sense. — 48 51 54 57 60	Sound judgment based on facts. — 63 66 69 72 75	
DISPOSITION AND ATTITUDE: Consider his willingness to work and get along with his fellows, and his attitude toward his boss and company's plans, policies, objectives and interests.	Antagonistic. — 3 6 9 12 15	Usually "sour." Reluctant to cooperate. — 18 21 24 27 30	Fair teamworker. Satisfied with company. — 33 36 39 42 45	Good teamworker and generally a booster. — 48 51 54 57 60	Goes out of his way to help fellows and the company. — 63 66 69 72 75	
PERSONALITY: Consider the way he impresses people. Consider the reaction his presence causes in a group.	Creates dissatisfaction. — 3 6 9 12 15	Unfavorable. Sometimes avoided. — 18 21 24 27 30	Fair impression. Accepted. — 33 36 39 42 45	Favorable impression. Well liked. — 48 51 54 57 60	A leader. Inspires associates to action. — 63 66 69 72 75	
SAFETY. Consider his reaction to the safety program, his interest in and adherence to safe practices and the safety suggestions he makes. Is he "safety conscious?"	A hazard to himself and his associates. — 3 6 9 12 15	Takes chances. Some "horse play". — 18 21 24 27 30	Usually does things according to practice. — 33 36 39 42 45	Works safely himself and considers others. — 48 51 54 57 60	Active in promoting safety. Makes suggestions. — 63 66 69 72 75	
HEALTH AND PHYSICAL CONDITION. Consider how his general health and physical condition, handicaps and other activities affect his work.	Poor health. Often in no condition to work. — 3 6 9 12 15	Abuses self. Reflected in his work. — 18 21 24 27 30	Usually satisfactory. Can hold his own. — 33 36 39 42 45	No noticeable handicaps. — 48 51 54 57 60	Always fit. Good condition. Lots of pep. — 63 66 69 72 75	

RATER _____ POSITION _____ DATE _____ TOTAL SCORE _____

Example 16

EMPLOYER RATING SHEET
Cranston High School

Rating Sheet for Nurse Aides

Cranston High School

Place a check mark in the column which best describes the typical behavior and
type of work performed. Whenever possible, it is desirable that check marks
be substantiated by a specific example or comment.

Name_____ Unit_____From_____To_____

	Always	Frequently	Infrequently	Never	COMMENTS
CONTACT WITH PATIENTS					
1. Is she courteous?					
2. Does she readily discuss other patients' and their conditions?					
3. Does she discuss her personal affairs?					
4. Does she tend to reject patients with cultural, religious, and or ethnic backgrounds different from her own?					
5. Is her language appropriate?					
6. Does she listen?					
7. Does she give equal service to all patients assigned her?					
8. Does she consider safety and comfort?					
ATTITUDE AND BEHAVIOR					
1. Does she carry out procedures as taught?					
2. Is it difficult to locate her when needed?					
3. Does she work without wasting time?					
4. Do co-workers report she is not helpful?					
5. Does she discuss work problems with the charge nurse?					
REPORTING AND ATTENDANCE					
1. Does she report promptly for duty?					
2. Is it difficult to locate her when needed?					
3. Does she leave the unit without reporting off?					
4. Does she report unfinished assignments?					
5. Does she report symptoms and changes in patients' conditions?					
GROOMING AND APPEARANCE					
1. Does she appear neatly dressed?					
2. Does she wear jewelry other than a wrist watch?					
3. Does she wear proper shoes?					
4. Does she chew gum?					
5. Does she have any objectionable body odors?					

Date_____

                    _____ Signature and title of person
                                                  doing the rating.

To: Mr. Gordon
     Cranston High School

Would you be willing to have this person as a member of your staff full time?

Example 17

STUDENT PLACEMENT FOLLOW-UP
Champaign Community Schools

PREVOCATIONAL EDUCATION
SPECIAL EDUCATION DEPARTMENT
CHAMPAIGN COMMUNITY SCHOOLS
Champaign, Illinois

PLACEMENT FOLLOW-UP

Name of Student Worker _____ Birthdate _____

Name of Employer _____

Type of Business _____

Job Description (D.O.T. No.) _____

_____

Date of Employment _____ Part Time _____ Full Time _____

Wage _____

WORKER TRAIT EVALUATION

	Excellent	Good	Fair	Poor	Comments
Dependability					
Honesty					
General Appearance					
Ability to understand directions					
Ability to follow directions					
Ability to get along with supervisor					
Ability to get along with fellow workers					
Motivation					

Do you feel the half-day instruction has helped the student worker do a better job?   Yes _____ No _____ Comments if desirable _____.

_____

Do you feel this student is making a satisfactory progress in this job?

Yes _____ No _____ Comments if desirable _____

_____

Areas in which the student needs to improve. (Be specific) _____

Appendix C

EXAMPLES OF

INSTRUCTIONAL UNITS

USED IN WORK-STUDY PROGRAMS

1 Instructional Unit, New York City Schools

Unit VII

YOUR FAMILY MEMBERSHIP

Many of the problems which have a serious impact on the educational growth and attitudes of potential early school-leavers arise from misunderstandings and inadequacies in the home environment. Group guidance sessions which study problems common to the group, without personal references, are effective in building wholesome changes and are very often followed up by the students in individual conferences with the teacher-coordinator. The effort in this unit is not to cover all the topics connected with family membership but to concentrate on the most pressing experience.

Objectives

1. To understand the elements of good family life.

2. To gain a better understanding of themselves and others in family living.

3. To develop an understanding of what is needed to build a satisfactory family life.

Content

1. What are families for?
   a. Feeling of belonging.
   b. Providing needs and wants.

2. How do you make yourself a part of a happy family?
   a. Learning how to give and take.
   b. Compromising.
   c. Discussing problems.
   d. Sharing responsibilities.
   e. Facing a problem.
   f. Extending encouragement to members who need it.
   g. Respecting others.

3. What are some important family problems?
   a. Financial.
   b. Medical.
   c. Emotional.
   d. Are you willing to take responsibilities?

    e. Do you give up readily?

    f. Are you ready to share?

4. How are you and your family a part of the community?
    a. Getting along with others.
    b. Helping to improve the community.

5. Where do you get extra help on family and personal problems?
    a. Community agencies (social service agency, religious centers).
    b. School guidance department.
    c. Social workers.
    d. Family doctor.

Suggested Approaches and Practices

1. Present typical problems in the form of case studies.
    a. "I work hard on my part-time job making $20 a week. I want all this for myself. Why should I give any to my parents?"
    b. "There's nothing wrong in staying out late tonight, 1 or 1:30 a.m. It's only once a week. I'm letting you know now, dad. Good night."
    c. "I'm old enough to take care of myself. I'm over 15. You may be my older brother but you're not telling me what to do!"
    d. "When John does his share of the housework, I'll do mine. Not before. I won't discuss it anymore!"

Students discuss what is wrong with each attitude, what advice they would give to help resolve the problem, and what additional important information is lacking in a, b, c, or d.

2. Enact scene in classroom to show how a closely knit family operates. Participants: parents, older brother, John. Problem: John wants to give up his present job as clerk and take a job closer to home. Point out the essentials of seeking advice, sharing ideas and information, democratic discussion, willingness to give full consideration to advice rendered, and acceptance of responsibility in making a decision. Students will keep these in mind for purposes of evaluating the presentation.

3. "If we had as much money as the Johnson family, our family would be happy too."
    a. Does this always follow?
    b. Does a happy family mean a family without problems?

4. How does the government show its interest in trying to make families happy in:
        a. Housing?   b. Health?   c. Welfare?

Students refer to facilities in the section and relate their experiences.

5. Use current events as reported in newspapers to give meaning to ideas developed on family membership. An example is "Soviet Boy, Homeless 16 Years, Gets To Know His Parents Here." (See Plan D)

6. Students evaluate the following reading selection:

"Here's the Way I Feel About It"

". . . now I know why when I was going to school a bunch of guys threw rocks at me and called me names. That was wrong! . . . Names can hurt. They can hurt you even more than sticks and stones.

". . . Take a brain from any man's head and no one can tell you positively from what race that brain came. Because every race produces men with big brains and geniuses, men with small brains, smart men, and fools; strong men and weak men. All human beings, from whatever race, have exactly 27 bones in their hands and 26 bones in their feet. The lungs, the liver, and other parts of all human beings are exactly alike.

". . . It's up to all of us to lay aside our unfounded hatreds and make the most of this wonderful country . . ."

Frank Sinatra in *This Way To Unity*

a. Consider the subjects you are studying: Science, Mathematics, English, History. How can they help to do away with feelings of hatred?

THEY DIED TOGETHER . . . SO THAT WE MAY LIVE TOGETHER

7. "I just can't seem to make friends," George complained. List 4 questions you would ask George in an effort to find out why he can't make friends.

8. Examine today's newspaper for pictures of local areas which need improvement.
   a. What improvement is needed?
   b. Does your section have this problem?

9. "I like to think of our country as one home in which the interests of each member are bound up with the happiness of all. We ought to know . . . that the welfare of your family or mine cannot be bought at the sacrifice of our neighbor's family; that our well-being depends on the well-being of our neighbors."

   F. D. Roosevelt

   If you had to set up a series of pictures or drawings on a poster to show the meaning of this statement, what pictures or drawings would you look for? Are there any sections in the U.S. where this statement is not applied in practice?

10. An employer of a large firm said: "It doesn't take me long to spot the fellow who is going to succeed on the job and outside of the job. In one day, I can tell his personality."

    Is it possible to learn about a person in so short a time? How could the employer tell how well the young man will do outside of his job?

    What are some of the things he could have noticed?
    a. Good grooming.
    b. Good manners.
    c. Application to work at hand.
    d. Cheerfulness.
    e. Willingness to accept advice.

TEACHING MATERIALS AND PLANS

Topic: TEAMWORK AND COOPERATION   Plan/Worksheet A

At least 2 periods should be devoted to this lesson which lends itself to full class participation in discussion and includes an appropriate reading selection. The main function of the teacher here, in addition to motivating and encouraging discussion, is in directing and aiding students in organizing their thoughts. Note-taking—especially the chart—should follow.

Aims

1. To impress students with the importance of teamwork and cooperation in every facet of living.
2. To relate current events to the theme.
3. To show how school training and record are helpful.

Materials

1. "Students' Record: Report to Employers" form. This form was developed with the cooperation of the Commerce and Industry Association of New York and is in use in hiring applicants from New York City public schools.
2. Cumulative record card of a graduate who is now doing well. Section — "Teachers Estimate" is read to class. For example, in this lesson the record of G. Pignitano (Major League baseball star) of Westinghouse Vocational and Technical High School was used.
3. Newspaper report on sports activities relating to theme.

Motivation

Motivate the lesson with these challenging thoughts:

1. The New York Herald Tribune (3/24/60) reported on an outstanding basketball game played by Boys' High School. In explaining why the game was unusual, the reporter gave some important statistics. "Their captain averaged 25.2 points per game, close to 20 rebounds and *passed off for almost as many baskets as he scored*." What does "passed off" mean? Why should it be as important as points scored?

2. In the Spring baseball training there are a number of players who do well when called upon to bat, to field, and to run bases. They're not afraid to play. They love baseball, but put them into a game and they can't make the grade. What's the trouble?

Word Study: solo, performer, amateur, audition, vacuum.

Development

1. What is the meaning of cooperation and teamwork? (Use phrases offered by students.)

Giving advice	Helping out when in need	Encouraging
Working together	Sharing information	

2. Organize a chart to show how cooperation and teamwork are carried out in the following areas:

School Shop	Home	Work	Armed Services
a.	....	....	....
b.	....	....	....
c.	....	....	....

3. Examine the employment form carefully. Find the places where ratings are given for cooperation and teamwork. Why do they belong on an employment form?

Application

1. Reading exercise, "From Quartet to Solo," (reproduced in this section).
2. Examine today's newspaper to find other items to show the importance of teamwork and cooperation.

FROM QUARTET TO SOLO
(Adapted from Practical English — 3/9/60)

Andy Williams is high on the list of television's up-and-coming stars.

Andy's start in the entertainment field was a family affair. Andy's father, an amateur musician, trained his four sons to sing for their church in Wall Take, Iowa. Having achieved local fame, Andy recalls, "We finally decided we were too good to stay home." The boys auditioned for radio station WHO in Des Moines and were hired. Andy made his start when he was eight years old.

In 1953, when his brothers gave up their group, Andy started out on his own as a solo performer. While he was in New York trying to market his first song, he landed a place on the Steve Allen Show — and stayed on as a regular performer for two and a half years.

Later on, Andy was on the Chevy Show and one hour TV specials. Andy believes he owes his success as an entertainer to learning, first of all, to be part of a team. In working closely with others, it's important to know how to give and take, to cooperate. You never work in a vacuum, even if you're a solo performer. According to Andy, if you can work well with other people, any job is more successful all the way around.

Like Andy Williams, you may appear to be a solo performer, but actually there are many hidden teams in your life: your family, your club, your class committee. How about it? Are you helping or hindering your team? It's important to develop your own abilities — but it's just as important that you are able to use these abilities with other people. If you can do it, you'll always be a valuable member of any team.

a. According to Andy, is anyone ever a "solo" performer?
b. Why is this titled, "From Quartet to Solo?" Can you suggest another title?

Topic: HOW TO SECURE HELP   **Plan/Worksheet B**
      FOR THOSE WHO NEED IT

This lesson makes use of simple research skills to obtain important information. It also aims to develop an appreciation for the many public and private agencies devoted to helping the needy. One of the problems is studied with the class, making use of the research materials. Students then continue individual work with the other problems. Center lesson around a series of problems.

Problems

1. You are walking in the park with a friend. He stumbles and hurts his foot so badly that he cannot walk. What do you do?

2. Your younger sister or brother would like to go to a summer camp. How can you help?

3. You applied for a job which you did not get. You feel sure you did not get the job because the employer did not like your religion . . . or color. Is there anything you can do?

4. You want to get a doctor at once. Would you call an ambulance?

5. Your neighbor does not have full power in his hands. Yet, he would like to get a job. What can he do?

6. The rent in your apartment has been increased. You don't think it is fair or allowed by law. What would you advise your parents?

7. You are being sued by someone who claims you owe him money. You would like to have a lawyer but cannot afford it. Where would you go?

8. A neighbor is so worried about problems at home that he cannot continue to work. He is very sad and has stopped speaking to people. What can the family do?

Research Materials

Students will have copies of the following:
1. "How to Secure Help for Those Who Need It" (Guide issued by Community Council of Greater New York)

2. Telephone directories to draw up a handy chart — "Important information for my home: name of agency, address, phone number."

Discussion

1. Why is speed and the right approach important in all these cases?

2. Have you ever experienced a problem similar to those presented? Tell the class about it and explain how you solved it.

Follow-Up

Use a film describing the work of one of the agencies discussed, e.g., Travelers' Aid Society, Tuberculosis Association. These films are available on loan.

Topic: OVERCOMING HANDICAPS   Plan/Worksheet C

Although many students are familiar with such names as Dr. Dooley and Dr. Salk, they have little appreciation of the character traits which made for their development and fame. Very few have given thought to possible applications to their own lives. The approach here is through a newspaper item which offers excellent areas for discussion.

Motivation

Elicit from students names of famous men in the field of medicine. Why do they have a right to fame?

Has anyone heard of Dr. Grant E. Ward? (Distribute copies of clipping.) Read this newspaper item about Dr. Ward and see if you think he should be remembered.

Word Study: countless, handicap, tumor, perseverance, adjustment, delicate.

EXPERT WHO SAVED MANY FROM CANCER IS DEAD OF IT
(Adapted from N. Y. Herald Tribune — 2/17/60)

Baltimore, February 16 (AP) — Dr. Grant B. Ward, sixty-one, cancer expert of Johns Hopkins University, died today of the same disease from which he had saved countless patients.

Dr. Ward overcame a tremendous handicap to continue his career after developing a tumor on the spinal cord of his neck in 1942. The tumor was non-cancerous but its removal cut a nerve and deprived him of the power to raise his right hand and to bend his elbow.

Although he could still use the fingers and forearm muscles of his right arm, Dr. Ward's career as a surgeon appeared ended. But with the help of experts in appliances, together with his own perseverance, Dr. Ward made a steel and leather harness equipped with springs to perform actions on his useless muscle.

To win over his handicaps, Dr. Ward developed certain special skills with his left hand. He asked for no special adjustments in the operating room, except that the table be raised to a higher level. The internationally known expert on head and neck tumors continued performing very difficult and delicate operations. He also continued his interest in swimming, gardening and motor travel.

Discussion

1. Do you think Dr. Ward deserves to be remembered?
                        Saved countless lives.
                        Overcame handicaps.

2. What was so remarkable about his continuing as a surgeon?

3. In what way can Dr. Grant be compared to Roy Campanella?

4. Do you think his hobbies helped him?

5. What lesson can younger people learn from Dr. Ward?

6. Suggest another heading for this newspaper clipping.

Topic: WHAT DOES A FAMILY MEAN?   Plan/Worksheet D

This lesson is also very useful for the unit dealing with the American Heritage in that it discusses how a dictatorship operates to destroy liberties. The motivation is directed not only to arousing feelings of sympathy, but also to building an understanding of the importance of the family unit.

Motivation

Have you ever been lost? What were your feelings? Is it possible to imagine what it is like to be homeless 16 years?

Word Study: combined, pleading, migrate, invade, reveal.

Reading

SOVIET BOY, HOMELESS 16 YEARS, GETS TO KNOW HIS PARENTS HERE
(Adapted from N. Y. Times, 4/24/60)

Eighteen-year-old Yuri Koral, until last Wednesday night an ordinary Soviet citizen, is living a dream come true here this weekend. But it took the combined pleadings of Vice President Nixon and Adlai E. Stevenson to produce what Yuri and the parents he had not seen in sixteen years consider something of a miracle.

In 1941 Yuri was born in the city of Ivanova, near Moscow, to Mr. and Mrs. Rubin Koral, Polish Jews who had fled their home when

What dangers faced these men? Would there be need of a leader?
Were you, as part of a group, ever faced with a very dangerous situation?
How did you react?

Word Study: barricade, conserve, ration, qualify, hospitality, pioneer.

Reading

In November, 1945, an explosion trapped nine miners in a Kentucky
coal mine. One of the men, Bud Townes, had special knowledge and
experience to fight the spreading gas and fire. He took charge and
after much work, the miners barricaded themselves in a side room
and sealed it. No man shirked his appointed task; the stronger
helped the weaker. The water and food were rationed, and to conserve the supply of oxygen, Townes had the others lie flat on their
backs. They hoped and prayed. Some time later they were all res-
cued — alive.

Bud Townes was proclaimed a hero, but he said: "It was teamwork
that saved us, the same teamwork we have when we are not in
danger." Bud Townes happened to be a Negro, but no one asked
him about his color as a qualification for employment or for living
in the Kentucky community. They were all interested in getting
along, and they found that team work was the way of doing it.

This same type of teamwork was shown by the early American
pioneers. In 1781, a Frenchman traveling through Connecticut
asked himself how it was possible to set up new settlements so
quickly. His conclusion was "that in America a man is never alone.
The neighbors, for they are everywhere to be found, make it a
point of hospitality to aid the new farmer."

Our country was built on faith in the people — people who came
from every stock — English, Scotch, Irish, French, Dutch, Germans, Swedes, and all religions. The meaning of democracy to
them was teamwork — the same teamwork and tradition for which
Colin Kelly, Meyer Levin, Dorie Miller, and others gave their lives.
How to get along with others? Teamwork. Practice it.

Understanding the Incident

1. Why was it necessary to seal the room?

2. Why was Bud Townes a hero?

3. Did Bud Townes save them? Explain your position.

4. Can you say the following about your neighborhood? "In my neighborhood a man is never alone. The neighbors make it a point to help out."

5. "Our country was built on faith in the people — people who came from

Hitler's army invaded Poland. He was still a baby when Soviet secret police arrested his parents and sent them separately to slave labor camps in Siberia and Arctic Russia.

When they were released separately after World War II and sent back to Poland in sealed trains, neither knew whether the other, or Yuri, was still alive.

The parents migrated separately to Israel where they met again, reestablished family life, and began to try and find him.

They went to Germany for a time, hoping it would be easier to find Yuri from there. Then they came to this country where Mr. Koral, a tailor, got a job with a clothing concern.

Meanwhile, Yuri had been sent to an orphan asylum where he was raised. After eight years of elementary schooling, he was sent to a vocational school to be trained as a locksmith.

At the same time, the director of the orphanage first revealed to the 14-year-old boy that he was a Jew, though Yuri had, and still has, little idea of what being one means.

The director knew because Mr. and Mrs. Koral had learned from Ivanova friends where Yuri was and had begun writing him. Yuri's parents appealed without success to the Soviet to return him to them.

Vice President Nixon and Mr. Stevenson came to the Korals' aid as a result of efforts by their New York lawyer, Marshall MacDuffie. Yuri became one of 200 similar cases that Mr. MacDuffie was pressing the Soviet to solve.

Discussion

1. How does this article show the importance of the family?

2. Why should Mr. Stevenson and former Vice President Nixon have shown so much interest in Yuri?

3. What problems face Yuri?

4. If Yuri were to attend this school, what preparations would you suggest the school or class make to receive him?

Topic: HOW TO GET ALONG WITH OTHERS   Plan/Worksheet E

Motivation

Write the following topic sentence on the blackboard: "November, 1945, an explosion trapped nine miners in a Kentucky coal mine."

every stock — English, Scotch, Irish, French, Dutch, Germans, Swedes, and all religions." Can you prove this statement by studying our class?

Research

Class committees visit library to get information on Colin Kelly, Meyer Levin, Dorie Miller. How did they show teamwork?

Topic: LIFE ON THE MIDDLE BORDER   **Plan/Worksheet F**

This is a good example of a brief, pointed reading selection adapted from a book which can be used to motivate extended discussion and, in some cases, develop a curiosity and taste for continued reading. It is well to have a copy of the book handy for examination by the students.

Reading

DO YOU THINK YOU "HAVE IT TOUGH"?

Life on the Middle Border (Adapted from *A Son of the Middle Border*, Hamlin Garland; Macmillan Co.)

> Winter mornings were most difficult. . . . It required a stern command to get us out of bed before daylight, in a room warmed only by the stovepipe, and draw on icy socks and frosty boots and go to the milking of cows. But our evenings were more cheerful. My sister, Hattie, was able to play a few simple tunes on the melodeon and friends came in to sing. . . . We took long walks to visit our boy friends or to borrow something to read. I was always on the trail of a book.

Discussion

1. What advantages do you have today over the "son of the middle border"?
2. Give two reasons for the changes which have taken place.
3. How did he spend his leisure time? Was it worth while? Entertaining?
  . Compare it with the way you spend your leisure time.

INSTRUCTIONAL FILMS AND FILMSTRIPS

The films and filmstrips listed in this section have been approved by the Board of Education. The films are available from the BAVI Central Loan Collection or from local film centers. For annotations and more details, see *Instructional Films and Tapes*, Curriculum Bulletin No. 14, 1958-59 Series; and 1959 *List of Approved Filmstrips and Supplements.*

The numbered topics in column 1 correspond with those in the *content section of this unit* for which the film or filmstrip is appropriate.

Films

CONTENT TOPIC (and *Filmstrip Title*)	PRODUCER	RUNNING TIME (*Minutes*)
1. What are families for?		
Friendship Begins at Home	Coronet	20
2. How do you make yourself a part of a happy family?		
Attitudes and Health	Coronet	11
Getting Along with Parents	E.B.	14
Griper, The	Young America	12
Mental Health: Keeping Mentally Fit	E.B.	12
Obligations	E.B.	18
Personality and Emotions	E.B.	13
3. What are some important family problems?		
Sharing Work at Home	Coronet	11
You and Your Family	Association Films	11
4. Are you grown up?		
Act Your Age	Coronet	12
Getting Ready Emotionally (For Service)	Coronet	11
Captains Courageous	T.F.C.	12
Developing Friendships	Coronet	10
Don't Get Angry	E.B.	12
Effective Criticism	Coronet	11
Feeling Left Out	Coronet	13
How to Say No	Coronet	11
Planning for Success	Coronet	11
Understanding Your Emotions	Coronet	14
5. How are you and your family a part of the community?		
Are You a Good Citizen?	E.B.	11
Belonging to the Group	E.B.	14
Brotherhood of Man	Brandon	11
Building Better Citizens	N. Y. Mirror	
Developing Leadership	Coronet	11
Developing Your Character	Coronet	11
Everyday Courtesy	Coronet	11
It's Up to You	Dr. Rosa Jordan	11
Make Way for Youth	Association Films	22

Filmstrips

Content Topic (and *Film Title*)	Vendor	Item No.
1 What are families for?		
Parents Are People, Too	McGraw-Hill	21800.31
Family Portrait	McGraw-Hill	22460.1
Future in Hand	McGraw-Hill	22460.11
The Family: A Changing Pattern	N. Y. Journal-American	
2. How do you make yourself a part of a happy family?		
Politeness Is for You	McGraw-Hill	21390.11
Yours for the Best	McGraw-Hill	21390.15
Home Ground	McGraw-Hill	21620.1
Personal Relationship	McGraw-Hill	21680.11
Your Family and You	Jam Handy	21790.14
Understanding Myself	McGraw-Hill	21800.13
4. Are you grown up?		
Popularity Comes to You	McGraw-Hill	21390.12
Stepping Out	McGraw-Hill	21620.13
Developing Social Maturity	McGraw-Hill	21620.32
Public Appearance	McGraw-Hill	21620.34
Your Feelings	Jam Handy	21790.15
How Can I Understand Other People?	McGraw-Hill	21800.14
5. How are you and your family a part of the community?		
As Others See You	McGraw-Hill	21620.12
Crime: Everybody's Problem	N. Y. Journal-American	
To Have a Neighbor, Be a Neighbor	McGraw-Hill	21800.32

2 Instructional Unit, New York City Schools

Unit IX
YOUR PREPARATION AS A DRIVER

This unit sets the groundwork for impressing the future driver with the importance not only of basic driving skills but also of reading ability and those character traits which contribute to safe and pleasurable driving. The *Content* section presents material designed to stimulate thinking and making judgments. Wherever possible, or indicated in the section, *Suggested Approaches and Practices*, visualization and modified performances are used to a maximum. Examples are the Skill Driving Tests, surveying the neighborhood, Snellen Chart Tests, etc. The suggested films are most valuable in studying problems facing the driver.

Future drivers should have more than superficial knowledge of the operation of an automobile and the reliability of senses (judging distances, fatigue, coordination, etc.). This area of information has been included and expanded in the unit, *Science in Daily Living*. The teacher will best decide when and how to weave it into the content which follows here.

Objectives

1. To stress the seriousness and responsibilities in operating a car.

2. To gain some of the basic knowledge demanded for a license.

3. To show the importance of reading in common activities.

4. To encourage observance of safety rules.

Content

1. Why is it necessary to license drivers?
   a. To protect the public from accidents.
   b. To obtain evidence of financial security.
   c. To cut down on hit-and-run drivers.
   d. Driving is a privilege not a right.

2. Would you license a driver who could not read a map, a sign, or the manual of instructions?
   a. Dangers in not knowing directions.
   b. Evidence of indifference.

c. Ignorance of laws and changes lead to accidents and traffic tie-ups.

d. Reporting accidents.

3. What are the common causes of automobile accidents? (Almost 40,000 deaths per year)
   a. Exceeding speed limit.
   b. On wrong side of road.
   c. Cutting in.
   d. Passing on a curve.
   e. Reckless driving.

4. Why do the automobile insurance rates vary?
   a. In different boroughs.
   b. For different age groups.

5. Under what conditions may you lose your license?
   a. If you disobey traffic laws.
   b. If you do not renew it in time.
   c. If you are convicted of certain offenses under the Point System, e.g., homicide, false statement in application.

6. How do traffic problems affect you?
   a. Coming to school.
   b. Going to work.
   c. Going to points of recreation.
   d. Why is the traffic problem more involved in city driving?

7. Why is the federal government interested in auto travel?
   a. National highway system.
   b. Interstate bus systems.
   c. Military needs in case of emergency.
   d. Aid to states (road building).

8. How does your physical condition affect your ability to be a good driver?
   a. Coordination.
   b. Control of muscles and senses in sufficient time for emergencies.
   c. The dangers in driving for those with a heart pressure ailment or epilepsy.
   d. Visual acuity.

9. Why is it necessary for you to learn how to share the road?
   a. The dangers in "hogging the road."
   b. The danger in "chiseling space."
   c. The danger in "blowing off."
   d. The danger in not helping motorists in distress.

10. Why must the driver think for the pedestrian?
    a. Two-thirds of all traffic fatalities in American cities are pedestrains.
    b. Twenty percent of the pedestrians killed are under fifteen years of age.
    c. About one-half of the pedestrians killed annually are fifty years of age or older.

11. What are the important safety precautions to remember when driving?
    a. Understanding and observing signals.
    b. Maintaining the car in good condition.
    c. Exercising skill in basic operations: starting, steering, braking, shifting, turning.
    d. Observing all traffic regulations.

Suggested Approaches and Practices

1. Class studies a photograph of an auto accident as reported in the newspaper and then listens to a reading of the report by a student. From the available facts, could this accident have been averted? How?

   Distribute *Heedless Horsepower* (Travelers Insurance Company) for examination of Table 3. Find the three most frequent reasons for casualties. Set up a chart showing the percentages.

2. Place on blackboard examples of road signs: symbols and words.

    a. What do they mean?
    b. Why is it important to be able to read them quickly?

3. Students learn how to fill out application for Operator's License. Do one section at a time, discussing common errors resulting from diffi-

culties connected with vocabulary and careless reading of directions. vocabulary to be studied will include: applicat, void, alteration, insurance, restrict, valid, pending, current.

4. The cartoon below is used for study by the class.

    a. Do you have to take a "head examination"?
    b. Suggest a good title for the cartoon.

5. Use N.Y. State Driver s Manual for reading and study exercises, adapting more difficult sections. Divide these exercises into short units with true-false examinations on the readings. Some of the more difficult words found in this booklet are: minimum, indicate, sufficient, infraction, persistent, miscellaneous, accumulate, deliberate, congest, prudent, obstacle, detect, moderate, destination, pedestrian, caution.

6. Students take Shell Driving Tests on skills and attitudes essential for safe driving. (Copies available from Shell Oil Company—an excellent series of modified performance tests.) Examples: Test Your Field of Vision, See How Fast You Can Move to the Brake, Can You Read These Signs at Arm's Length?, Are You A Patient Driver?

7. A committee does a neighborhood survey and reports results to the class.
    a. What recent improvements have been made to ease traffic problems?

b. Where is improvement necessary?

c. Are there any dangers to safe driving?

8. The traffic toll each year is close to 40,000 killed, 2 million injured, and financial losses of over 4 billions of dollars. Think of these facts, then study the statement: "Accidents happen to the other fellow—not to me." Do you agree? How would you reword the statement?

9. The modern car requires very little use of physical labor and is easy to operate. Why then is good health required of applicants for licenses?

10. Read the Motor Vehicle Law on visual acuity requirements. Conduct Snellen Chart Test in class.

11. The famous baseball star, Ted Williams, said: "Whether you are in the batter's box on the baseball diamond, inside the cockpit of a jet plane, or behind the wheel of your car, alert attention, sound judgment, and smooth skill are vital for the best performance."

    a. Show exactly how comparisons could be made with baseball and auto-driving in:

        1) Alertness.

        2) Sound judgment.

        3) Smooth skill.

    b. In what way is auto-driving different from playing baseball?

TEACHING MATERIALS AND PLANS

Topic: DRIVING SAFELY   **Plan/Worksheet A**

In this lesson, students learn through a variety of activities the importance of safe driving. It should take a minimum of 3 periods.

Aims

1. To analyze the main causes of automobile accidents.

2. To stress the importance of alertness and safe driving.

3. To engage in simple research skills making use of government publications, e.g., manuals, instruction.

Motivation

1. On February 16, 1961, the National Safety Council reported that motor vehicle accidents were the leading cause of deaths — 38,200 — the largest figure since 1957. Why are these figures mounting?

2. Place a newspaper photograph of a recent auto accident on a poster and draw a question mark beneath it. Students suggest words, phrases, or sentences to go with the question mark.

Procedure

1. Students report on auto accidents they have witnessed: the nature of the accident, where it occurred, and probable causes. The causes, in the students' language, are written on the board. For example:
   a. "He was traveling at high speed. He jammed on the brakes but it was too late."
   b. "The wheels were wobbling, something was wrong with the steering."
   c. "He was getting the other drivers nervous by weaving in and out."
   d. "When he turned the corner, I didn't see any directional signal flashing."
   e. "The auto crossed the street slowly but the sign said 'stop'."

   After all the causes are written, they are then coordinated and classified by the students into a more meaningful unit.

   Causes of Accidents
   a. Speeding.
   b. Disobeying sign.
   c. Signals, directionals not working.
   d. Defective equipment.
   e. Reckless driving.

2. Provide students with copies of N.Y. State Driver's Manual and "New York State Says . . ." Divide the class into 3 committees, each committee to find specific reference to 3 assigned causes of accidents. Their worksheets will be headed *Causes of Accidents* and will contain the following:

Cause	Page Reference	What It Says
1.		
2.		
3.		

   When the assignment is completed, the committees pool their information and add to their worksheets.

Application

Students read their mimeographed copies of the poem which follows and prepare to answer questions about it.

EPITAPHS FOR THE SPEED AGE
Leonard H. Robbins

Strangers pause and shed a tear
    For one who leaves no mourners.
D.F. Sapp reposes here;
    He would cut corners.

Here lie G. Whilliken's friends, all five.
He took them along when he learned to drive.

Hic jacet* now what little remains of Aleck McFee.
He let her up and raced with trains R.I.P.**

Under this mound is Goofus Green.
    His chemistry few extol.
He filled his tank with gasoline
    Himself with alcohol.

1. Do any of the causes listed on your worksheet appear in this poem? Where?

2. By studying source of the names, how did the author of the poem express his opinion about certain drivers?

3. Under the recent revision of auto insurance liability rates in February, 1961 the new rates for drivers under 25 years of age (2-C) is about $350 for New York City inhabitants and $215 in north Westchester. Is such a difference justified? Why?

Follow-Up

Film: *And Then There Were Four* (Socony Vacuum)

1. In what way is this film a good companion to the poem, *Epitaphs for the Speed Age?*

2. Prepare a short, descriptive paragraph in which you state whether or not this film is to be recommended for high school students.

Topic: WHAT DOES SAFE DRIVING MEAN?   Plan/Worksheet B

Although the comic book (*Tommy Gets the Keys*—H. F. Goodrich Co.) used here is filled with striking illustrations in color and a meaningful text, it is still important to motivate the lesson in advance in order to direct the read-

---

* (This is in the Latin language and means—'here lies')
** (This is an abbreviation in Latin which means 'May He Rest in Peace')

ing for instructional value. Students know, in advance, the questions they will be expected to answer.

Motivation

1. "Dad, may I have the keys to the car?" When should dad give the keys to the car?

2. Newspaper item: "I didn't mean to hurt anybody when I drove off. Maybe I was showing off. The fellows on the block said I was 'chicken'." Has anything similar to this happened in your neighborhood?

Reading

Tommy Gets the Keys

Understanding What You Read

1. Why was Tommy disappointed in his first lesson with Skip?

2. What does "driving defensively" mean?

3. Why did Tommy have to learn to think about the other fellow?

4. Where do you find sportsmanship in driving an auto?

5. List 4 good rules for safe driving.

Application

Students study the graph to the right. Does it help to explain why Tommy's dad hesitated to give him the auto keys?

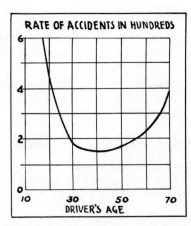

ACCIDENTS AND AGE

(Chart from Federal Bureau of Public Roads and New York Herald Tribune, 1/6/61)

INSTRUCTIONAL FILMS AND FILMSTRIPS

The films and filmstrips listed below have been approved by the Board of Education. The films are available from the BAVI Central Loan Collection or from local film centers. For annotations and additional information, see *Instructional Films and Tapes*, Curriculum Bulletin No. 14, 1958-59 Series; and the 1959 *List of Approved Filmstrips and Supplements*.

The numbered topics in column 1 correspond with those in the *content section of this unit* for which the film or filmstrip is appropriate.

Films

CONTENT TOPIC (and *Film Title*)	PRODUCER	RUNNING TIME (*Minutes*)
1. Why is it necessary to license drivers?		
Safe Driving: Streets and Highways	Coronet	11
You Bet Your Life	Progressive Pictures	10
3. What are the common causes of automobile accidents?		
And Then There Were Four	Socony Vacuum	27
Crash Research	Ford Motor Co.	10
Dick Wakes Up	Ford Motor Co.	8
Driving at Night	Ford Motor Co.	8
Driving in the City	Ford Motor Co.	12
Driving on the Highway	Ford Motor Co.	12
7. Why is the federal government interested in auto travel?		
Freedom of the American Road	Ford Motor Co.	27
10. Why must the driver think for the pedestrian?		
On Impact	Ford Films	10
Pedestrians	Ford Motor Co.	10
11. What are important safety precautions in driving a car?		
Care of the Car	Ford Motor Co.	12
Safe Driving: Advanced Skills and Problems	Coronet	11
Safe Driving: Defensive Driver, The	Coronet	11
Safe Driving: Fundamental Skills	Coronet	11

Filmstrips

Content Topic (and *Filmstrip Title*)	Vendor	Item No.
1. Why is it necessary to license drivers?		
You and the Automobile	N. Y. Journal-American	
2. Would you license a driver who could not read a map, a sign, or the manual of instructions?		
Driving Signs — A	Bowmar, Stanley	25240.1
Driving Signs — B	Bowmar, Stanley	25240.11
Information Signs	Bowmar, Stanley	25240.12
Warning Signs	Bowmar, Stanley	25240.14
11. What are important safety precautions in driving a car?		
Science of Automobile Safety	McGraw-Hill	25220

3 Topical Outline, Cranston High School

SUGGESTED TOPICS (Daily) FOR COOPERATIVE NURSING (Home Economics)

Types of Hospitals and Services	Etiquette for Hospital Workers	Your Health and Personality

Grooming

The patient-nucleus of the hospital	The patient as a person

Taking care of patients personal needs-hair, nails, flowers, cards

Understanding and following directions	Keeping Patients' Record

General procedures for hand care, the coverall, care of thermometer, ice bag hot water bag, etc.

Food & Nutrition	Choosing Foods for health	Kings of Diets House--soft--liquid--special

Feeding the Patient	Trays with eye appeal	Remembering "Special days" birthdays, anniversaries, "going home"

Mental Health	Rationalization	Compensation	Projection

The Art of Conversation	Week spent in role playing. What and how to talk to patients.

Art principles	Lab work making tray favors--floral arrangements

Meeting Expenses of Illness	The subscription plan. The community and patient's responsibility. Limits of service. The Out-patient dept.

Spiritual needs of the patient.	Get outside help from rabbi, minister, priest

Saving the Nurse's strength	Class demonstrations of what they have learned. (also use time saving from Home Management)

The Art of Detachment	The Nurse as a person--time for work, play and personal development

Plans for all times	simplicity, completeness, flexibility, workability

4 Resource Unit: School-Work Level I
City School District, Rochester

TRUCKING IN NEW YORK STATE

(Sample Unit Outline for Classes for Slow Learners, Secondary Schools--
Tentative)

I. SCIENCE & MATHEMATICS

1. Materials used in manufacture of
   trucks and in road building.

2. Expansion & Contraction of Roads
   a. Natural elements - heat, cold,
      moisture (rain, snow, sleet &
      flood)
   b. Causes and prevention of weak-
      end & pock-marked roads
   c. Properties of concrete and other
      road surface materials
   d. Salt and other de-icers
   e. Slab joint maintenance and other
      road repair work

3. Problems of Weight & Overloading
   a. Trucks made of aluminum, stain-
      less steel, steel
   b. Math problems on gross weight,
      net weight, truck weight, etc.

4. Types of Trucks
   a. Refrigerated, milk, oil, lumber,
      carryall, automobile haulers,
      furniture vans, gas, cement, ink,
      etc.
   b. How refrigerated trucks work

5. Mileage & Fuel
   a. Road map reading
   b. Computing gasoline consumption
      and mileage traveled
   c. Types of gasoline (octane content
      and additives)
      Diesel fuels

6. Bridges and Highways
   a. Single, double, 3 and 4 lane
      roads leading to bridges
   b. Types of bridges
   c. Restrictive weights and head-room
      limitations for trucks

II. SOCIAL STUDIES & ENGLISH

1. Sources of materials in manufacture
   of trucks and in road building

2. Early roads of New York State

3. The Erie Canal era to the New York
   State Thruway

4. Toll roads vs. Free ways

5. Map study of roads in the areas of:
   Niagara Frontier, Genesee Valley,
   Central New York, Mohawk Valley,
   Capital District, Mid-Hudson, Met-
   ropolitan District, Southern Tier

6. Trucking on New York State Highways

II. SOCIAL STUDIES & ENGLISH (cont'd)

Rules and regulations on maximum
weight and overloading. Penalties
for violations. Weighing stations

7. Gasoline and Highway Taxes
   Local, State and Federal

8. Highway Signs for Safety
   Driver training reading skills and
   requirements for chauffeur's
   license

9. Legal Rights and Responsibilities
   Obeying safety rules.
   What to do in case of accidents,
   arrest witnesses, etc.
   Lawyers - personal and company

10. Insurance
    Fire, theft, collision, liability

11. Intra & Inter State Truck Travel
    License Plate Regulations
    The ICC-PSC

12. Biography of John L. McAdam, the
    Scotch road builder for whome
    "macadem" roads were named

    The McAdam report of 1823 to the
    London Board of Agriculture.

13. Contribution of Modern Trucks and
    Modern Roads to Modern Living -
    Develop concepts of
    a. 50% of truck farm
       products - corn, cucumbers,
       lettuce, celery, tomatoes, etc.
       travel by truck to 15 major
       markets
    b. 99% of live poultry & fresh eggs
       hauled by trucks to 10 major
       markets.
    c. 75% of livestock, 69% of gravel
       and 20% of coal from mines
       hauled by truck
    d. 69% of all new automobiles
       hauled by truck
    e. Most of country's furniture,
       drugs, clothing, toys and fuel
       hauled by truck
    f. There are 8,000 ambulances-
       30,000 fire trucks and 15,000
       Railway Express Co. trucks in
       use daily in the U.S.

14. Major Manufacturers of Trucks and
    Plant Sites

    Freuhauf, Mack, Diamond T, White,
    Ford, Broackway, Chevrolet

15. Secure information regarding
    Analysis of Trucking Industry

from Home or Local Offices of -

ATLANTIC COAST FREIGHT
LINES - AKRON-CHICAGO
TRANSPORTATION LINES -
CARGO-IMPERIAL FREIGHT

CENTRAL N.Y. FREIGHTWAYS
COAST TO COAST

MOTOR FREIGHTWAY SERVICE-
EASTERN FREIGHTWAYS

EAZOR EXPRESS SERVICE-
MID-STATES FREIGHT

MUSHROOM TRANSPORTATION CO. -
NORTH AMERICAN

VAN LINES - N.Y. CENTRAL
TRANSPORTATION CO.

RED STAR EXPRESS LINES -
TRANS-AMERICAN

FREIGHT LINES - WESTERN EXPRESS
COMPANY (also from smaller local or
area truckers)

III. HEALTH TEACHING

1. General care of body for maintenance of good health

2. How our skeletal and muscular
   systems operate

3. Cautions to observe in lifting
   of heavy cartons, crates, etc.

4. Proper care of eyes and ears and
   their importance for good driving

5. Proper diet, rest and sleep for
   safe driving

IV. RELATED HAND WORK

1. Building models of trucks and
   trailers - wood, sheet metal

2. Building models of roads, highways, bridges

3. Mixing concrete and observing
   its properties

4. Making a New York State Highway
   map

(Some of the topics suggested might be included in an occupational reading-social studies
unit, similar in format to the Rochester Occupational Reading Series, but stepped up in
content and ability level to approach interests of dull-normal and borderline pupils.)

5 Resource Unit: School-Work Level II
City School District, Rochester

SOCIAL STUDIES

THE MATERIALS LISTED IN THIS GUIDE ARE SUGGESTED. IT IS NOT INTENDED THAT THE TEACHER
COVER IN DETAIL EVERY ITEM MENTIONED, NOR FOLLOW THE EXACT SEQUENCE PRESENTED.

DEVELOPMENTAL AREAS   SUGGESTED ACTIVITIES

I. ROCHESTER AS IT IS:
   A CITY FOR LIVING AND WORKING

   Getting acquainted with Rochester
   (to be used as a short introductory
   unit reviewing materials covered in
   S.W. I)

   A. City background and development   Films on Early Rochester may be used
      1. Early Rochester
          a. History
          b. Development

      2. Factors determining growth   Discuss:
          a. Location   Zoning laws, availability of power
          b. Industries   resources, tax assessments, connecting
                                                commercial lines, etc.

      3. Present day city   Slide series on city growth - from City
          a. Compared to early times   Manager's Office may be used
          b. Compared to other cities
             in the state

      4. Future growth   Obtain information on new Civic Center,
          a. City construction   port plans, proposed recreational pro-
          b. Port development   grams, inner-loops and other highway
          c. Highway development   and public construction programs

   B. Citizens' rights and responsi-   List freedoms, privileges and opportuni-
      bilities   ties - compare with communist and other
      1. Privileges   totalitarian systems
          a. Freedoms earned
          b. Opportunities available

      2. Guarding rights and privileges   Discuss obligations of citizenship -
          a. Preventing misuse   neighborhood duties, care of home and
          b. Assuring continuance   yard - civic responsibilities

                                            Mock political party convention

                                            Find out how a voting machine works

                                            Compare citizenship in the community with
                                               citizenship in the school

                                            Hold election of class officers and rep-
                                               resentatives

                                            Film "Don't Be a Sucker" may be used

II. Rochester as it is: a city for busi-
    ness and work

   A. Job situation organization
      1. Function of business   List the materials needed for the school
          a. Need of product   year - discuss where they come from and
          b. Employment of people   where we get the money to pay for them -
                                                make a diagram of the business cycle and
                                                explain simply and in a manner that is
                                                meaningful to the students the princi-
                                                ple implied

      2. Worker's rights and benefits   Discuss school marks - how do we earn
          a. Good work - good pay   good marks - compare this with pay on job

b. Other benefits	List other benefits you may get from working - payroll deductions a. Compensation insurance b. Paid lunch c. Work clothes and uniforms d. Tools e. Life insurance plans f. Medical insurance plans g. Retirement plans h. Discounts i. Vacations j. Unemployment compensation k. Seniority benefits l. Laundry service for work clothes m. Recreational facilities n. Overtime o. Incentive programs p. Schooling and other education q. Suggestion programs
B. Choosing a job 1. Types of jobs	Have class list jobs available in the Rochester area at which they would like to work
a. Qualifications of low skilled workers (Usually routine work - may be repetitive - worker must be vigilant and alert - some decisions made by others - training period may be short, usually 6 months or less)	Give examples of this class of worker i.e. machine operator, meat cutter, bus driver Compare wages among jobs in this area Stress throughout the dignity and value of low skilled and unskilled work - cite examples of prominent men in these fields
b. Qualifications of unskilled workers (jobs require little or no training - apt to be repetitive - require from little to heavy physical exertion - no previous experience needed - possibilities of advancement are present)	Legend of such workers as: Johnny Appleseed - seed planter Paul Bunyan - lumberman John Henry - railroad worker
c. Job areas (see outline on pages 6a,b,c,d for job areas)	Discuss what is meant by the title of each job area - service occupations, agricultural occupations, etc. Have class list jobs with which they are familiar in each area Have members of class give oral reports on farm experiences, etc. List advantages and disadvantages of each job area
2. Education needed for the job	Have class discuss the importance of education in our lives - its application to the world of work - what they feel they must know on the job Have businessmen talk to class about job requirements
3. Physical ability necessary for work	Stress importance of good health proper diet, proper habits Have class list health requirements: height, weight, strength, knowledge of lifting, eyesight, hearing, etc.

4. Age requirements for a job
   12-16 part time after school
   4 hrs. per day on school
   days
   8 hrs. on Saturdays or
   holidays
   16-18 - 28 hrs. per week as
   stated above if person is
   in school - or full time
   if not in school
   over 18 - factory work allowed - full time and
   overtime allowed

Study State and Federal Child Labor
Laws (see: "An Abstract of Laws
Governing the Employment of Minors
in New York State" from Department
of Labor, State of New York

Discuss limitations set regarding
hours of work, wages, age, etc.

Discuss reasons for state and federal
regulations - working conditions of
years gone by

6 Resource Unit: School-Work Level III
City School District, Rochester

SCIENCE

The following is a suggested outline of the possible methods in which science can be adapted for functional use within the core program. It is expected that the S.W. teacher will make similar adaptations to suit the circumstances within his own class.

DEVELOPMENTAL AREAS	SUGGESTED ACTIVITIES
I. The science of the body	Compare the eye to the camera - show similarities of function and parts
A. The human eye	Obtain model of eye from the science department - demonstrate to class
1. How the eye works	
2. How the eye adapts to various situations	Visit Rochester Association for the Blind and sight saving classes
3. Proper protection and care	Show effect of light on light sensitive materials - film
	Show the spectrum with the help of prisms discuss rainbows and harmony of colors
	Stress care of eyes
	Show optical illusions and explain simply principle involved
B. The human ear	Beginning with the description of the human ear the teacher could build a unit around the science of sound
1. The ear we don't see	
2. Functions of the ear	Discuss what is Hi Fi and stereo sound
3. Safety precautions	Show how dancers and skaters overcome dizziness by fixing sight on an object while they are twirling
4. Proper care	
	Demonstrate correct method of cleaning ear
C. The body muscles	Show advantages of levers, pulleys, block and tackle, ratio, etc.
1. The job they do	
2. Their growth and development	From a discussion of the "Roller Coaster" the meaning of gravity and its effect on people and things can be developed
3. Helping them function	
	Show ways of overcoming gravity, friction, inertia
II. The science of the elements	Keep weather chart daily of temperature and weather forecast
A. Effect of elements on: 1. The area around us a. Soil b. Crops c. Types of construction	By the use of maps and globes discuss the reason for seasons, climatic zones, etc.
	Visit weather bureau to observe weather instruments
2. Our living habits a. Types of homes b. Living conditions	Write to U.S. Weather Bureau for weather maps of this area
3. Our lives a. Type of work b. Way of life	Reference sources - "Science and You," Fowler, Collister and Thurston "The Earth Then and Now," Craig, Johnson and Lewis
	Relate effect of elements to the scenic beauty spots - Niagara Falls, Letchworth Gorge, Yellowstone Park, etc.

B. Man's attempt to control the ele-   Discuss future possibility of predicting
   ments   weather in advance

   1. Cloud seeding   Show effect of dry ice in closed contain-
                                            er
   2. Changing course of tornadoes
                                            Read stories of airplanes flying into
   3. Weather satellites   "eye" of tornadoes and hurricanes

                                            Attempt to read about weather forecasting
                                            instruments carried by satellites

III. Household science   Obtain labels from various household
                                            products - make a list of chemical in-
   A. In the kitchen   gredients

   1. Chemical we use   Show action on some products, i.e., lye
                                            in water (Caution - do not get on fin-
   2. Type of action involved   gers or clothing - use enamel container)

   B. In the food we eat   Learn effect of various ingredients in
                                            the cooking process - i.e., baking pow-
   1. Preparation   der, yeast, food coloring

   2. Digestion   Test various foods with litmus paper -
                                            acids turn litmus red - bases turn lit-
                                            mus blue

                                            Make simple test for starch in food

   C. In the laundry   Show effect of laundry starch on clothes

   1. Detergents   Use of dyes on various cloths

   2. Starches   Removal of stains from various cloths

   D. The clothes we wear   Meaning and effect of soft water and hard
                                            water
   1. Synthetics
                                            Why does bluing turn clothes white
   2. Blends
                                            Meaning of color-fast and non-fast arti-
                                            cle

   E. In our hobbies   Have pupils visit photography club in
                                            school to see film developing
   1. Photography
                                            Encourage students to start a hobby -
   2. Animal collection   suggest such hobbies as - rock col-
                                            lecting, animal care, etc.

                                            Build and stock an ant farm

        ADDITIONAL SUGGESTIONS FOR PRESENTATION AND DEVELOPMENT

                              SCIENCE

1. Pupils working in various businesses may contribute subject matter according to the
   type of process involved on the job

2. Learn how such fabrics as nylon and rayon are made

3. Discover how Kodak makes vitamins and synthetic fabrics with by-products from film department

   _____

   The above list is not complete. You may wish to add other suggestions.

REFERENCE AND SOURCE MATERIAL

SCIENCE

Reference text: Craig, Arey, and Sheckles, <u>Learning With Science</u>, Ginn and Company,
                 Book 7

                 Fowler, Collister and Thurston, <u>Science and You</u>

                 Craig, Johnson and Lewis, <u>The Earth Then And Now</u>

                 "Mr. Wizard's Experiments in Science," Prism Productions, Inc., 220 East
                 23rd Street, New York 10, New York. Subscription price $1.00 for 8 is-
                 sues per year. Offers many simple science suggestions.

The above list is not complete. You may wish to add other references.

REFERENCE AND SOURCE MATERIAL

SCIENCE

<u>Audio-Visual Aids</u> - Board of Education

<u>Films:</u>
Heritage We Guard
Water Cycle
Water Supply
What is Science
What Makes Day and Night
What Makes Rain
Choosing Clothes For Health
How Weather Helps Us
Learning About Our Bodies
Learning About Your Nose
Learning About Sound
We Use Power
How To Improve Your House
How To Avoid Muscle Strains
Nose, Throat and Ears
How The Eye Functions
Rest And Health
Body Defenses Vs. Disease
Exercise And Health
Gateway To Health
How To Control Bleeding

<u>Filmstrips:</u>
Good Health series
 534 You And Your Clothes
 536 You And Your Food
 537 Your Posture

General Science Why series
 610 Why Does It Rain
 611 Why Does The Weather Change
 612 Why Does The Wind Blow
 613 Why The Seasons

Basic Science series
 614 Air About Us
 615 Our Ocean of Air
 616 Living Things

The above list is not complete. You may wish to add other audio-visual aids. Consult
the Audio-Visual Co-ordinator in your school for ordering these films and also the
films available at Rundel Library.

7 Introduction and Resource Units:
The Work-Study Curriculum, Kansas City

INTRODUCTION

This proposed tentative curriculum for eighth grade boys is an experimental program under the direction of the Work-Study Project of the Practical Arts Division and the Secondary Curriculum department of the Instructional Division.

The aims of the research project are to:

1. Build better pupil self concepts and self understandings by establishing more realistic goals.
2. Improve basic skills in reading, speaking, listening, writing and computation.
3. Develop success habits and attitudes toward work and job activities.
4. Provide a functional curriculum that will meet pupil needs.
5. Establish a school climate that will help improve pupil social and emotional adjustment to our democratic culture.
6. Encourage the pupil to explore wholesome recreational and vocational opportunities.
7. Develop a functional knowledge of our government and the American heritage.
8. Recognize the importance of science in daily living.
9. Develop an understanding of the pupil's role as a consumer and as a worker in industry.
10. Encourage worthy home and family relationships.

The curriculum is to be structured in flexible patterns to meet the needs of each individual pupil. However, the curriculum base should relate to the general eighth grade curriculum according to the pupil's ability, to the end that he may not be set apart from his peer group in the junior high school setting.

In identifying and understanding these pupils, teachers should be alerted to the following pupil characteristics:

        —poor reading abilities and habits
        —poor work-study habits
        —lack of interest in school and school work
        —poor attitudes
        —irregular school attendance
        —poor mental ability
        —poor achievement record

Teachers should carry on a guidance-centered approach to the class group and a counseling-centered approach to the individual pupil. Anecdotal records and accounts for each pupil should be kept with the focus upon growths and progress made. Such growths should be known by the pupil and can serve well as a basis for personal conferences.

Teachers in the Work-Study Project should feel free to seek the assistance of their school administrators and staff personnel. The Secondary Curriculum and all of the departments will lend any assistance that can be of value to the teachers as the project advances.

Work supervisors and assistant supervisors in the work part of the project will strive to bring out and develop desirable potentials of these pupils. The goals of the program are to stimulate in the individual boy the following qualities:

—neat personal appearance
—punctuality
—dependability
—ability to work with others
—personal application on the job
—cooperativeness and initiative
—enthusiasm for work and its rewards

These qualities will tend to equip each individual to better meet the challenge of today's social world.

Finally, it is essential that the classroom teacher and the work supervisors consult and plan cooperatively so that the best results may be attained for both the in-class learning activities and in the pupil work experience.

General Objectives

I. To establish within these boys self-realization by
   —formulating proper attitudes
   —developing full potentials
   —creating a climate which will establish a sense of personal security
   —teaching them to live more successfully with their families

II. To develop within these boys a desire to establish good human relationships through their growth
   —mentally
   —morally
   —physically
   —emotionally
   —socially

III. To help these boys to see the need for assuming civic responsibilities to better their
   —home
   —school
   —community

IV. To cause these boys to see their need for specific work experiences

V. To instill the desire within these boys to participate in wholesome leisure-time activities by
   —recognizing needful family life activities
   —establishing proper home and community behavior patterns
   —developing reading as a necessary and leisure time activity
   —introducing them to wholesome private and public cultural facilities

Suggestions to Teachers

The following are suggested methods and techniques for teaching the slow learner:

1. Eliminate fear, be sympathetic, give praise, be patient, never be sarcastic.

2. Develop confidence, give recognition, provide for success by giving attainable assignments.

3. Establish goals, larger and intermediate goals must be known, a need must be felt.

4. Vary assignments, be specific, make sure the pupil understands, encourage questions, suggest answers to a few of the beginning problems to get students started, keep specific written assignments short, and give much *general reading at proper level.*

5. Develop good habits, stress punctuality, insist upon regular time to study, insist upon class participation, do not permit delayed homework.

6. Stress personality development through group work and personal counseling, and give responsibility commensurate with ability.

7. Vary teaching procedure, demonstrate often, utilize visual and auditory aids of all kinds, use simple language, make each step simple, test often and use short tests, give much practice, repeat often, and promote competition with student's self and between teams.

8. Adjust courses, lengthen period of study where possible in order to give personal attention to counseling.

9. *Use Visual Aids and Provide Opportunity to Manipulate Concrete Materials.* Visualize your instruction—don't tell them, show them. Research has shown us that the slow learner needs *more* varied visual aids and *more* opportunity for repeat practice with concrete materials.

10. *Laboratory-Type Teaching and Practice.* Arrange class laboratory periods for the slow student in order to provide extra teaching and student practice. This may be the "key" to opening the door to occupations for these students.

11. *Individual Assignments.* Make assignments according to individual ability—do not give the same assignment as given the bright pupils. (The slow pupil will only copy it. What else can he do if it is beyond his ability?) If the first question is: "How will I grade them?" the answer is simple. Don't worry about *grading*—worry about *teaching* them.

12. *Understanding the "Slower Than Average" Boy.* The most effective technique with the "slower than average" teen-ager is the teacher's enlightened, sympathetic understanding—kindness, patience, and encouragement. Being surrounded by the above qualities, each boy whose life you are helping to build will be more likely to achieve self-realization, economic independence, and worthwhile participation in civic life.

COMMON LEARNINGS—Grade 8

Resource Unit I: Understanding My School, My Program *and* Myself.

Overview

The purposes of this resource unit are to make students more actively
aware of the part each must play in an effective school organization; to
aid each in gaining a better understanding of some of the problems and
responsibilities he will meet and must assume as he merges into his social
world; to have each student further the process of self-evaluation in determining his needed skills in communication, problem solving and
group living and to take stock of the special abilities, aptitudes and interests, which each should develop; and to help each to organize and
utilize his time and energy for achieving the most satisfactory results.

It is suggested that 2-3 weeks might be necessary to consider the listed
problem areas and to carry out some of the activities which would develop important skills and understandings. The skills, concepts, and the
thinking developed in this unit should be kept alive and active throughout the year. Focus should be upon:

1. How can I adjust to new school situations and get the most out
   of the work-study program this year?

2. How does the school help and serve me and what are my responsibilities to the school and the work-study program?

Specific Objectives and Problem Areas

A. How can I make and keep worthwhile friendship among boys, girls,
   and adults? What experiences do we have in school which will help
   us develop the meaning of:

   1. thoughtfulness
   2. consideration
   3. patience
   4. sharing
   5. cooperation
   6. sincerity
   7. loyalty
   8. companionship
   9. appreciation
   10. diligence
   11. responsibility
   12. honesty
   13. courtesy

B. How can we effectively organize our classroom for efficient living
   this year?

   1. Who are the members of our class?
   2. What class organization do we need?
   3. What are each member's responsibilities in our class organiza-
      tion?
   4. Dependability.
   5. Sense of pride.
   6. Ability to accept criticisms.

7. Perseverance
8. Cooperation

C. What is the proper attitude toward the school *personnel?*

   1. Who are the members of the school personnel?
   2. What are their duties?
   3. How can we cooperate with them?
   4. Respect for authority
   5. Attitude to leadership.

D. What are my responsibilities in helping to take care of the school property and equipment?

   1. What school equipment is available for our use?
   2. What is the correct procedure for using each type of equipment?
   3. Techniques of good work procedures.
   4. Relate their school work to job experience.
   5. Care and selection of tools.
   6. Safety procedures.
   7. Efficient utilization of tools, time and material.

E. How can I cooperate and contribute to the work of the school?

   1. What are the purposes of the Student Council and School Patrol?
   2. What is the role of the individual student in these organizations?
   3. What school clubs are available for my individual interests?
   4. Develop personal insights.
   5. Identify limitations.
   6. Ability to accept criticisms.

F. What skills will we need to develop to get the most from our work this year?

   1. What are the skills necessary for planning?
   2. What are the skills necessary for gathering information?
   3. What are the skills necessary for sharing information?
   4. What are the skills necessary for recording and organizing information?
   5. What techniques can we use for successful committee work?
   6. How can we effectively evaluate our work?
   7. How do all of the above fit into the problem-solving approach to learning.
   8. Develop a sense of productivity.
   9. Dignity of being able to work.
  10. Develop a sense of accomplishment.

G. What are some of the areas of study which 8th graders will find interesting and profitable?

   1. How can a quick recall of 7th grade learnings help us to determine our next steps in rounding out our study of common learnings for democratic living in American society?
   2. Planning of units of study for the year—class discussion of some of the major units of study.

3. Proper time for the use of proper materials.

4. Relate their school work to job experience.

Outline of Content—Understandings and Skills to be Developed

  A. Understandings

    1. Good citizens in a democratic society try to understand and get along with others.

    2. A good citizen practices respect for the rights and property of others.

    3. With every privilege goes a responsibility.

    4. A well-adjusted person can always maintain self-control so that he doesn't interfere with the rights of others.

    5. A public-spirited citizen should take good care of school property and equipment.

    6. Much time can be saved for widening our interests and leisure activities if we learn and practice good study habits.

    7. One gets out of a thing what one puts into it. This applies to school, as well as to other phases of life. (Group discussion)

    8. Students should work to develop their potentialities rather than to measure their achievements by those of others.

    9. Good speech, writing and listening habits are important to one's success in life activities.

    10. Problem solving is a very effective way of learning and is usable in most daily activities throughout life.

    11. If we set worthwhile goals and work to fulfill them, we will achieve personal satisfaction.

    12. Planned and controlled use of initiative, imagination and the materials at hand will contribute to progress.

    13. We will enjoy and appreciate "work assignments" if they are closely related to our daily activities and in turn contribute to our total achievement.

  B. Skills to be Developed

Developing an overall view of all skills which will be used throughout the year and setting the general goals for the year.

    1. Using correct speech and speech habits—practice in explaining simple directions to others.

    2. Improving sentence and paragraph structure.

    3. Using proper punctuation and capitalization.

    4. Emphasizing correct spelling of words in daily use.

    5. Learning and using new words—words peculiar to the job situation.

    6. Improving library procedures and improving reading.

    7. Increasing the amount of reading done for information and for pleasure.

    8. Taking notes and following directions.

    9. Making oral and written reports of activities and take notes on information about different jobs.

    10. Evaluating oral and written reports—use care in enunciation—listening carefully to directions.

11. Writing letters—business and social. (Applications)
12. Increasing ability to organize materials into written compositions. Transcribing oral instruction to clearly written directions.
13. Increasing daily news reading and understanding. Scan newspaper for articles similar to your work—oral and written reports.
14. Develop interest in writing—write up daily activities on work experience.
15. Reviewing and using names in relation to world locations.
16. Using *World News Map of the Week*.
17. Helping plan an attractive classroom. Follow principles of neatness and order in the job environment.
18. Improving printing and poster work.
19. Using rules of order for informal and formal group procedures.
20. Setting up and carrying out responsibilities of officers in group organizations. Have work organization such as assistant foreman, foreman, and superintendent.
21. Conducting elections and committee appointments.
22. Manipulating figures concerned with daily costs—job estimates on material and time.

C. Learning Activities

1. Find out the cost of desks, books, globes, maps, record players, window shades, etc., and discuss reasons and ways for being intelligent consumers.
2. Make individual lists of communication skills which need special attention.
3. Set up class organization using parliamentary procedures for the purpose of handling group business, news periods.
4. Study list and practice good group procedures.
5. Develop individual study and work schedules.
6. Start a class student file and lists of materials related to the year's program.
7. Plan to read and share many books and short stories with class and parents.

Culminating Activities

1. Set up a code of ethics for the class regarding attitudes toward school personnel and classmates, care of property and equipment, and economical study skills and habits.
2. Invite the Physical Education supervisor to talk to the boys about understanding and controlling their emotions.
3. Review *"Major Types of Study Skills."*
4. Discuss and list some general goals to be reached during the year.
5. See available films related to the unit.

Evaluation

1. How have we solved problems that arose at the beginning of the unit?
2. What understandings have we gained through the study of this unit?

3. What new skills have you as an individual developed?
4. What new skills has the "class" group developed?
5. How has this study changed former opinion and ideas?
6. Has each individual made worthwhile contributions to the solution of problems in this unit of study?
7. Other evaluative techniques can be developed as the teacher and pupils realize need, e.g. written exercises may be developed in the class period.

Resources for Pupils

Heavey and Stewart: *Teen Age Tales,* Book A,
D. C. Heath and Company, 1959.
>   "Kindness of Jenny" (story)

Heavey and Stewart: *Teen Age Tales*, Book B,
D. C. Heath and Company, 1959.
>   "Play to Win" (story)

Lodge and Braymer: *Adventures in Reading,*
Harcourt, Brace and Company, 1958.
>   "Introduction by Jesse Stuart"
>   "Trademark"
>   "Off the Track"
>   "Ah Love, Ah Me"

Ross, Thompson and Lodge; *Adventures in Reading*
Harcourt, Brace and Company, 1957.
>   "The Thread That Runs So True"

Strang and Roberts; *Teen Age Tales,*
D. C. Heath and Company

Billett and Yeo; *Growing Up,* Second Edition
D. C. Heath and Company, 1958

Brown, Howard E.; *Getting Adjusted to Life,*
J. B. Lippincott Company, 1955

Hanna, Lavone A.; *Facing Life's Problems,*
Rand McNally and Company, 1957

Jenkins, Bauer, Shacter; *Teen-Agers,*
Scott, Foresman and Company, 1954

Roth and Hobbs; *Your World and You*
Laidlaw Brothers, 1954

Audio-Visual Aids

Films available from the Department of Audio-Visual Education:

00-167	Act Your Age
00-7	Aptitudes and Occuptaions
0-487	Attitudes and Health
0-476	Brotherhood of Man
0-654	Bully
0-656	Cheating
0-657	Choosing Your Occupation
00-416	Control Your Emotions
00-236	Dating Do's and Don'ts

0-915   Developing Self-reliance
0-537   Everyday Courtesy
00-4   Citizenship and You
00-421   Facing Reality
00-353   Good Loser
0-917   Good Sportmanship
0-1040   Griper
0-203   How to Read a Book
0-1031   How to remember a Book
0-920   How to Say "No"
0-204   How to Study
0-921   How to Succeed in School
00-527   How to Think
0-1032   How We Learn
0-542   Improve Your Reading
0-1039   Making Friends
00-393   Making Yourself Understood
00-626   Mr. Chairman—Fundamentals of Parliamentary Law
00-66   Make Way for Youth
0-460   Name Unknown
00-400   Parents are People Too
0-674   Outsider
0-709   Procrastinator
0-931   Overcoming Worry
0-672   Other People's Property
0-671   Other Fellow's Feelings
00-110   Shy Guy
00-510   Social Acceptability
0-680   Social Courtesy
00-256   Social Development
0-944   Why Study Industrial Arts
00-178   You and Your Parents

Filmstrips available from the Department of Audio-Visual Education:

F-1770   Are You Adaptable
F-1866   Discovering Your Interests
F-1768   Don't Know? Look it UP!
F-238   Etiquette Series, Set I (Kit of 5)
         I — As Others See You
         II — Home Ground
         III — School Spirit
         IV — Stepping Out
         V — Table Talk

F-1857   Etiquette Series, Set II (Kit of 5)
         I — Table Setting
         II — Perfect Party
         III — Public Appearance
         IV — Away From Home
         V — Developing Social Maturity

F-1199   Etiquette Series, Set III (Kit of 5)

Resource Unit II.   We Belong To A Team

Overview

Mathematics and science will play an important part in the lives of these boys no matter what directions their future lives may take. In this unit, very practical topics will be suggested to make these boys more efficient citizens who will have greater opportunities for happiness as they enter further training, and finally enter upon adult life with the satisfactions of making real contributions to their communities.

Objectives

Here we are developing an attitude of cooperation and fairness, and at the same time presenting material that will get the boy's attention and interest.

Outline of Content	*Learning Opportunities*

(A team can carry on classroom activities according to the rules of the classroom. It can play baseball according to the rules of baseball.)

I. To throw a ball we give it a push. The harder the push, the farther and the faster the ball goes.

Measure the distance around the bases of a baseball field.

Find the distance between the bases.

II. When we catch a ball, the ball pushes on our hands. If the ball is thrown hard, we may have to wear a glove or mit so that the ball will not hurt our hands. We sometimes call a push or pull a FORCE.

What is the shape of a baseball infield?

Draw a picture of the baseball infield. (What is the shape of this picture?)

III. Pitchers may throw a ball very fast. In catching fast balls, the catcher needs a heavy mit, a chest protector, and a face mask so that

On the baseball infield, throw a ball from home plate to first base —now, throw ball from home plate to second base. In which case do you have to push the harder on the ball?

In this case why do you have to

the ball will not hurt him.

IV. When you hit the ball with a bat, the ball is given a harder push than when you throw the ball. This is why batted balls may go farther than a ball that is thrown. If the bat is not held properly, this force may break the bat.

V. After the batter hits the ball, he must push very hard on the ground to get himself started toward first base. The heavier the boy, the harder the push needed to get him started.

VI. To run fast around the bases, boys lean to the left at the bases so that they can push themselves in the new direction toward the next base. Thus, we see that FORCE is necessary to make us turn corners.

VII. If the wind is blowing toward the batter, it is difficult to hit a home run. If the wind is blowing from home plate toward the pitcher, it is easier to hit a home run. This is because the moving air, or wind, pushes on the ball, helping or hindering.

VIII. If the wind is blowing from third base toward first base, pitched and batted balls may curve toward first base. Balls will also curve if you cause them to spin when you throw them. Balls can be made to curve right, left, or down, depending on the direction of the spin of the ball.

IX. The sun may help or hinder boys playing ball because the sunlight shining in the players' eyes may make it dif-

push harder on the ball?

If it takes 11 seconds to run from one base to another, how long will it take to run all the way around the bases?

Measure the distance from the pitcher's mound to home plate.

Which is the farther, from home plate to first base or from home plate to the pitcher's mound?

In this case what is the difference in the distances?

If the distance around the bases is 320 feet, what is the distance from one base to the next?

On the baseball diamond, you will find that you don't have to push hard to get started if you don't want to start quickly. If you wish to get there before you are put out at first base, you must start quickly. See how quickly you can get to first base.

Find out how long it takes you to run all the way around the infield.

Go out on the ball diamond and see how far you can throw the ball when the wind is blowing in the direction that you are throwing the ball. Now, go to where the ball is, pick it up, and then see if you can throw it all the way back to the place from which you threw it on the first throw.

Try throwing the ball in a strong cross wind. Does the wind make the ball curve? When the wind is not blowing, try to make the ball curve by giving it a spin.

If the sun is shining in your window, hold your hand or a book in the sunshine to see where the shadow is and what it looks like. Perhaps you can use your hands and fingers to make shadows that look like animals.

ficult to see the ball. When
there are no clouds, the sun
may cast shadows that will
make it difficult to see the
ball.

Culminating Activities

Give boys an opportunity to describe the rules of some game other
than baseball. If science is involved, let them indicate where it is involved. If practical, this might be written.

Evaluation

Give an informal, short test on the rules of baseball, and the science
and safety precautions involved.

Audio-Visual Aids

0-728   Force of Gravity

Resource Unit III.   From Indians to Industry
(Industrial Growth in the United States)

Overview

The growth of our industry has been mainly responsible for the growth
of our country.

Objectives

To help each boy gain an understanding of and a feeling of a personal relationship with industry.

To help each boy learn how industry has influenced life and history
of people.

Outline of Content	*Learning Opportunities*
I. A quick trip around the world A. Continents B. Major bodies of water C. Major countries	Make a chart called "Above and Beyond the Call of Duty" whereby a boy can get credit for extra work done Develop a word list or picture dictonary on the unit study Obtain a collection of library books for the unit study Use globes, charts, and maps extensively Use student maps for individual study Check distances (in miles) from Kansas City to various places Draw a map of the local community (compose a legend to mark schools, churches, businesses, and homes)

II. A quick trip around the United States
- A. Review location of states
- B. Review location of states bounding Missouri
- C. Review major cities of the United States
- D. Review names and locations of major waterways
- E. Review major mountain ranges

Develop a series of maps from local to world

Order current events reading material

Make individual jigsaw puzzle maps and put them together

Have oral or written reports on various states

Visit local points of interest

Discuss industrial areas of our cities and plan visits

Have team work on state reports, listing important facts about the state

Tell or write of their visits to various states

Make a map of our country, showing locations of various places

Make a state map including surrounding states

Draw a map of Missouri including places of historical interest

Develop a jigsaw map of Missouri

Discuss skin diving, swimming, and fishing in connection with waterways

Give an assignment in connection with the T. V. show "Sea Hunt"

III. Man's needs and how they are satisfied
- A. Physical
  1. Food
  2. Clothing
  3. Shelter

Discuss personal needs and the proper way to satisfy them

Draw of collect pictures to illustrate man's needs and how they are satisfied

Discuss the idea that everyone else has needs

Lead the class in making a list of common needs

- B. Social life
  1. Group living
  2. Early explorers and exploration

Write their viewpoints on social life or society

Talk about group life—stress advantages, disadvantages, and adjustments necessary for *all*

Discuss the influence of T. V. on our life

Suggest how our friends set our standards

Discuss public opinion vs. my opinion

Make maps and trace routes of early explorers

List the qualities of early explorers and discuss development of these qualities

Make a list of important early discoveries and discuss their importance to us

C. Experiments
  1. Discoveries
    a. Fire
    b. Wheel
    c. Growth of seeds

Draw an illustration and write an explanation of an early discovery

Make a list of things we have now that people did not have fifty years ago

Construct or draw a wheel and tell of its importance to us

Plant seeds and report on their growth

Discuss importance of growing to our nation and the world

  2. Inventions
    a. Cotton Gin—Whitney
    b. Steamboat—Fulton
    c. Telegraph—Morse
    d. Airplane—Wright brothers
    e. Diesel engine

Express in drawing, writing, or building some of their own inventive ideas

Discuss the machines needed today

Relate influence of inventions to industry

Illustrate or tell about modern machines (coke machines and game machines)

Write reports on inventions

Draw or build some known invention and explain it

Read stories about inventors

List the characteristics of inventors

Visit the airport or railroad station

Tour an airplane or automobile factory

  3. Important scientists

Give oral or written reports on scientists

Discuss the qualities that made success possible for these scientists

Draw pictures showing the lives of people before and after certain inventions

IV. The last frontier is settled   Ask the student how many times he has moved

A. People move West

  1. Homestead Act   Make a list of reasons why people moved fifty years ago and why people move today

  2. Transcontinental railroad   Build or draw (in miniature) ways people moved West in early days

Give a report on the T. V. program "Wagon Train" (stress realism of program)

Draw colorful pictures of the Indians

B. Peace with the Indians   Build a small Indian village

  1. Indian territory   List foods that the Indians contributed to American life (sample these foods)

  2. War with the Indians   Discuss the problems of the Indians (stress the idea that *all* people have problems)

Visit museums which emphasize early West

  3. Indian reservations   Watch T. V. shows on Indians and discuss the errors in depicting them

Read stories about Indians

V. The United States becomes a great industrial nation   Discuss industries according to apparent student interest

A. Communication   Draw a time card and tell its use

  1. Telegraph
  2. Cable   Discuss importance of communication

  3. Telephone
  4. Radio   Build models of communications

  5. Television   Relate influence that radio, T. V., and telephone have on our lives

Give oral or written reports on inventors

Discuss the qualities of inventors

Visit a radio or T. V. station

Read stories about inventors

Draw with explanations a series about an invention

Make a chart with drawings and explanations of inventions

B. Transportation   Build a model railroad and explain importance

  1. Railroad
  2. Automobile   Set up field trips to the Union Station and to a bus terminal

Outline of Content	*Learning Opportunities*
3. Airplane	Draw, write, and/or build a series depicting the car from the "tin lizzie" to the "hot rod"
	Build a model car or airplane
	Tour an automobile or airplane factory
	Construct a chart comparing transportation today and yesterday
	Make a report on the T. V. program "Pony Express"
C. Other factors contributing to development	Display raw materials
1. Vast natural resources	Show resource areas by means of graphs and charts
2. Know-how	
3. Foreign money	Exhibit foreign money (real or drawn)
4. Inventive spirit	Discuss the inventive spirit
	List and discuss employment opportunities available (emphasize the ones available to the individual's needs)
	Make a sample chart of the minerals of Missouri
5. New methods	Discuss the advantages and disadvantages of mass production
6. Labor	
a. Skilled	Visit factories and industries
b. Semi-skilled	Discuss significance of *all* labor
c. Unskilled	List manufacturing terms

Culminating Activities

1. Display work and invite others to see it.
2. Give additional stress on points in which the group shows greatest interest.
3. Prepare review questions and have a simple contest.
4. Exhibit pupil work in school display cabinets.
5. Compose a class scrap book with maps that have been made by pupils.

Evaluation

1. Give a test over United States geography, covering location of principal cities and states.
2. Discuss to determine the formulation of new ideas on proper satisfaction of needs.
3. Extend by discussion the idea that all jobs are important no matter how small or large the job may be.

Textbooks (Pupil)

America's Frontier, Lyons and Carnahan

Homelands Beyond the Seas, Thurston and Hankins
The Missouri Citizen, Karsch
My America, Ames-Ames-Staples
Our Country's Story, Eibling-King-Harlow
Our Homeland and the World, Thurston and Southworth
Our United States, Eibling-King-Harlow
Our World and Its People, Kolerzon
The Story of American Freedom, McGuire
Story of Our Country, Baker-Alsager-Webb
Story of Our Land and People, Moon and MacGowar
This is America's Story, Wilder-Ludlum-Brown

Audio-Visual Aids (Films)

00-182	America the Beautiful
0-184	Cities: How They Grow
0-97	Development of Communication
0-957	Great Lakes
00-317	History of Aviation
00-454	Inland Waterways
00-426	Johnny Appleseed
00-499	Navajo—People Between Two Worlds
0-96	Our Earth

Filmstrips

F-260	Covered Wagon Days
F-2106	Globe, The
F-259	Trail Blazers and Indians
F-2000	Trucks Work for Us
F-2103	Using Common Maps
F-2107	Using the Globe
F-2101	What a Map Is
F-749	Why We Pay Taxes

Resource Unit IV.   Living Things Need Each Other

Overview

All living things have some importance in maintaining the balance of
nature. We should have an understanding of the relation of living
things to the environment and to one another.

Objectives

To develop an appreciation of all living things and their contribution to nature. We can also show that we can not live without other
living things.

Outline of Content	Learning Opportunities
(Living things need us and we need them)	
I. The animals in this room are interesting. Watch the day-to-day activities of fish and plants in an aquarium, birds in a cage, turtle in a pen, or a dog.	Keep the animals fed and keep their surroundings clean—observe them each day
	Germinate bean and corn seeds
	Grow some plants that we like be-

II. Wild animals need protection

III. Plants may need protection

IV. Animals that live in our classroom need us to feed them, to give them water and exercise, and to keep them and their surroundings clean.

V. There are times when wild animals need our protection. During those times of the year when fish and other animals are having their young, there may be laws that protect them.

VI. We use some animals for food. You may see several different kinds of animals in meat markets.

VII. Plants are important to us. We use them for food, to build houses, for clothing, for their flowers and foliage, for shade, and for the protection of the soil from being washed away when we have heavy rains.

cause they have beautiful flowers or attractive leaves

Make a trip to a vegetable garden

Make a trip to the school gardens

Call attention to some of the things that we can do to protect animals and plants

Find a place where rain has washed away the soil that plants need

If you bought a bird for 75¢, a turtle for $1.00, and a dog for $2.50, how much change would you get back from a $5.00 bill?

If a bird can fly 78 miles in three hours, what is its average speed in miles per hour?

If a plant grows 3 feet a year, how many feet will it grow in 4 years?

Make a list of the animals that we use for our food—make a trip to a meat and fish market

Go to a food market to see how many foods you can find that come from plants

Culminating Activities

1. Make a list of foods we could have if there were no animals.

2. Make a list of foods we could have if there were no plants.

Evaluation

Using one of the bird booklets, ask pupils to write the names of four of the birds as you hold the picture where they can see it.

Audio-Visual Aids (Films)

0-236	Life on a Dead Tree	0-785	Kangaroos
0-1087	Your Eyes	0-891	Life in the Desert
0-435	Water for the Community	0-850	Mammals are Interesting
0-1049	Bushy the Squirrel	0-276	Moths
0-335	Our Senses: What They Do For Us	0-326	Pond Insects
0-93	Deer and Its Relatives	0-351	Robin
0-1035	Exploring Your Growth	0-378	Snapping Turtle
		0-392	Spiders
0-838	Fish are Interesting	0-862	Understanding Our Earth: Glaciers
0-165	Gardening		
0-195	Honey Bee	0-670	Mother Mack Trains Her Seven Puppies
0-475	Ice Cream		

0-227	Killers of Insect World	0-317	Plant Traps
0-892	Life in the Forest	0-610	Ruby-Throated Humming-bird
0-1086	Your Ears		
0-24	Butterfly Mystery		
0-376	Elephant (Nature of Things)		
0-403	Heart, Lungs, and Cir-culation		
0-141	Flowers at Work	0-556	Snakes
0-150	Frog	0-468	Work of Rivers
0-918	Grasshopper	0-197	Horse and Its Relatives

Filmstrips

F-1990	Story of West Coast Lumber		
F-1972	Birds We Know	F-1976	Oil from Earth to You
F-299	Green Plants	F-300	Seeds
F-310	Roots	F-302	Stems
F-303	Leaves	F-304	Flowers and Fruits
F-2100	Audubon's Birds (with guide)		

Resource Unit V. I'm a Partner With My Family

Overview

The family is the foundation of American society, and one must learn to become a useful member of the family.

Objectives

To learn the importance of the family circle.

To gain a knowledge of the relationship between the family group and community life.

To gain a better understanding of other families in the community.

To realize the rights and responsibilities of a family in a democracy.

Outline of Content	Learning Opportunities
I. The family circle	Discuss the meaning of the term family
A. Meaning	
	Tell what you think is an ideal family circle and why
	Illustrate and discuss pupil family history
B. Purposes	List the purposes of the family
1. Love	Discuss the effects of family living
2. Cooperation	Give examples of how the boy can help to fulfill the purposes of the family
3. Security	
4. Personal care of children	
	Report on a T. V. show which you think shows the best family circle
	Tell or write a story about pleasant

home living and discuss it

Display on the bulletin board pictures or drawings of the pupils' families

C. Cooperation efforts
   1. Duties of each member
   2. Personal responsibilities

List on the board qualities of family members that produce cooperation

Read and discuss stories about people with good qualities

Discuss the idea that family life can be fun

Discuss a family schedule and the cooperation necessary for its success

List your family's time schedule and how it might be improved

Tell of examples of how individual members have met or should meet their family responsibilities

Dramatize or draw the effects of good family behavior in one living experience

D. Assuming family responsibilities
   1. Physical
   2. Emotional

Write a paragraph telling how one family member can make the entire family unhappy

Make a chart showing duties in the family and who should assume each duty

Discuss the assumption of a responsibility by another family member

Tell how the individual can improve family life

Draw a picture to illustrate courtesy in the family

List the proper attitudes toward accepting home resposibilities

Discuss the qualities we like to see in other members of our family

Give reasons why the family must have a leader

Read and report on books showing ideal family life

Make a list of desirable characteristics found in books or stories and discuss development of them

E. My family responsibilities

Tell or list what you believe your family responsibilities are

1. Financial
2. Home duties
3. Cooperation
4. Love
5. Respect

6. Interest
7. Concern

II. The family in community life
   A. Activities
      1. Church attendance
      2. P. T. A.
      3. Social clubs
      4. Politics

   B. Responsibilities
      1. Support
      2. Concern
         a. Individual
         b. Group

III. The family cooperates with family groups that differ
   A. Religious
   B. Racial
   C. Economic
   D. Social
   E. Political

IV. The family's rights and responsibilities in a democracy

List the things you have done for your family this week

Draw a chart (individual or class) to illustrate how one grows in family responsibilities as one becomes an adult

Discuss the ways the home helps us

Write a paper on what results if I don't assume my family responsibilities

Discuss making useful furniture, etc., in shop

Draw a map of the community showing places of family activity

List the organizations to which your family belongs or relates (note —must be a family project)

Give reasons why a family should participate in community activities

Tell about the organizations to which a family may belong

Illustrate activities your family does together

List ways in which the famlly supports the community

Draw pictures to illustrate what pupil might do to help a neighbor

Discuss how the student might help his family become more aware of their community responsibilities

Give examples of ways you have helped or might help other families

Collect pictures showing family community activities

List ways in which your family differs from other families

Tell how you want to be treated by other families (stress the idea that they want fair treatment, too)

List the various religious groups or churches in your neighborhood

Discuss the idea that differences in politics is the American way

Discuss the importance of voting and a knowledge of political issues in relation to the family

A. Rights
1. To assemble
2. To worship
3. To vote
4. To speak
5. Others

B. Responsibilities
1. To participate
2. To be informed
3. To defend
4. To work

List the freedoms the family enjoys in a democracy

Draw a picture to illustrate *one* right all members of a family enjoy in a democracy

Report on a T. V. news broadcast as to content, length, personal opinion injected, and knowledge gained

Discuss the idea that democracy is *not* free, but we have responsibilities

Tell ways you can be informed

Suggest ways one may be informed in a democracy

Draw a picture to show how members of a family might defend our democracy

Give a report on work in a democracy compared to a dictatorship

Discuss the idea that military service is a responsibility

Culminating Activities

1. Set up desirable home and family goals for the year.
2. Discuss problems which have been solved by the family this year.
3. Tell how new concepts about home and family have been learned.
4. Tell about individual improvements in personal habits, conduct, and sanitation in the home.
5. Have the pupils learned how to contribute to the family group?

Evaluation

1. Written reports from each student explaining activities in the home.
2. Written statements concerning how each boy feels about his home and family.
3. Oral presentations to the class of interesting family trips or activities.

Textbooks (Pupil)

America's Frontier, Lyons and Carnahan
Homelands Beyond the Seas, Thurston and Hankins
The Missouri Citizen, Karsch
My America, Ames-Ames-Staples
Our Country's Story, Eibling-King-Harlow
Our Homeland and the World, Thurston and Southworth
Our United States, Eibling-King-Harlow
Our World and Its People, Kolerzon
The Story of American Freedom, McGuire
Story of Our Country, Baker-Alsager-Webb
Story of Our Land and People, Moon and MacGowar
This is America's Story, Wilder-Ludlum-Brown

Audio-Visual Aids (Films)

    0-722   Don't Get Angry

    0-538   Family Life

    0-877   Are Manners Important?

Filmstrips

    F-1774   Who Do I Want To Be?

    F-1866   Discovering Your Interests

    F-1739   Making Your Money Work For You

    F-1818   Manners At Home

    F-752   Danger of Narcotics

Appendix D

PROCEDURES AND TABLES

1 Mount Diablo

The following list, distributed by the program co-ordinator at Mount Diablo Unified School District, guides the selection of student work stations.

SUGGESTED TASKS FOR STUDENTS ENROLLED IN
INSIDE WORK EXPERIENCE

I. Construction, Repair, and Remodeling of Buildings

    a. Washing and varnishing woodwork
    b. Painting walls
    c. Preparing a room for special activities
    d. Building observatory
    e. Building greenhouse
    f. Refinishing floors

II. Construction, Repair, and Remodeling of Public Facilities

    a. Building a rifle range
    b. Building an archery range
    c. Constructing stage scenery
    d. Making extra backboards for basketball practice
    e. Constructing bleachers
    f. Constructing scoreboards
    g. Constructing bulletin boards
    h. Constructing bicycle racks
    i. Planning, laying out, and maintaining parking lot
    j. Planning, laying out, and maintaining tennis courts
    k. Repairing scenery

III. Construction, Repair, and Remodeling of Equipment

    a. Repairing and refinishing furniture
    b. Making coatracks and other special furniture
    c. Mending and taking care of swimming suits and team suits
    d. Washing and ironing gymnasium suits and towels
    e. Laundering and reconditioning shop aprons
    f. Building ping-pong tables
    g. Building a telescope for the school
    h. Building benches for gymnasium and dressing rooms
    i. Building shuffleboard sets
    j. Installing buzzers and bells
    k. Building playground apparatus

IV. Improvement and Maintenance of Grounds

    a. Clearing and grading play area
    b. Landscaping: setting, pruning, and caring for trees and shrubs
    c. Placing bulbs and caring for flower beds
    d. Making and placing signs for safety in street
    e. Picking up papers, other debris
    f. Caring for athletic field

  g. Constructing nature trail
  h. Building additional walls
  i. Cutting grass
  j. Reforestation and soil conservation

V. Building Maintenance

  a. Sweeping
  b. Dusting
  c. Cleaning washbowls
  d. Cleaning blackboards and erasers
  e. Cleaning buses
  f. Sterilizing drinking fountains
  g. Sterilizing shower-room floors

VI. Clerical Assistance Service

  a. Copying reports, other papers
  b. Filing
  c. Telephone calls and switchboard
  d. Typing
  e. Attendance report work
  f. Messenger service
  g. Issuing supplies
  h. Inventorying supplies
  i. Acting as secretary or clerical assistant to teachers and department heads
  j. Assisting faculty treasurer of special funds
  k. Keeping records
  l. Indexing records of graduates and nongraduates

VII. Library Service and Book Repair

  a. Repairing books
  b. Rebinding books, binding magazines
  c. Cataloging new books
  d. Inventorying and checking
  e. Lending and receiving books
  f. Assisting in public library
  g. Assisting students in finding references
  h. Collecting free teaching material
  i. Making cross references
  j. Collecting material for vocational guidance
  k. Making paper boxes for magazines
  l. Taking care of bulletin boards and making book displays
  m. Keeping records of due slips and sending notices to delinquent students
  n. Collecting fines and accounting for cash
  o. Keeping tables and chairs in order
  p. Maintaining reserve shelves
  q. Preparing bibliographies
  r. Typing and stenography
  s. Messenger and errand service

    t. Research work for subject areas such as occupations

    u. Gathering free materials

    v. Filing pictures

    w. Keeping records of book circulation and numbers using library

VIII. Duplicating work

    a. Typing stencils and copy work for teachers

    b. Running duplicating machines

    c. Printing school paper

    d. Preparing and blueprinting shop instructions

IX. Departmental Services

    a. Physical Education

      1. Record keeping and reporting

      2. Running intramural games

      3. Assisting physical director in care of locker and shower rooms

      4. Assisting on gym floor

      5. Refereeing for smaller children

      6. Cleaning, repairing, and checking equipment

      7. Supervising playgrounds, marking fields

      8. Printing schedules for athletic activities

      9. Making posters for games

     10. Setting up and supervising game room

     11. Making posture charts

     12. Keeping posture records

     13. Inspecting equipment

     14. Maintaining lifeguard service

     15. Making armbands, leis, stripes, or jackets for team identification

     16. Keeping game records

     17. Maintaining bulletin board

     18. Drawing diagrams of stunts, plays, and tactics

     19. Collecting tickets

     20. Cleaning and repairing equipment

     21. Taking inventory of supplies

     22. Assisting with supervision of playgrounds

     23. Conducting grade-school hikes

     24. Servicing basketball hoops and backboards

    b. Shops

      1. Checking and replacing tools

      2. Sorting, checking, and storing lumber and other supplies

      3. Printing materials needed for shop

      4. Repairing tools and equipment

      5. Servicing machinery and equipment

      6. Making designs for classroom use

      7. Maintaining stockroom

      8. Servicing various school departments, building equipment, and tools

    9. Repairing board of education equipment such as school buses, trucks, and other mechanical equipment

   10. Constructing and repairing metal play equipment

c. English Department

    1. Making library lists
    2. Maintaining reference files
    3. Keeping cross-reference files
    4. Maintaining filing system
    5. Mounting pictures
    6. Making charts and graphs
    7. Making dolls to illustrate characters of literature
    8. Collecting teaching materials
    9. Conducting school "Use of English" campaign, keeping statistics, posting error lists
   10. Maintaining bulletin board service
   11. Making bibliographies
   12. Preparing "Better Speech" posters
   13. Maintaining special displays of attractive books

d. Social Studies Department

    1. Making reference lists
    2. Collecting pamphlets
    3. Making topical scrapbooks
    4. Maintaining current events file
    5. Conducting surveys
    6. Preparing illustrated card series for world history
    7. Making and costuming dolls to illustrate periods of history
    8. Arranging materials for classroom use
    9. Drawing, painting, or constructing charts, graphs, and maps
   10. Building a file of photographs and illustrations
   11. Arranging bulletin boards
   12. Preparing radio program guide lists of posters

e. Mathematics Department

    1. Maintaining bulletin board service
    2. Filing, typing, stenography, and making copies of charts
    3. Repairing and maintaining equipment
    4. Constructing models, such as wire models for solid geometry, transits for trigonometry
    5. Compiling descriptions of use of mathematics in vocational life

f. Cafeteria and Home Economics Department

    1. Preparing food in cafeteria
    2. Serving in cafeteria
    3. Cleaning tables and dishes
    4. Running power dishwasher
    5. Cashier for cafeteria
    6. Preparing hot dish and carrying it to grade school
    7. Making band and other uniforms

8. Checking and placing material in homemaking rooms
9. Assisting in planning menus
10. Maintaining milk and sandwich shop
11. Typing menus and place cards
12. Setting tables
13. Keeping stockroom in order
14. Keeping inventory of stock and supplies
15. Putting utensils away
16. Keeping equipment in order and repair
17. Arranging tables and chairs
18. Working at lunch counter
19. Serving as lunchroom supervisors
20. Keeping statistics on food types selected by pupils
21. Making school insignia

g. Medical Department—Health and Hospital Work

1. Assisting nurse with records
2. Helping in office, especially when nurse is out
3. Giving out milk
4. Serving free lunches with surplus foods
5. Making bandages, swabs for local hospital
6. Checking dental and medical charts
7. Checking reports on tests, inoculations
8. Checking daily school sanitation
9. Assisting in vision and other tests
10. Maintaining health bulletin board

h. Art and Drama, Music

1. Working on school paper
2. Making posters publicizing safety and other subjects
3. Making stage settings
4. Caring for music library
5. Making artistic signs for room doors
6. Assisting in art department, taking care of materials
7. Making maps and charts for instructional purposes
8. Assembling pictures
9. Making props for stage
10. Designing costumes for dramatics
11. Arranging displays and exhibits
12. Designing book covers
13. Preparing exhibits
14. Providing photographs of school activities
15. Repairing and painting stage equipment; painting stage scenery
16. Making scrapbooks and other teaching materials
17. Painting murals for temporary use in halls and classroom
18. Keeping music library
19. Caring for minor repairs on instruments
20. Maintaining file of illustrations of technique, stage appearance, and posture
21. Building music stands

22. Making musical arrangements
23. Making music inventory
24. Assisting with maintenance and operation of public address system
25. Mounting and framing pictures
26. Preparing visual aid material
27. Photographic service
28. Binding books
29. Transcribing and copying music
30. Providing lunch-hour music

i. Chemistry

1. Collecting teaching materials
2. Making models, such as atomic models and manufacturing models
3. Checking lockers
4. Setting up apparatus
5. Arranging materials for classroom work
6. Maintaining pamphlet library
7. Repairing apparatus
8. Cleaning apparatus
9. Checking and keeping a laboratory inventory
10. Maintaining stores in order
11. Checking experiments

j. Biology

1. Collecting specimens
2. Caring for living animals in the laboratory
3. Caring for living plants in the laboratory
4. Constructing cages, display cases, and mounts
5. Preparing, labeling, and caring for microscope slide files
6. Conducting museum displays
7. Collecting teaching materials
8. Conducting surveys
9. Preparing charts, graphs, maps
10. Making slides for projection
11. Gathering photographs, clippings
12. Setting up apparatus
13. Maintaining pamphlet library
14. Testing milk

k. Physics

1. Making charts and graphs
2. Constructing models, such as optical bench, small electric motors, insulating boxes
3. Setting up equipment and apparatus
4. Keeping supplies and equipment
5. Compiling descriptions of applications of physics for everyday life
6. Collecting photographs, news items, teaching materials
7. Maintaining physics bulletin board

8. Arranging displays
9. Repairing apparatus

l. Commercial Department

1. Typing materials
2. Duplicating
3. Maintaining filing system
4. Operating school savings system
5. Taking care of machines
6. Scheduling services to other departments
7. Making teaching charts and graphs

m. Agricultural Department

1. Testing milk for local farmers
2. Repairing, cleaning, adjusting, and sharpening farm machinery, tools, and equipment
3. Arranging and filing farm bulletins and periodicals
4. Working on school farm or forest enterprises
5. Doing departmental clerical work
6. Constructing, remodeling, repairing, and improving departmental equipment and buildings
7. Performing special community services such as spraying, pruning, trimming, and planting of shade trees and shrubs
8. Performing special services in times of fire, flood, drought, disease, insect attack, or similar emergencies
9. Making charts
10. Collecting and testing seeds
11. Testing soil for local farmers

n. Guidance Department

1. Maintaining filing system
2. Checking folders
3. Maintaining guidance library
4. Maintaining guidance bulletin board
5. Compiling statistics
6. Maintaining student suggestion or request files
7. Conducting surveys in the community
8. Publicizing guidance library
9. Making student appointments

X. Research, Statistical, and Survey Work

a. Keeping card file of work record, extracurricular activities, hobbies, and other information for each pupil
b. Recording present address and other information of last year's graduates and dropouts
c. Charting standardized test results
d. Cataloging of graduates and dropouts
e. Preparing material for yearbook
f. Doing clerical work in connection with studies such as causes of absence, causes of dropouts, costs of attending school, follow-up of alumni, types of occupations in the community

g. Assisting in the preparation of curriculum materials
h. Putting records in usable form
i. Investigating local school history

XI. Elementary School Services

a. Arranging material for grade teachers
b. Correcting objective tests
c. Storytelling and other activities for kindergarten
d. Conducting games for small children
e. Helping primary teachers with remedial work
f. Repairing and building toys and furniture

XII. General School Services

a. Operating moving picture projectors
b. Making transportation maps
c. Operating book and stationery store
d. Operating ticket booth for games and plays
e. Checking lockers
f. Maintaining lost-and-found department
g. Reading for sight-conservation pupils
h. Tutoring pupils needing help

2 Santa Barbara

CHART 1

JOBS HELD BY WORK-EXPERIENCE
EDUCATION STUDENTS, SANTA BARBARA, CALIFORNIA, IN 1955[1]
(In one middle-sized high school)

JOBS FOR PAY AND CREDIT	NUMBER OF STUDENTS	JOBS FOR CREDIT BUT NOT FOR PAY	NUMBER OF STUDENTS
Market stock boy	5	Teacher assistant	6
Groom	4	Nurse assistant	5
Service-station attendant	3	Mechanic assistant	3
Salesclerk	3	Bookkeeping assistant	2
Janitor assistant	3	Secretarial assistant	2
General office assistant	2	Lawyer assistant	1
Dry-cleaning assistant	2	Physical-therapy assistant	1
Ranch hand	2	Merchandising assistant	1
Gardening assistant	2	Farm assistant	1
Pantryman assistant	1	Butcher assistant	1
Typist	1		
Mechanic assistant	1		
Usherette	1		
Waitress	1		
Carhop	1		
	$\overline{32}$		$\overline{23}$
22 boys; 10 girls		8 boys; 15 girls	

---

1. Clarence Feilstra, *Work-Experience Education Program in Santa Barbara County High School Districts* (Santa Barbara: Rood Associates, 1961), p. 4.

CHART 2

JOBS HELD BY NONPAID STUDENTS IN WORK-EXPERIENCE
EDUCATION PROGRAM, SANTA BARBARA, CALIFORNIA[2]
(Large high school—February 1955)

JOBS HELD BY STUDENTS	NUMBER OF BOYS	NUMBER OF GIRLS
Office assistant (Filing, typing)	0	8
Teacher assistant	0	6
Library assistant	0	5
Nurse assistant	0	5
Salesclerk	1	3
Switchboard operator	0	3
X-ray assistant (hospital)	0	3
Psychologist assistant (school)	1	1
Receptionist assistant	0	1
Legal-secretary assistant	0	1
Veterinarian assistant	1	0
Laboratory assistant (for M.D.)	0	1
Laboratory assistant (dairy)	1	0
Dental assistant	0	1
Totals	4	38

---

2. *Ibid.,* p. 21.

CHART 3

PROFESSIONAL AND BUSINESS ESTABLISHMENTS EMPLOYING STUDENTS
IN WORK-EXPERIENCE EDUCATION PROGRAM, SANTA BARBARA, CALIFORNIA[3]

PROFESSION OR BUSINESS	NUMBER	PROFESSION OR BUSINESS	NUMBER
Public school	8	Engineering company	1
Insurance agency	7	Farm machines	1
Bank	5	Hardware store	1
Retail food store	5	Hospital	1
Department store	5	Interior decoration company	1
Gasoline service station	5	Ice-cream store	1
Automobile dealer	4	Jeweler	1
Automobile service shop	3	Justice court	1
Doctor's office	3	Library	1
Dental laboratory and office	3	Light and water department	1
Law office	3	Lumber company	1
Pharmacy	3	Massage and steam bath	1
Newspaper publisher	2	Machinery company	1
Radio and TV sales and service	2	Museum	1
Medical clinic	2	Outdoor supply company	1
Office supplies	2	Public accountant	1
Bookstore	2	Publishing company	1
Beauty school	1	Restaurant	1
Blood bank	1	Retail clothier	1
Camera shop	1	Saddlery	1
Carbon corporation	1	Savings and loan association	1
Chiropractor	1	Seafood dealer	1
Credit bureau	1	Sports goods store	1
Dairy	1	Transfer and storage company	1
Day camp	1	Travel agency	1
District agriculture association	1	University	1
Dry cleaner	1		100

3. *Ibid.*, p. 37.

3 Kansas City

WORK-STUDY PROGRAM TO PREVENT JUVENILE DELINQUENCY
Kansas City Public Schools

ANALYSIS OF RESEARCH OPERATIONS FOR 1963–65

*A Two-Year Period When the Experimental
Groups Will Be in Full Operation*[1]

Research associate B—based in the schools—to collect the following data:

Achievement test data during the boys' fifteenth year, roughly six months before they reach the age of sixteen so as to minimize through dropouts. Tests to be given, scored, and recorded in reading, arithmetic, and general knowledge. 350 boys.   ONE MONTH

Secure teacher reports with something like the Behavior Description Chart on all 350 boys. Score and tabulate.   ONE WEEK

Secure attendance records and make a record of absences of all 350 boys. Also school grades.   ONE WEEK

Administer and score a personality inventory and a projective personality test for all 350 boys.   TWO MONTHS

Devise and administer a sociometric test to get data on social adjustment of all 350 boys.   ONE MONTH

Interview work supervisors and academic teachers once every three months to collect their diaries, to supplement the diaries if necessary; code and record the interview information.   ONE WEEK

Make systematic observations on the work groups at various points in the project, as a basis for evaluation of progress.   THREE WEEKS

Co-operate with research associate A on interviews with parents of control and experimental groups.   FIVE MONTHS

Research associate A—based in the community—to collect the following data:

Interviews with parents of control and experimental groups when boys are approximately fifteen and a half years old. 350 interviews—three hours to interview and record.

If assisted by associate B   SEVEN MONTHS

Get information on each boy's social contacts in the community—friends, gang membership, club membership, etc.   ONE MONTH

Set in progress a system of post-dropout interviewing to be made six months after a boy drops out of school. 100 per year from 1964 on.   SIX MONTHS

---

1. School District of Kansas City, "A Work-Study Program to Reduce Juvenile Delinquency" (December 12, 1960), pp. 26–27.

Interview employment co-ordinator-supervisors once every three months to collect their diaries and to get supplementary information; code and record the interview information.   TWO WEEKS

Collect delinquency data from police court and other places when necessary on experimental and control groups.   TWO WEEKS

Observe systematically the community activities of the boys in the experimental and control groups—gangs, street-corner locations, roller-skating rinks, drive-ins, pool halls, etc.   TWO MONTHS

Chronologically, this calendar was planned for staffing the program:

DETAIL OF PERSONNEL IN OPERATIONS AND RESEARCH[2]

Jan. 1961–Aug. 1961:
Director, two research associates, work program supervisor start training program.

Sept. 1961–Aug. 1962:
Director, two academic instructors, two work supervisors, two assistant work supervisors, two research associates.

Sept. 1962–Aug. 1963:
Director, four academic instructors, four work supervisors, four assistant work supervisors. One employment co-ordinator-supervisor starts work in January 1963 and commences placement of a few boys in Group X_1. Two research associates.

Sept. 1963–Aug. 1964:
Director, four academic instructors, three work supervisors, three assistant work supervisors. Second employment co-ordinator-supervisor starts work in January 1964. Two research associates.

Sept. 1964–Aug. 1965:
Director, three academic instructors, one work supervisor, one assistant work supervisor, three employment co-ordinator-supervisors. Two research associates.

Sept. 1965–Aug. 1966:
Director, one academic instructor, two employment co-ordinator-supervisors. Two research associates.

Sept. 1966–Aug. 1967:
Director, one employment co-ordinator-supervisor. Two research associates.

Sept. 1967–Aug. 1968:
Two research associates.

Sept. 1968–Aug. 1969:
Two research associates.

---

2. *Ibid.*, p. 25.

Summary:

14 academic instructor years; 10 work supervisor years; 10 assistant work supervisor years; 8 employment co-ordinator-supervisor years; one director, 6.5 years; and two research associates, 8.5 years.

All personnel assigned to the project receive salaries from the school system in accord with the district's regular salary schedule.

Appendix E

NAMES AND ADDRESSES OF THE DIRECTORS OF THE WORK-STUDY PROGRAMS REPORTED

CEDRIC BOESEKE
Santa Barbara High School
Santa Barbara, California

PAUL DRISCOLL
Chairman, High School Division
Board of Education of the
  City of New York
110 Livingston Street
Brooklyn 1, New York

GEORGE W. EYSTER
Communication Services
The Mott Program of the
  Flint Board of Education
923 East Kearsley Street
Flint 3, Michigan

HERMAN GOLDBERG
Board of Education
13 South Fitzhugh Street
Rochester, New York

GERALD GORDON
Co-ordinator of Co-operative
  Employment Program
Cranston High School East
Park Street
Cranston, Rhode Island

BERNARD C. GREENE
Director, Work-Study Program
Board of Education
1211 McGee Street
Kansas City 11, Missouri

MRS. MERLE B. KARNES
Director of Special Education
705 South New Street
Champaign Community Schools
Champaign, Illinois

PHILLIP H. MAHONEY
Director, Special Services
Board of Education of the
  Moline Public Schools
1619 Eleventh Avenue
Moline, Illinois

MILAN WIGHT
Co-ordinator,
  Work-Experience Education
Mount Diablo Unified
  School District
1936 Carlotta Drive
Concord, California

Selected Bibliography

ALPENFELS, ETHEL J. "Children at Work—Foreword," *Childhood Education,* 37 (April 1961), pp. 364–65.

ANDERSON, STUART A. "High School Work Experience Program in Action," *American School Board Journal,* 123 (August 1951), pp. 18–19.

BARBER, GERTRUDE A. "Guiding the Low-Ability Student," *National Education Association Journal,* 50 (March 1961), pp. 38–39.

BROWN, MARION A. "Oakland's Work-Study Plan," *School Executive,* 64 (October 1944), pp. 49–51.

BROWNE, E. C. "Petersburg High School Work Experience Program," *Occupations,* 25 (January 1947), p. 231.

CALIFORNIA STATE DEPARTMENT OF EDUCATION. *Handbook on Work Experience Education.* Sacramento: the Department, May 1959.

CAMPION, H. A. "Work Experience in Secondary Education," *California Journal of Secondary Education,* 30 (January 1955), pp. 4–10.

CHILDREN'S BUREAU. *A Look at Juvenile Delinquency,* (U.S. Department of Health, Education, and Welfare.) Washington, D.C.: Government Printing Office, 1960.

CONANT, JAMES BRYANT. *Education and Liberty: The Role of the Schools in a Modern Democracy.* Cambridge, Mass.: Harvard University Press, 1953.

————. *Slums and Suburbs.* New York: McGraw-Hill Book Co., 1961.

DICK, ARTHUR A. "Work Experience Programs," *American Vocational Association Journal,* 27 (March 1952), p. 17.

DILLON, HAROLD J. *Work Experience in Secondary Education: A Study of Part-Time School and Work Programs.* New York: Publication 394 of National Child Labor Committee, 1946.

DRESDEN, KATHARINE. "Current Materials in a Work Experience Program," *School Review,* 57 (March 1949), pp. 165–67.

EGGERT, MARY MCMILLAN. "Children at Work—School Is Work," *Childhood Education,* April 1961, pp. 365–68.

FIELSTRA, CLARENCE. "Values of Work Experience Education," *Educational Leadership,* January 1961, pp. 231–35. Also in *California Journal of Secondary Education,* 35 (December 1960), pp. 495–501.

FORKNER, HAMDEN L. "Work Experience—A Must in Education," *Teachers College Record,* 48 (April 1947), pp. 435–39.

FRAZIER, A. "The Case Against Work Experience," *Nation's Schools,* 38 (October 1946), pp. 20–21.

HANDY, MARY. "Willingly—to School," *National Education Association Journal,* December 1955, pp. 544–45.

HAVIGHURST, ROBERT J. *Developmental Tasks and Education.* Chicago: University of Chicago Press, 1948.

———— and COREY, S. M. "Work Experience for High School Youth," *School Review,* 50 (May 1942), pp. 331–32.

HILL, ARTHUR S.; MILLER, LEONARD M.; and GABBARD, HAZEL F. "Schools Face the Delinquency Problem," *Bulletin of the NASSP,* 37 (December 1953), pp. 181–221.

HORACE, REGIS A. "Work Experience or Just Plain Work?" *UBEA Forum,* 5 (February 1951), pp. 19–20.

HUNT, DEWITT. *Work Experience Education Programs in American Secondary Schools.* (U.S. Department of Health, Education, and Welfare, Bulletin 1957, No. 5.) Washington, D.C.: Government Printing Office.

IVINS, WILSON H. "Contributions of Work Experience to General Education," *The High School Journal,* 37 (April 1954), pp. 214–20.

———— and RUNGE, WILLIAM B. *Work Experience in High School.* New York: Ronald Press, 1951.

JANSEN, M. L. "Small Community Plans for Work Experience," *Nation's Schools,* 51 (May 1953), pp. 77–78.

JOHNSON, ELIZABETH S. "From School to Work with Help," *Vocational Guidance Quarterly,* Spring 1955.

Juvenile Delinquency Facts and Facets, 11 (1960).
Washington, D.C.: Government Printing Office, 1960.
1. "The Children's Bureau and Juvenile Delinquency"
2. "Sociological Theories and Their Implications for Juvenile Delinquency"
3. "Selected, Annotated Readings on Group Services in the Treatment and Control of Juvenile Delinquency"
4. "Delinquency Prevention: The Size of the Problem"
5. "Identifying Potential Delinquents"
6. "Family Courts, An Urgent Need"
7. "Co-ordination of the National Effort for Dealing with Juvenile Delinquency"
8. "Current Needs in the Field of Juvenile Delinquency"
9. "How Effective Are Services for the Treatment of Delinquents?"
10. "Comparison of Expenditures and Estimated Standard Costs for Selected Juvenile Delinquency Services"

11. "Delinquency and the Adolescent Crisis"

12. "State Agencies and Juvenile Delinquency"

13. "Staff and Training for Juvenile Law Enforcement in Urban Police Departments"

14. "Community Programs and Projects for the Prevention of Juvenile Delinquency"

15. "Survey of Probation Officers"

KVARACEUS, WILLIAM C. *Delinquent Behavior: Principles and Practices.* (National Education Association Juvenile Delinquency Project.) National Education Association, 1959. Vol. II.

LONG, WILLIAM C. "Let's Put Our Teen-Agers to Work!" *The American Magazine,* 160 (October 1955), pp. 84–88.

MACKIE, ROMAINE P., and others. *Preparation of Mentally Retarded Youth for Gainful Employment.* (U.S. Office of Education, Bulletin 1959, No. 28, and Office of Vocational Rehabilitation, Rehabilitation Service Series, No. 507.)

MILLER, LEONARD M. "Education for Work," *Review of Educational Research,* 20 (October 1950), pp. 287–93.

———. "School Work Programs Keep Youth in School!" *Occupations,* 29 (January 1951), pp. 281–84.

MOORE, BERNICE M. (ed.). *Juvenile Delinquency, Research, Theory and Comment.* (Association for Supervising and Curriculum Development.) National Education Association, 1958.

OFFICE OF EDUCATION. *Vocational Education in the Next Decade: Proposals for Discussion.* (U.S. Department of Health, Education, and Welfare, January 1961.) Also in *Industrial Arts and Vocational Education Journal,* 50 (April 1961), pp. 14–16.

O'LEARY, M. J., and BLUME, F. L. "How Can Work Experience and Cooperative School Work Plans Become Effective in the Education Program?" *Bulletin of the NASSP,* 38 (April 1954), pp. 92–94.

OLIVERIO, MARY ELLEN. "The Experience of Work—Prerequisites to Its Success," *American Vocational Journal,* 36 (January 1961), pp. 15–16.

OLSON, MYRON S. "Students Work To Learn, Not Earn," *School Executive,* 74 (May 1955), pp. 58–59.

Report to the Congress on Juvenile Delinquency. Washington, D.C.: Government Printing Office, 1960.

RIDGWAY, J. M. "Work Experience Program," *National Education Association Journal,* 41 (March 1952), pp. 166–67.

SAMPSON, BILL A., and JACOBSON, PAUL B. "Controversial Issues Involved in Work Experience Programs," *Bulletin of the NASSP,* 34 (January 1950), pp. 215–18.

SPLAVER, SARAH. "Work Experience of High School Students," *Personnel and Guidance Journal,* 32 (February 1954), pp. 353–54.

STINCHCOMB, KOMA. "Part-Time Employment Programs for Slow-Learning Adolescents," *Baltimore Bulletin of Education,* 32 (December 1954), pp. 5–13.

"These Students Try on Jobs for Size," *Good Housekeeping,* 148, No. 5 (May 1959), pp. 166–67.

THURSTON, LEE M. *A Community School Work-Learn Camp.* Lansing, Mich.: Department of Public Instruction, 1951.

TYLER, HENRY T. *Report of the Study of Work Experience Programs in California High Schools and Junior Colleges.* Sacramento: Bulletin of State Department of Education, Vol. XXV, No. 3, July 1956.

WERT, JAMES E., and NEIDT, CHARLES O. "The Education for Work Movement," *Review of Educational Research,* 17 (June 1947), pp. 202–8.

Index